The Falls

Graeme CM Smith

Paperback ISBN 978-1-80424-122-6
e Pub ISBN 978-1-80424-123-3
PDF ISBN 978-1-80424-124-0

Published by MX Publishing
335 Princess Park Manor, Royal Drive, London, N11 3GX
www.mxpublishing.co.uk

Cover design by Brian Belanger

Contents:

Map Table:

Pictures:

Dedication

This is story is dedicated to my children who through the years were only given bits and pieces of my story, and I am sure often wondered what I was thinking as they tried to work out exactly the person that I am.

It's complicated.

It is also dedicated to those who didn't "run-away" during that long hot summer of 1940 as we battled for mere survival in the face of overwhelming odds.

Particularly, to those who didn't make it home, and to those who ended up giving five years of their young lives simply trying to survive.

Prologue

As a boy, Dad and his pals used to run through the fields to catch sight of the steam trains at full steam speeding through the Lanarkshire countryside on their way to Glasgow Central.

It was quite a sight, son.

Well, why don't we go down to Corfe Castle and see if we can catch site of a steam train on the old Swanage railway?

It was a few years since we had been to Corfe with Mum and Dad, but on this occasion, it was just Dad as we lost our Mum a couple of years before. We stood on the platform at Corfe Castle and right on queue a steam train came down the newly opened track from the main line at Wareham and drew to a halt right in front of us. It was a rare sight. The train was pulling a couple of passenger carriages, but apart from the driver, the fireman and a trainee driver, the train was completely empty.

I asked the driver on the footplate, "Could we take the train to Wareham?" but he said we couldn't, "because it was a training exercise and passengers weren't covered by normal insurance."

"Never mind," he said, "come up onto the footplate and we'll show you how we drive it."

So, Dad and I climbed aboard, and we were given a full "tour" of the footplate and how it all worked. I could see Dad thinking about what it must have been like on the Flying Scotsman.

After a while we stood down from the footplate to watch the train get up a head of steam to slowly pull out of the station.

As the train inched forward, Dad was looking down at the steam billowing out from between the drive wheels below the platform.

I said, "What is it?"

"See that wheel there son?"

Looking at it, I guessed it was a good couple of meters in diameter.

He said, "The last time I saw one of them it had half an axle attached to it and was flying through the air heading straight for me. I was transfixed by the sight of it as it arced slowly towards where we stood in a field and buried itself into the ground some 100 metres away."

"Good God! Dad, where were you?"

"We had just evacuated Halberstadt as the air-raid sirens went off and no sooner had we been put into a field, about a kilometre from the railyard where we had been working, when the US Army Air Force came over and flattened the place."

"The rail engine sheds took a direct hit that more or less turned it to shrapnel and a tangled heap of metal ruins. The human carnage was indescribable as body parts rained down around us."

As I stood there, it was a story that was difficult to comprehend.

The horror of it all.

What else had he seen that he hadn't told us about before?

This is his story.

Chapter 1: Fall Weiss – The Call Up

The common consensus at the time was that the signatories to the Versailles Treaty on 29-Jun-1919, brought to an end the "War to End All Wars." Little did they know that as they were signing peace terms to conclude the First World War, the terms of the treaty would in fact be the genesis for the Second World War.

Ferdinand Foch, the French general and military theorist who served as the Supreme Allied Commander during the First World War, famously called the treaty, "an armistice for twenty years" and in an interview with a British newspaper in April 1919, he predicted that, "Next time the Germans will make no mistake. They will break through into Northern France and will seize the Channel ports as a base of operations against England."

At the time of the treaty, I was just two months old.

Throughout the 1920s, the British and French active armies reverted to the role of a colonial police force, while domestically the economics of the time contributed to the neglect of the reserve forces at home.

Their respective armed forces were both prosecuting traditional low-intensity conflicts fighting small brush-fire operations around the globe. Britain gained control over Iraq after the First World War and considerable effort was expended turning this country into a British client-state to assure access to its oil resources.

Like the French Army, the British Army spent much of the inter-war period focused on low-intensity conflicts rather than thinking about conventional warfare.

By 1926, the Reichswehr had more than 48,000 NCOs, which gave General Hans von Seeckt, the then-chief of staff, a solid, professional core of trainers when the time for expansion arrived. Entrance into the Reichswehr's enlisted ranks was so competitive that there were 15 applicants for every slot, ensuring high-quality armed services.

By the mid-20s some were beginning to realise that the restrictions of Versailles placed on the Germans were allowing the Germans to focus on quantity, not quality. Indeed, the conditions created a greenhouse environment that provided ideal conditions for General Seeckt to set about rebuilding German ground combat power.

Seeckt was Chief of Staff for the Reichswehr from 1919 to 1920 and Commander in Chief of the German Army from 1920 until he resigned in October 1926. He occupied this role by intensively studying the lessons of the First World War.

In particular, the 4,000-man Bundeswehr officer corps was the pick of the former Kaiser's army.

He concluded that offensive action through mobile warfare was the key to success on the battlefield. Although the General's Staff was forbidden by the Allies, Seeckt connived to create a hidden staff within the army bureaucracy and placed the most talented officers within its ranks.

Seeckt also established a covert group known as Sondergruppe R to conduct German–Soviet military technical collaboration and put individuals in it he could trust, like Oberstleutnant Fedor von Bock and Major Kurt von Schleicher. This collaboration was in part enshrined in the Treaty of Rapallo that normalised German-Soviet relations in 1922, and Seeckt began moving towards his goal of establishing secret testing facilities in the Soviet Union, out of sight of Allied inspectors.

In 1926, the Lipetsk flying school was opened, where the Germans used 50 Dutch-built Focke Wulf fighters for flight training and ground attack experiments. The role of the Lipetsk facility was crucial in shaping future German doctrines for the use of fighters in close air support of ground troops.

The Franco-Prussian war imbibed a deep sense of grievance that was to fuel French nationalism and in turn a desire to recalibrate the balance of power in Europe in French favour, particularly after the loss of Alsace and Lorraine following their defeat (Romano, 2014).

Britain was not immune from this movement that began to permeate political discourse throughout Europe, as the first challenges to British imperialism began to surface in Ireland and India.

As we entered the '30s, France's primary wartime partners, the British, and the Americans, political focus drifted away, choosing to focus on their own issues and reluctant to engage in new security commitments on continental Europe. The Entente Cordiale, the basis of the wartime Anglo-French alliance, was allowed to wither and die; Anglo-French military collaboration virtually ceased to exist.

By now some facts realised by the Versailles agreement were beginning to gain political weight. American and British political leadership were beginning to regard French efforts to financially punish a defeated Germany as unnecessarily harsh and this difference helped to drive a wedge between the former allies. Later, when France and Belgium decided on their own initiative to occupy the Ruhr industrial area in Jan-1923, in response to the failure of the Weimar Republic to deliver coal as part of war reparations, Paris was stunned by sharp Anglo-American criticism of its actions. After this, it was clear that the old wartime alliances were moribund.

Even the hushed tones of my parents listening to this play out on the radio could not hide the fact that this narrative was beginning to gain a wider audience and the right-wing media in Britain didn't even attempt to hide their support of a growing political movement taking place in Italy, Spain and Germany. Tensions were rising.

As a family we were unfortunate.

Quite rare for those days, my Mum was a qualified gardener and held many posts alongside my father on some of Scotland's grandest estates.

My mother died when I was 14, I was the second eldest of five.

I left home at the age of 17, and I departed on bad terms with the Old Man.

With the Old Man, this became a repeating pattern with my brothers and sisters also, probably because my father was left with a young family of five where the eldest was just 15, in what was called the "hungry thirties."

So, the home had split up and the two girls had left home; one went into the nursing, and the other went to the Air Force.

In 1933, as soon as he could the Old Man took me out of school and found me employment. At the age of 14 I was gardening in Lanark with my father who was the head gardener at a local sanatorium.

And next, one of my younger brothers had been sent away to garden the same way as I had been put out of the house. Since it was the hungry 30s, perhaps I could see why it was done, but I had my doubts.

I was a general apprentice inside the glasshouses there and did two years with my dad before deciding to move onto a private estate at Lockerbie to gain more experience.

After nearly a couple of years I got itchy feet and moved on again to gain wider experience and the head gardener there said he didn't want to lose me and there was an outside position coming up, would I like that?

I said, "yes" and took the position, I was about six months in that.

Due to recession and austerity across the British political landscape it would seem that my dreams of flying and serving in the RAF were stillborn. I followed developments in the RAF with a keen interest and my sister, Dorothy, gave me some insights as well.

In 1934, the Air Ministry looked to develop requirements to support the army with a new dive-bomber resulting in the Hawker Henley that was never used in that role. This was closely followed by the Westland Lysander, designed primarily for artillery spotting and not close air support. Hardly the direct ground air support the British Army could count on from the RAF.

However, things seemed to gather pace after the creation of the Luftwaffe in early 1935 that seemed to reignite my ambitions to get into the RAF.

As Chamberlain and Baldwin became uneasy about the potential for enemy bomber raids on England, they prodded the Air Ministry to bolster home defences. Consequently, the Air Ministry issued specifications for a new high-speed monoplane fighter armed with eight machine guns, which would eventually result in the Hurricane and the Spitfire, but with the great British talent for missing the point, both were optimised for intercepting bombers not enemy fighters.

"So, maybe my pilot career could take off after all!!!"

On the ground military learning seemed no less promising.

Obrest Heinrich Kiesling's treatise on the training inadequacies discusses how the French Army dropped the ball on training its non-commissioned officers and reserve junior officers. Having poorly trained privates is one thing but having poorly trained NCOs and platoon leaders deprives an army of its backbone.

Many were questioning the much-maligned Maginot Line for costing too much and "infecting" the French Army with an overly passive mentality as a form of entropy on the French Army. Yet the Maginot Line fitted well into France's overall defensive strategy because its presence would deter the Germans from attacking directly into Alsace-Lorraine as others argued that it bolstered French morale. There was a lot of propaganda creating a false sense of security, particularly in the British media.

That said, few discussed the fact that the Germans invested heavily in their own West Wall during 1934–39, pouring twice as much concrete and four times as much steel into the project.

Something I personally witnessed during the Battle for France was the size of investment the Germans had made to upgrade tactical communications, at infantry division level for use by regimental commanders and the division artillery and as a radio pack at infantry battalion level.

By now the British and the French claimed to recognize the need for a combined arms approach to modernisation, but in fact they focused too heavily on tanks and neglected or deferred modernisation for infantry weapons, field artillery, air defence and communications. Little was afforded in the way of funding.

Other arms of the field services equally suffered. In 1940, most French engineer units still moved their equipment with horses and wagons, as the Wehrmacht was becoming increasingly motorised.

The Germans took the correct approach of studying the lessons learned from the First World War, using these lessons to formulate a new doctrine, and then developing the weapons to meet the requirements of the new doctrine. German military modernisation efforts in the 1930s reflected a balanced alignment of doctrine and technology, unlike the Anglo-French who placed much more emphasis upon technology while neglecting doctrinal improvements.

As a teenager life was quite comfortable away from home. I had a decent job, was learning a trade and more to the point earning a wage through dependable employment that looked like it had prospects. Socially I was active, particularly in sport where I enjoyed and played golf, but football was my real passion as I was pretty good at it. My ideal position was left wing as a forward because I could run very fast and was good at holding my own in possession of the ball. I used to have a knockaround with my local pals and our team was the Briaryhill Skinlifters.

I played for local teams both in Lanark and at Lockerbie; at that time there were some football scouts who were taking an interest in me and on a couple of occasions I was playing for the Scottish Junior side Loch Maben Rangers where I played a full season 1938-39. The Doonhamers showed an interest and were on the point of inviting me to train at Palmerston Park the home of Queen of the South who had joined the Scottish Football League at the start of the 1923–24 season some 12 years previously.

By 1933-34 season they were in the Scottish First Division giving a very good account of themselves when they finished fourth in the league. In May 1936 Queens were on an eleven-game tour to France, Luxembourg, and Algeria. The tour included competing in a four-team invitational tournament in Algiers. Queens worked their way through four matches all the way to the final. In the final Queens faced Racing de Santander who had just finished fourth in Spain's La Liga. Norrie Haywood's goal saw victory for La Belle Equipe Ecossaise. The trophy can still be seen in the Queens club museum today.

But by Jun-39 I got warning that my call-up was imminent.

I feel disappointed about my football career for the simple reason that my father wasn't interested in football, my father was only interested in work. He had no other diversions, no pastimes or anything like that. It was work, work, work. And we were to do the same.

And that's when I got called up to the Army.

By now Hitler was privately confiding that the intent of his rearmament was to "utterly crush France."

Lieutenant-Colonel Guderian's experimental tank team included a platoon of light tanks, two platoons of armoured cars, a motorcycle platoon for reconnaissance and a motorised platoon equipped with Pak anti-tank guns. In April 1934, he demonstrated his mechanised team to Hitler, who enthusiastically exclaimed, "That's what I want! That's what I mean to have!"

Despite advance warning from German spies, the French were stunned when the German Heer boldly conducted Operation Winter Crossing on 7-Mar-1936, marching three infantry battalions into the Rhineland. The German reoccupation of the Rhineland was a flagrant violation of the Versailles Treaty and exposed the fact that France and Britain had no means of opposing it.

While others were willing to give Hitler a pass, Georges Mandel was one of the few leaders in either Paris or London who early on realised that Hitler was not going to stop. Mandel was an economic conservative and an outspoken opponent of Nazism and Fascism. In the 1930s, he played a similar role to that of Winston Churchill in the United Kingdom, highlighting the dangers posed by the rise of Adolf Hitler in Germany.

While the French military and political leadership made many mistakes in the inter-war period, Britain's failure, perhaps driven by a right-wing press supportive of Hitler, even to consider the possibility of another European war until 1934 was divorced from reality and made it easier for Hitler to achieve his early aggressive coups.

On 15-Mar-1935, Hitler announced the reintroduction of conscription and his intent to increase the army to 36 divisions with 500,000 men.

By the time of Munich, Hitler had a larger army than the French and a larger air force than the British.

The RAF was outnumbered about 2–1 by the Luftwaffe and Hitler was not in the least bit deterred. The fact that the British Army was unprepared for a European war made the French skittish and afraid to stand up to Hitler alone. Recognising that he had no useful military options, Neville Chamberlain opted instead for a diplomatic solution which sacrificed Czechoslovakia.

Indeed, the commander-in-chief of the French Armed Forces at the start of World War II and his political masters suddenly realised that Hitler had a taste for revanchism and that the French Army needed to be modernised quickly if it were to be able to respond to the next crisis.

Britain and France had begun talks after the Rhineland Crisis in 1936, but these discussions focused primarily on broad political issues and avoided military details.

Actual planning and co-ordination between the two general staffs was studiously avoided until the Munich Crisis made clear that Hitler would only listen to force. In February 1939, Chamberlain's cabinet finally agreed to military talks between the two staffs. The first session was held 29 March–4 April and it discussed the likely result of a German offensive against Poland; the British military representatives concluded: If Germany undertook a major offensive in the East there is little doubt that it could occupy Rumania, Polish Silesia, and the Polish Corridor.

Another result of the staff talks was that the French finally learned that the British intended only to make a token commitment to the continent of just four regular divisions and about 200 RAF aircraft within 33 days of mobilisation. The French CSG was shocked to learn that Britain was not going to make a large-scale commitment to assist French operations in the west.

On 06-Apr-1939, the Anglo-Polish agreement was signed, which unequivocally stated that, "If Germany attacks Poland, His Majesty's Government in the United Kingdom will at once come to the help of Poland."

After years of trying to avoid a continental military commitment, Britain made a commitment against the advice of its General Staff and then urged the French to do the same. A week later, the French affirmed their military alliance with Poland and provided a similar security guarantee.

The scene was set for my future over the next six years.

The Cabinet stuck with the decision to send only four regular divisions to assist France but informed the French that this initial BEF would eventually be supplemented with two armoured divisions and six or seven TA divisions. The British General Staff did not expect the BEF to be fully formed until at least one year after mobilisation, since the TA units would start from zero, without training or modern equipment.

Closer to home, in May-1939, the first group of men aged from 20 to 22 years of age reported for 6 months full-time military training as part of a "militia." Other recruits joined, either voluntarily or via conscription papers, in September. Six months later I was in the second group of conscripts when we were called.

I received my calling up papers to go for my medical in the Old Mill in Dumfries, towards the end of the summer of 1939; they give me the option of what part of the armed services you wanted to join.

I wanted to go in the air force.

I had previously, when I left school, wanted to go into the RAF but my father and my employer wouldn't sign the papers for me.

After the medical, although my family home was in Lanark I was staying in Lockerbie, I just went back to work.

I finally got my calling up papers in October 1939 and I had to go to Berwick for training in the King's Own Scottish Borderers (KOSBs), just as Third Lanark held the mighty Glasgow Rangers to a draw and then finally went down 2-1 to them in the semi-final of the Glasgow Cup. A portent perhaps?

I spent six weeks there; all those called up in May 1939 were then transferred to Dorset. There was about half a dozen of us kept back in Berwick to do camp fatigues.

The reason I didn't initially follow the 1ˢᵗ Battalion was because they were all in the first May draft while I and few others were in the second October draft.

With the introduction of the National Service (Armed Forces) Act, Britain by Dec-1939 had added an additional one and a half million men to the armed forces.

We stayed behind at Berwick until the end of April 1940 and there was an outbreak of meningitis which actually killed a few poor souls. They actually had to set up a mortuary. We were all vaccinated and all the big tough guys over six foot kept passing out while us little guys just took it in stride.

At the end of April, I was given embarkation leave before going overseas. Just in time to get home and see Third Lanark lose to Dumbarton 3-1.

Meanwhile, in Europe there was a serious deterioration in the political field. Before I got to Berwick the German Army had crossed the border into Poland on 01-Sep, in what the German operation called Fall Weiss (Operation White), and by the 08-Sep were on the outskirts of Warsaw.

They were joined two weeks later by the Soviet Red Army which invaded eastern Poland.

Once this occurred, General Gamelin knew that Poland's fate was sealed.

French efforts to issue a formal condemnation of the Soviet action were dissuaded by the British, who chose to ignore it.

By now Chamberlain's foreign policy had become completely incoherent since he had been willing to declare war on Germany for invading Poland but was then unwilling to declare war on the Soviet Union for the same offence.

Lord Halifax, foreign minister, led the obfuscation by proclaiming that Britain's security guarantees to Poland were only to defend it from aggression by a "European power," which excluded the USSR.

Once again, traditional British indifference to the fate of Poland took hold.

Two months later, Chamberlain would change his mind again when Stalin attacked neutral Finland, a country to which no security guarantees had been provided, as appeasement simply shifted from Hitler to Stalin.

Squeezed between the Germans and the Soviets, Polish resistance was now hopeless, and Warsaw surrendered on 27-Sep. However, as the last of Poland's military surrendered to the Germans in Poland, German Navy command suggested to Hitler the need to occupy Norway.

The French General Laury managed to escape Warsaw and reach neutral Romania, where he helped establish a conduit for escaping Polish troops to reach France through the Balkans.

Initially just a trickle, the flow of Polish expatriate military personnel to the West quickly grew into tens of thousands.

These military refugees included combat troops and aircrew, and more importantly the Polish Army's Cipher Bureau, complete with two Enigma machines.

The origins of Fall Weiss went back to 1928, when Werner von Fritsch started working on it.

Fall Weiss was developed primarily by Günther Blumentritt and Erich von Manstein while the two were serving as staff officers under General von Rundstedt with Army Group South in Silesia.

As the Germans joined the Soviet Union, occupying the territory east of the Curzon Line as well as Bialystok and Eastern Galicia, the British aircraft carrier HMS Courageous was torpedoed and sunk by U-29 on patrol off the coast of Ireland, causing the death of 514 aboard; it represented the first major warship to be sunk in the war (Mawdsley, 2019). !

In response to these events the British and French Parliament approved an emergency war budget and agreed to issuing an ultimatum to Germany the following day and as the French Army begins its general mobilisation, at 9 a.m. the British ambassador to Berlin Ivan Henderson delivered an ultimatum to Germany which went unanswered and therefore Britain was at war with Germany.

Closer to home the 1st Battalion of the KOSBs had embarked for France as part of the British Expeditionary Force (BEF) towards the end of Sep-39.

Safe passage across the Channel for both men and machinery was secured by the Royal Navy by the end of October. Some 7,000 mines had been laid across the Channel effectively blocking it through the Straits of Dover with a mine barrage.

It was a well-executed operation, but not without incident. During the operation one U-boat managed to slip through and laid mines off both Dover and Weymouth, two were eventually sunk. Towards the end of the operation a third U-boat tried to slip through but ran aground on the Godwin Sands and once exposed was dealt with by the Navy.

After that the enemy abandoned attempts to pass through the Channel, through which the BEF was being maintained, until it in turn occupied the French coasts.

By the end of October, the BEF had some 158,000 men in France, which was increasing daily. And in mid-March 1940 the BEF had doubled in size to some 316,000 men; 50, 000 vehicles; 700 tanks; and 500 aircraft.

The Army by now had to provide for all the needs of a community of British men in France the size of a large city dispersed across some 200km of Normandy, Picardy, and the Pas de Calais. This army had to be distributed, housed, and fed, and vast stores for its immediate use and its future operations had also to be accumulated and conveniently disposed south of the Somme in and around Le Havre and Rouen.

I remained at Berwick all the way through what became known as the Phoney War, and I was there until the beginning of April 1940, and then suddenly thing's started moving in France and they needed more manpower.

The six months that followed the invasion of Poland made many wonder if there would be a war in the west at all.

It was all pretty surreal.

Due to the German invasion of Poland both Britain and France declared war on Germany as part of a peace treaty. It was a brave act, for Britain or France was equipped for such a fight, as other free nations applauded the Allied mobilisation on the French Belgian border.

And so, we waited while Germany conquered Poland and divided the spoils with Russia.

Then, we waited while Germany moved their armies to the west and disposed ports, routes, and lines of communication (rail) for them to attack us.

Then, we waited, for Hitler to choose the time and place for his assault.

And all the time we waited, we accepted the applause, that stroked our ego, of a world which did not know how ill-prepared we were

And all the time Germany was allowed to mass her armies without interference on the western frontiers while the Allies prepared to defend themselves.

For six months after the BEF took its place in the Allied line of battle beside the French, it had neutral Belgium between it and the enemy.

In those six months it had time to prepare for the coming battle, to build up its strength, to perfect its training, to strengthen the defences of the front it was to hold, and to develop rearwards organisation for eventual expansion. And the time was put to good use.

By the end of 1939 it had proved possible to form another regular division in France, the 5th Division. In Jan-40, the first Territorial Division arrived. In February came the 50th Division and the 51st Highland Division, and in April the 42nd and 44th Division. All territorial divisions.

By the 09-Apr a third corps was operational, under the command of General dam, and by the beginning of May-40 the BEF had been increased from four regular divisions in two corps to ten divisions: (half regular and half territorial) in three corps and GHQ reserve.

Three incomplete territorial divisions were also sent out in Apr-1940 for labour duties and to complete their training.

It was to this last group that I belonged, and my fate was tied up with those behind the main fighting force of nearly a quarter of a million.

There were more than 150,000 men in the rearward areas preparing bases, depots, and installations for the maintenance of the much larger fighting force which was to build up as rapidly as possible. Many of them were skilled tradesmen with little or no military training.

By the end of April, the strength of the British Army in France had increased to 394,165. Of this total, 237,319 were with GHQ and in corps and divisions, that is the main fighting force; 18 347 were in the territorial divisions sent out for labour duties and further training; 17,665 were reinforcements held at bases; 78,864 were on lines-of-communication duties; 23,545 were in HQ of various services and missions, hospitals, and miscellaneous employment; 9,051 were in drafts en route; 2,515 were not yet allocated (Karslake, 1979).

My battalion had been one of the first to embark for France in September and was placed in the BEF between the French 7th Army to its left and the 1st Army to its right occupying the front line between Armentieres and Maulde on the Belgian border with its HQ in Arras.

Before we were to move in that direction, back in Blighty we were earmarked for Operation Claymore, which was a British commando raid on the Lofoten Island, on 04-Mar, designed as a feint to the real intention that was to build up British forces in France.

German prisoners were taken in Lofoten, and they became the first POWs to enter the POW camp at Glenbranter in Argyll.

Not reported at the time, was the recovery from the trawler Krebs of a set of spare rotors for a German Enigma coding machine. They were dispatched to Bletchley Park, the top-secret code breaking establishment near Milton Keynes in southern England, where they were examined in the hope of gaining some advantage in the battle to intercept German military communications.

We were all equipped to go to Norway and at the last moment we were sent on embarkation leave. When we got back, embarkation orders had been changed from Norway to France, and we were transferred from Berwick to West Hartlepool.

We were in an old school there and we were met by a regimental sergeant major there out of the Royal Scots Fusiliers. As KOSBs we were welcomed by an RSM from the Royal Scots Fusiliers and he wanted to give us a lecture, so he welcomed us and he said, "You KOSB's have always been classed as better than the RSF's so I'll bloody well make sure that it stays that way."

"Great, just what we need, a medal hunter."

While the British Army debated whether to send me to Norway or France, the 51ˢᵗ was deployed as the Saar Division to take over part of the frontier defences manned by French troops while French forces retreated from their adventure in the Saarland in Germany and returned behind the Maginot Line. The French had occupied the Saarland as part of their pact with Poland to try to take pressure off the Polish Army.

By 01-May the Allies begin evacuating Norwegian ports.

The whole Norwegian campaign was fought until 10-Jun-1940 by which time King Haakon VII evacuated to the United Kingdom with the heir apparent, Crown Prince Olav.

The campaign was an attempt to defend northern Norway with the support of Norwegian forces' resistance to the German invasion. From the German point of view main strategic reason for the invasion was to seize the port of Narvik and guarantee the iron ore needed for the critical production of steel.

A British, French, and Polish expeditionary force of 38,000 soldiers landed in the north of Norway where it had moderate success.

However, events were not going so well in France and a rapid strategic retreat took place after Germany's quick invasion of France on 10-May. The Norwegian government were exiled in London, and the campaign ended with complete occupation and exiled Norwegian forces escaping to continue the fight from overseas.

In the meantime, Prime Minister Chamberlain formally declined Hitler's peace offer in a speech held in the House of Commons and by now an estimated 158,000 British troops were in France. The French Premier Daladier also declined Hitler's offer of peace so things by now were not going great.

As the French settled down for Drôle de guerre, the Germans entered their Sitzkrieg to recoup their strength and look at lessons learned in Poland while Britain planned my future during the Phoney War.

French troops were settling down in the Maginot line's underground barracks and tunnels; the British were building new fortifications along the "gap" between the Maginot Line and the Channel. Meanwhile large portions of Poland were being integrated into the new Germany; as the first Jewish ghetto was established at Lublin (Anon, 1939: Key Dates, 2013).

Germany further annexed the former Polish regions of Upper Silesia, West Prussia, Pomerania, Poznan, Ciechanow (Zichenau), part of Lodz, and the free city of Danzig and created two new administrative districts, Danzig-West Prussia, and Posen (later called District Wartheland or Warthegau); the areas of occupied Poland not annexed directly by Germany or by the Soviet Union were placed under a German civilian administration called the General Government (Anon, 1939: Key Dates, 2013) (Mawdsley, 2019).

While Belgium announced that it was neutral in the conflict, for all the good it did them, Germany remained in a revanchist mood brooding over various formulations for the battle in the west to settle old scores with Britain and France. German General von Manstein proposed that Germany should attack through the Ardennes rather than through Belgium the expected attack route.

As Manstein's plans were being discussed Jews in Austria and Czechoslovakia were being deported to Poland under the direction of Adolf Eichmann, a key architect in what was to eventually become the 'Final Solution' (Anon, 1939: Key Dates, 2013).

The British government released a report on concentration camps being built in Europe for Jews and anti-Nazis.

During the winter of 1939-40 British troops rotated tours of duty on the Maginot Line, to give them terrain experience and that of close contact with the enemy. The much-respected troops of the 51st who made their name in WW1were deployed on the Saar Front at the end of Apr-1940.

The sector they occupied lay to the south of the Ardennes, holding three sectors each with its own battalion with one held in reserve for contingency.

As a first line division the command was larger than usual than the number of units which normally form a division, including a mechanised cavalry regiment; artillery; machine-guns battalions; and other units such as a number of French troops. All under the command of General Fortune including a composite squadron of the RAF and army cooperation flight and a flight of fighters.

The comparative quiet of the "Phoney War" persisted throughout the winter and into the early spring of 1940 although enemy's patrols were increasingly active and there was some larger-scale skirmishing near Hartbusch in which the artillery exchanged salvos.

At the beginning of May these exchanges died down and an uncanny quiet fell the central sector. The same couldn't be said at either end of the 51st sector. Here the Germans were a bit more inquisitive probing the Highland positions, but without success. In early May the situation gradually changed as the Germans were observed ranging and registering key British positions with their artillery.

After our embarkation leave we were all back in West Hartlepool in the first week of May 1940 and we immediately were locked in a school, doors were bolted, guards were on the doors in case we escaped, but the next day we got all our equipment together and marched to the station and straight on to an overnight train to Southampton.

We reached Southampton at 9 o'clock in the morning and were given breakfast in one of the big sheds there and I always remember the ham and eggs; it was lovely.

The mood amongst us all was one of anxiety. Because you didn't know what was coming next. We didn't even know where we were going.

After a very fine breakfast we were loaded onto a ship at Southampton Docks, we departed at midday and the ship started off down Southampton Water and we thought, right, this is us going to France, but it wasn't, at least not yet, as we stood off the Isle of Wight and waited for out escort out of Portsmouth. We then waited there until midnight and dashed across the Channel in darkness.

Under a grey leaden sky, we slipped into Le Havre at the mouth of the Seine just down river from Rouen.

"My war had started."

Chapter 2: Fall Gelb – First Battle for France

As we docked at Le Havre, we were looking over the side of the ship, and I turned to my mate, "They call it La Belle France, but Le Havre doesn't look that much different to Greenock."

The port was busy with the movement of the instruments of war as we were ushered off the ship onto the quayside. There were a good number of passenger trains on the quayside, and we were assigned to board one of them without a clue as to where it was going.

We were never told anything as to where we were or where they were sending us to.

I had an idea that I would soon be with the rest of the 1ˢᵗ Battalion KOSBs who had come over to France six months earlier, which was a bit of a worry as I knew by now that they held a sector of the allied line somewhere up in Belgium and this much, I knew, we were a few kilometres away from there as we approached Rouen in the early morning.

In the centre of Rouen, we were ordered off the train and ordered to fall in outside of the main station; we shouldered arms and marched to an assembly point with hundreds of bell tents in the Rouen Hippodrome where we were billeted for the next three days.

As we did so I turned to my mate and said, "If Le Havre was Greenock, then Rouen was Glasgow only just a bit cleaner."

We were given passes to take leave for a few hours and a group of us decided to have a look at what downtown Rouen had to offer.

I had never seen anything like it. The centre of Rouen was heaving with activity and the noise of a major industrial city centre, trams, buses, lorries, cars, people, and it was all quite exciting.

A group of us entered a café. There were three of us, a fella Willie from Dumfries and another from Stranraer; we were mates, and we're sitting at the table and we're looking at the menu card and not being able to speak French. Willie decided that he would have a go.

We couldn't speak French or anything like that but with a bit of sign language and pidgin French and English being exchanged, we realised that we were in a 'hostelry' that was offering more than just coffee.

We were wanting eggs and chips and this young girl came over and asked us what we wanted to order. Willie, in his pidgin French was doing his best to make her understand what he was wanting, and, in the end, he had to ask for it in English.

She put us right with better English than we had.

Once our eyes adjusted to the dim lighting inside, you could tell that there was a bustling trade going on.

We sat down for a while as others were battering with youngish French girls on what was on offer; after a while some of us remembered what our sergeant major sternly told us about what was contactable in such places, and the perilous condition that that may leave you in and so on.

While some, around us succumbed and stayed, I and my mates paid our bill and left for more the loftier pursuit of sight-seeing in this historic city, as we were having a good laugh over what we saw in the café, and then started our way back to camp.

By now it was early evening, and we found a Church of Scotland restroom.

At least it offered a common language, even if it was in pitch perfect BBC English.

There was one particular young girl there who seemed to take a keen interest in us and turned her head from serving tea and cakes towards us on hearing our accents. She came over to talk to us and she was a stunning beauty, very posh accent but clearly Scottish.

She sat down with us for a while and chatted to us, her name was Marnie MacLachlan, and she was in nursing at the time and when she was off shift, she would come down to the Restroom and speak to the British soldiers.

It was only after the war that I found out who she was.

When I moved to Glenbranter I discovered that she was the owner of a neighbouring highland estate on the shores of Loch Fyne, the clan seat of the MacLachlans. During the war she had succeeded to the title of Clan Chief on the death of her father.

Next day we were on a troop train to Amiens.

After three days in Rouen, we were on the move again as our train slowly meandered through the countryside toward Forges-les-Eaux and Amiens. We continued to rattle through the French countryside and by now the sun had burned away the early morning mist to reveal some beautiful farming countryside redolent with spring growth that was by now tipping into the early summer.

The train drew to a halt at a little village called Saveaumare where we were all ordered off the train and lined up on the platform in good order. We shouldered arms and fell-in as we had a 5-mile march ahead of us. Marching north through the French countryside seemed quite agreeable although it was rather warm; we were not being rushed and after a couple of hours we reached a little hamlet just outside the small town of St. Saens.

The terrain was fairly flat and near St. Saens a huge supply depot came into view bustling with activity, officers, and NCOs, barking orders and all manner of vehicles being loaded and unloaded coming and going with the instruments of war.

We spent a few days there doing fatigues, moving items from A to B and then back again from B to A in typical British Army fashion. Then the balloon went up, the Germans had finally pushed west on a broad front.

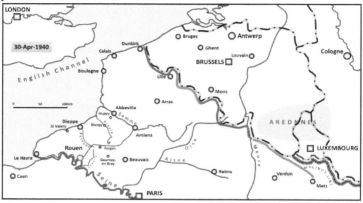

Map 1 :Opening Allied Position on the Eve of Fall Gelb

On the Saar Front a number of German aircraft passed over the 51st positions on the night of 09-May heading towards targets well behind the front line and in the morning, news arrived that the Germans had crossed the Dutch and Belgian borders. The Germans attack at several point on the Saar Front and these were driven off. Up and down the front-line troops were ordered to stand too, but the day passed quietly, meanwhile French and British troops themselves moved forward into Belgium to blunt the German advance.

The codename Operation David initiated the British part of the Dyle Plan. The British vanguard, spearheaded by the armoured cars of the 12th Royal Lancers, crossed the border at 1 p.m. on 10-May, cheered on by crowds of Belgian civilians who lined their route.

For months the BEF had been deployed along the Franco-Belgian border between Armentieres and Maulde. The BEF performed a rapid advance across strange country to pre-planned positions which had been photographed from the air but had not been reconnoitred.

This involved complex movements and required careful planning if it were to be carried out smoothly and without congestion of traffic on the roads; and the move might take some days to complete. But British plans for an advance to the Dyle had been carefully prepared and rehearsed and as a result all went well.

The 12th Lancers arrived first followed by other dragoon detachments, and the armoured reconnaissance units allocated to I and II Corps reached the Dyle that night and deployed across the front between Louvain and Brussels. These were all mechanised but still fulfilling the old role of a cavalry screen moving ahead of the main force.

My battalion, which I was about to join, 1st Battalion KOSBs followed with others and were greeted warmly by the Belgian people and saw nothing of the fear and confusion which was soon to choke the roads with refugees. Whereas I was stuck at St. Saens south of the Somme doing supply depot fatigues.

One unit of the 3rd Division had a frontier barrier closed against them because they could not show the faithful but ill-informed Belgian official in charge "a permit to enter Belgium."

But they charged the barrier with a 15cwt truck, and the advance of the division proceeded.

The remaining BEF divisions were positioned to provide defence in depth all the way back to the River Escaut. The riverbank to the north of Louvain was already occupied by Belgian troops, who refused to give way to the British, even when General Brooke appealed to the King of the Belgians and had to be ordered out by General Georges.

In Belgium, German glider troops captured Fort Eben-Emael by noon on 11-May and the disaster forced the Belgians to retreat to a line from Antwerp to Louvain on 12-May, far too soon for the BEF and French 1st Army to arrive and dig in.

Within two days of the start of hostilities, on 12-May General Heinz Guderian's Panzers were overlooking the banks of the river Meuse having travelled 100km from their start position.

Meanwhile in central Belgium the first tank battle of the war was playing out on 12-May around Hannut between the German 3rd and 4th Panzer Divisions and two French armoured divisions; French Sumas and Hotchkiss tanks overwhelmed their German counterparts, destroying large numbers of their Panzer I and II tanks (Chen, 2008).

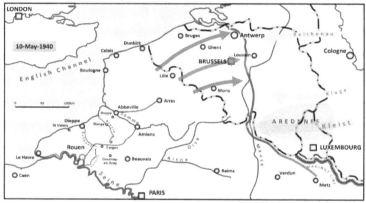

Map 2: Allies Respond and move into the Low Countries.

As Rommel's 7th Panzer Division joined Guderian on the Meuse the bridges had already been destroyed. Rommel immediate set about trying to establish river crossings that were initially unsuccessful due to a very heavy response by the French on the other side of the river.

We were stationed more than 300km away in the huge British depot in St. Saens, and we knew nothing of the dire situation unfolding on the front and in many respects it all still seemed so far away.

Approximately 120km up the front line at Louvain the British and the French were hard pressed, now that it was becoming apparent that the main weight of the German attack was coming through the Ardennes. In the early hours of 13-May heavy artillery fire opened on the central and northern sectors. It lasted for half an hour and was answered by French and British artillery.

As soon as the German artillery stopped, they attacked along a Saar sector south of the Ardennes. The 2nd Seaforths and the 4th Black Watch held their ground. North of the Grossenwald the enemy made other attacks, but these too were defeated. While in the French sectors were attacked.

Early next day heavy shelling preceded renewed attacks on the and fighting at close quarter lasted for several hours. All attacks were defeated except a small lodgement in the north of the Grossenwald. Two hours later a third barrage was laid down by the enemy and a third attack followed.

Meanwhile, my regiment in Belgium with the aid of our artillery broke up the enemy concentrating in Hermeswald orchards and pursued the retreating formation. The KOSBs were holding their own.

South on the Saar Front shelling and machine-gun fire renewed on the 14-May, but the attacks were half-hearted, and driven off. In and around the Grossenwald the 7th Argyll and Sutherland Highlanders (Argylls) spent the afternoon burying enemy dead.

The first organised German attacks commenced on the BEF's front on 15-May, the reconnaissance troops of three German infantry divisions having been dispersed on the previous evening to their positions. Attacks on Louvain by the German 19th Division were repulsed by the 3rd Division. Further south, the river was only about 4.5m wide, enough to prevent tanks from crossing but less of an obstacle to infantry. During one attack at the south of the BEF line, Richard Annand of the Durham Light Infantry earned a Victoria Cross. German bridgeheads across the Dyle were either eliminated or contained by British counterattacks helped by my own 1ˢᵗ Battalion KOSBs (Thompson, 2009).

By 15-May the whole of the British front line was engaged with the enemy as the Germans made small penetrations that were quickly cleared by counterattacks. Next day the Germans made a more determined attempt to take Louvain preceded by a two-hour bombardment that gave them initial success, this time the KOSBs pressed home a counterattack to restore the original line.

While the British held the line, their French allies on the right flank were so pressed that a 5km breach in their front line occurred. The French only restored their position by shortening their defensive position by withdrawing in good order to restore and close the breach. Things were much more serious on the British left flank as catastrophe overtook the Dutch, Belgian, and French positions which were becoming increasingly pressed in that sector.

Within five days the Commander of the Dutch Army ordered a ceasefire; Holland had surrendered.

On 15-May the whole of the British front between Brussels and Louvain was quiet except in the extreme north where a heavy attack on the neighbouring French sector spilled over on to a post held by the 5ᵗʰ Gordon Highlanders, who drove off the first assault but were eventually overrun (Ellis, 1953).

In the south things looked much more serious.

The Germans took advantage of French strategic inaction on the front facing the Ardennes, which they deemed as impractical to armoured attack.

The Germans had other ideas.

Here the French Army was in a much weaker position due to strategic French thinking wedded to the conventional wisdom of expectation that any German attack would come through the Low Countries via Holland and Belgium.

This meant that the better-trained French troops and armour were in that part of the front. The Germans had put all their best assets against the French on the Ardennes front.

The Manstein Plan was one of the alternatives used to describe the plan of the German initial strategic moves to gain a quick decisive victory in the opening phase of the battle for France in 1940.

The original strategy was a compromise between various schools of conventional wisdom at the time and as such satisfied no one and left General Halder the Chief of Staff at OKH (Oberkommando des Heeres) in a rather isolated position. In effect, Halder's version had been overtaken by the learning gained in Code Weiss, the invasion of Poland the previous year.

One does wonder if Halder's plan was compromised deliberately.

What didn't help Halder either was the unfortunate circumstance of the plan falling into Belgian hands in the Mechelen incident of 10-Jan and the plan was therefore in need of some major revision. Each revision giving more emphasis to an attack by Army Group A through the Ardennes, which progressively reduced the offensive by Army Group B in the north through the Low Countries to that of a diversion.

The final version of the plan, diverted the main thrust of the German invasion through the Ardennes, the weakest part of the Allied line, where the French defence was left to second-rate divisions on the assumption that the difficulty of moving men and equipment through such difficult forested terrain would give the French plenty of time to send reinforcements if the area were attacked.

The French 7th Army was the most powerful part of the French strategic reserve was committed to the north to defend a German rush through Belgium and join with the Dutch Army as part of the Allied deployment plan (Jackson, 2003).

On the Saar Front there had been some action and patrolling across the front line, but on 10-May the Germans opened an artillery barrage; the 51ˢᵗ withstood a heavy attack in the area of Grossenwald. To conform with the French, the 51ˢᵗ was ordered back to the next line of defence. On the afternoon of the following day further small attacks on posts of the 4ᵗʰ Black Watch were all repulsed. And on the 12-May complete calm rested on the whole front.

The next day the expected attack began in earnest.

News from the French front grew worse by the hour. The breach of the Meuse front led to further withdrawal of the French 1ˢᵗ Army, my battalion along with the rest of our troops east of Brussels were threatened by a dangerous salient on either side of Louvain.

On the night of 16-May the French 7ᵗʰ Army (to the left of the British line) moved south.

The outline of the strategy to withdraw was to move back to the starting positions on the Belgian border. Belgium had been lost due to the German offensive through the Ardennes and pressure on the Meuse. A breach was inevitable, and a response became more urgent.

British General Headquarters (GHQ) knew little of these German moves; indeed, even less about what was happening on the French front. Throughout the campaign, information of what was happening to the French was scanty, vague, contradictory, and often inaccurate.

What became very apparent, very quickly was that a huge gap had formed in the French front and was growing bigger and the German penetration deeper.

GHQ had no information that any effective steps were being taken by the French to close the gap. The area in which the breach on the French front occurred was quite outside the area of Gort's responsibility, defined anew in an order issued on this day by General Georges (Ellis, 1953).

This order described the southern boundary of the territory to be held by the BEF as running back from Maulde, through Orchies, Raches and Henin-Lietard (8km east of Lens).

This whole series of movements back to the start positions on the Belgian border was bedevilled as much by the lack of information from the French as that that was self-inflicted by a poorly designed communication of intelligence at Gort's HQ that hampered the transmission to the frontline in time to be used effectively.

The Germans followed up closely the Allied withdrawal but did not press any advantage.

What was the point at this stage?

The main thrust was further south as the Germans crossed the Meuse and benefitted greatly from the lack of a coordinated Allied command structure whose main difficulty was in effective and efficient communication of information and intelligence.

By now the Germans were in more or less open countryside heading west straight for the Channel coast.

On 17- May Brussels fell.

From our depot at St. Saens on 18-May we were detailed to go to Amiens on the Somme where there was another depot at Saleux, in an attempt to shore up the breach on the French front and stop the German dash to the Channel. Supply lines to the BEF in the north from the Somme, at this stage, remained open as we reached Amiens.

Around 02 p.m. a train up ahead of us carrying the 7th Battalion Royal Sussex Regiment (RSR) stopped at St. Roche station, 2km outside of Amiens, as it coincided with a heavy air raid on Amiens by the Luftwaffe.

We were further down line by about 5km.

As our train drew to a halt on the edge of a wood between Creuse and Prouzel to the west of Amiens, we began to get up and stretch our legs and move around and as we looked out of the windows in the carriage, we could hear the air raid.

It was the first time I had ever heard the scream of a Stuka.

Away in the distance we could see them drop out of the sky into a vertical dive and as they did so their siren started off as a low-pitched noise that increased to a crescendo, a scream in intensity as it gathered speed heading for its target.

Suddenly you could actually see a little black dot drop from the underside of the Stuka and the noise of the siren would quickly tail off in intensity as it pulled out of the dive.

As the bomb struck its target there was a mushroom shaped plume of smoke could be seen rising.

It was the first time that any of us had seen such a thing and it left a deep impression on most of us.

German pilots had always selected troop trains as priority targets and consequently a Stuka targeted the train that the Sussexes were in up ahead of us and bombed the train. One bomb fell on the engine tender and another on the first coach which contained all the officers.

For us the bombing of the train effectively prevented any further movement northwards.

In the bombing, eight officers were killed, and some were wounded, including the commanding officer. He ordered the battalion to de-train and to withdraw some 700m to the north of the railway as he felt that it would be safer to have the men deployed until the line was cleared.

Later he moved the men to higher ground in case the Stuka dive bombers returned, which they did at 4 p.m. and bombed the train again. After the first raid, rescue parties had been organised and the killed and injured were removed from the train. The number of casualties, including the eight officers killed, was eighty.

Of the 581 men that boarded the train at Buchy, the remaining 500 now took up defensive positions each side of the Poix to Rouen Road. The ground they occupied was rising ground, slightly wooded with some farm buildings and a few hedgerows breaking up the open ground. Here the Sussexes waited, not expecting any direct confrontation.

Just after 5 p.m. the train bearing the 6th Battalion RSR approached the St. Roche station but as another air raid was in progress the train was stopped.

Amiens was taking a bit of a pounding.

At the end of the raid the Sussex train was switched to the up line and passed through the station. At the sight of the damaged train the men of the 6th Battalion did not connect it with that of their sister Battalion, the 7th, as their train proceeded into the marshalling yards.

Later the train started off again but the track ahead had been badly damaged, so no further progress would be possible for some time. The Sussex train was switched to the south side, and it passed us going south in the opposite direction.

It then went on to Paris and further on to Nantes and St. Nazaire where the men worked stacking petrol and stores until 17-Jun.

Similar problems were faced by the train we were on. Our train engine began to shunt us back down the line heading back to the main depot at St. Saens.

On the way back we were ordered off the train at Serqueux and trucks took us to a sub-depot at l'Epiney near Forges-les-Eaux the depot was hidden under nets, canvas, and trees in the Bois de l'Epinay forest.

We were billeted in an orchard where there were a large number of bell tents.

The team or the detachment I was with was placed under to orders of a sergeant. I have no idea where he came from. I'd never seen him before but he was in charge and kept an eye out for curfew to make sure there were no lights, not even a cigarette could be seen.

As we were lying down in the bell tents every now and again, we heard something falling onto the canvas of the tent making small dull thuds.

"Is it raining?", asked one of my mates.

I said, "Don't be silly, it's the middle of summer and it's been belting hot all day."

We both got up and went outside as if to confirm the fact, it turned out that in the orchard there are big beetles, and they were in the apple tree above us. They we're dropping off the apple tree and hitting the tent

Next day we were outside the tent and the sergeant had his own chair alongside a small table and one hit him on the head and bounced off and went down behind him on the chair.

He jumped up startled and said to me, "Get it!"

I dived at it with the rifle and bayonet and attacked the chair with the beetle on it and upended everything, chair, table, the lot.

"Idiot!" he said sorting through the debris.

We had a good laugh over that.

This rural idle all seemed far away from what was unfolding around Amiens.

As things turned out that would not last long for us.

General Guderian's troops pressed their advantage on 19-May and besieged Amiens and by now were more or less rampant along the north bank of the Somme capturing Amiens at 9 a.m. on 20-May, Abbeville at 1900 hours, and Noyelles-sur-Mer on the English Channel coast at 10 p.m..

At 16:00 hrs on 19-May the enemy appeared and gave battle until 18:00 hrs when they disengaged, and overnight regrouped and made good his losses.

In the meantime, things were not looking great for the 7th Battalion RSR.

At 03:00hrs 20-May, the enemy re-appeared, coming from the east. A column of motorised infantry accompanied by tanks approached the positions of the 7th RSR. Their positions had previously been detected and noted by German spotter planes. The Germans had decided that it was essential to eliminate this possible threat to their advance.

It should be remembered that the 7th RSR, in common with all battalions of 12th Division, had very few arms. Each man carried a rifle and 50 rounds of ammunition and their experience of handling these was very limited.

The battalion's supply of ammunition was minimal as no effort had been made by their divisional staff to ensure that they were properly equipped before they were sent into battle.

Nevertheless, the 7th RSR engaged the enemy as if they were a well-founded battalion. The enemy was quite unaware of the weakness of the force against them. From behind every bit of cover these gallant but doomed men fought their one-sided battle. A lucky shot from one of the few anti-tank rifles put a tank out of action.

This caused the enemy to become wary.

The German infantry deployed heavy mortars and a battery of field artillery was bought into action to add to the deluge of shells being poured out by the encircling tanks.

Against the Germans, the 7th RSR had 6 Boyes anti-tank rifles with 32 rounds and 10 Bren guns.

The ammunition was soon gone; there was no reserve, they had no mortars and no artillery support or signals platoon to help them.

When the fire from the 7th RSR slackened, the enemy was reluctant to advance for the kill, so they called up the Stuka dive bombers to help them.

The outcome was never in doubt.

As the afternoon wore on the casualties increased, and finally at 20:00hrs with every round fired, the survivors reluctantly surrendered.

Of the 581 men that had left Buchy on 18-May, only 70 men survived.

Not even during the murderous engagements on the Somme or at Passchendaele in World War I had any unit suffered such casualties.

Their sacrifice had not been in vain: It so discouraged the enemy from penetrating south of the Somme that it had saved their sister battalion, the 6th RSR, from a similar fate and that of a Moroccan Regiment that was not far off. Of those men taken into captivity, the adjutant of the battalion, a Major Cassels, had refused to raise his arms in surrender and was promptly shot.

During the action Sergeant Glover (Carriers) shot down two Stukas with a Bren gun. He would have had three, but in the confusion of battle he forgot to remove the safety catch and the target had passed by before he realised his error. The 7th RSR had delayed the advance of the German Army Group 'A' for nearly a whole day.

The Allied lines of communications had effectively been cut between those fighting north of the Somme and the logistics and communications lines south of the Somme where we were.

Effectively the BEF had been cut in two.

At the same time Rommel's forces surrounded the British frontline troops of the BEF at Arras.

For us the transport situation between the Somme and our bases was becoming increasingly confused. The roads were hugely congested, and progress was made with great difficulty owing to the huge congestion of traffic, the flight of refugees, interference by enemy bombing, and such trains that came through from the north were largely filled with French and Belgian troops.

The roads were thronged with civilian refugees and a varied crowd of troops and transports moving away from the battle area as the Germans thrust forward along the north side of the Somme valley.

Brigadier Beauman was unable to communicate directly with BEF GHQ in Arras or to discover whether any attempt was being made by French or British troops to establish a line of resistance on the Somme (Ellis, 1953).

After taking Amiens and Abbeville, the Germans pushed out south of the Somme to create bridgeheads at those points. The appearance of their patrols was enough to cause the wildest rumours to circulate and to spread alarm, for the want of exact information.

By 23-May the Germans reinforced the bridgeheads with their motorised infantry and consolidated their positions to gain a firm hold on the Somme crossings.

To answer this threat at the bridgeheads Beauman took steps to strengthen the defences of the rear area south of the Somme for which he was becoming increasingly responsible for.

A small mobile force, the "Beauforce," was formed consisting of the 2nd and 6th East Surreys who were under orders to join the 51st on the Saar. The 4th Buffs were added as machine-gun platoons along with the 212th Army Troop Company and Royal Engineers.

A second "Vicforce" (Karslake, 1979) was also formed, and consisting of battalions raised from reinforcements in the infantry and general base depots with officers and men available, though shortage of arms and equipment severely limited their deployment as a fighting force.

By now I hadn't a clue as to who I was fighting with and only a little less clue what I would be fighting for.

Things must have been bad.

By now I was stationed was in and around Forges-les-Eaux immediately south of the Somme and constituted the northern district of our lines of communication; it contained two sub-areas at Dieppe and Rouen which were of prime importance to the BEF up north from Belgium to the Saar.

The Dieppe location was the chief medical base, with valuable medical stores. Le Havre was a different proposition entirely as the main supply base, with large quantities of supplies and ordnance stores distributed to sub-depots in the St. Saens/Buchy area, northeast of Rouen, and up the line where I was now stationed, in a large forest at Bois de l'Epinay near Forges-les-Eaux next to a large railway junction, halfway between Rouen and Amiens at Serqueux.

Beauman's operational responsibilities were the security of the BEF supply line depot's in and around Le Havre and Rouen and forward supply lines all the way to the British troops on the Belgian frontier. In addition, he had operational security of RAF airfields in north-east France

Troops available to him came from specialist corps such as the Royal Engineers, the Royal Army Ordnance Corps, and the Royal Corps of Signals; formations of older men, fit only for garrison duties; and soldiers who arrived late and required further training.

That would be me.

Our situation was an unhappy story, relieved only by the loyalty of our intention to do what we could with all we had until larger forces could re-join the battle.

General Hoth's Panzers reached Arras on 20-May and received orders that the town should be bypassed and therefore isolate the British within it.

He ordered Rommel's 7th Panzer Division to move to the west flanked by the SS Totenkopf to the east.

The following day the British launched a counterattack, deploying two infantry battalions supported by heavily armoured Matilda Mk I and Matilda II tanks in the Battle of Arras. The German 37 mm anti-tank gun proved ineffective against the heavily armoured Matildas; however, once a battery of 88 mm anti-aircraft guns was called in the British withdrew (Anon, 1939: Key Dates, 2013). This short reversal unnerved the Germans.

By now south of the Somme, Beauman was labouring against an operational vacuum in the absence of any firm command structure. In extremis, he decided to use what troops remained in organising a defensive position along the rivers Bresle, Bethune, and Andelle. In turn, from east to west, none of these are large rivers in the summer, but together they provide a fairly effective tank should the Bresle be crossed.

To improve the defensive position, orders were given to prepare the bridges for demolition and to erect obstacles where needed.

Meanwhile the 1st Armoured Division under the command of General Evans had arrived in France. Advance parties had reached the neighbourhood of Arras where it was originally intended to concentrate the division, when the approach of the Germans slicing down the north bank of the Somme made it clear that this would be impossible as Le Havre was rapidly being rendered unusable by enemy bombing and mining.

This was the first armoured division ever to be formed in the British Army (Evans, 1942-1943). Its arrival in France was haphazard to say the least. It arrived in Cherbourg one tank regiment short; without supporting artillery; it's infantry support was in Calais; deficient of some wireless equipment; and it had only a small supply of spare parts, no reserve tanks, and no bridging material. It comprised 114 light tanks and 143 cruisers.

An inauspicious start to motorised divisional warfare that didn't instil much confidence in the rest of us.

German armoured divisions reaching Boulogne and St. Omer confirmed their hold on the Somme valley forming a new front facing us to the south and cutting the supply lines to the BEF in the north and its main base ports at Cherbourg and Le Havre.

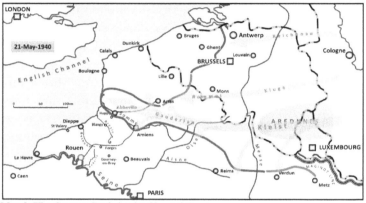

Map 3: The German Dash for the Channel Coast

During the evening of 21-May General Evans received a message from GHQ which instructed him to seize and hold crossings of the Somme from Picquigny to Pont Remy inclusive, and concentrate the remainder of the leading brigade in rear areas south of the Somme.

When this had been done, he was to prepare to move either eastwards or northwards according to circumstances to operate in the German rear area towards the BEF north of the Somme valley.

It was pie in the sky as far as we were concerned as we did not have the troop resources in terms of numbers, armour, nor training for this kind of frontline combat

A few hours later Lt-Col Briggs arrived by aeroplane bringing a confirmation of these instructions. On arrival at HQ in Rouen, he digested the reality of latest intelligence defining the German held crossings of the Somme and was feeling their way towards the Seine crossings towards Rouen.

We knew the situation was very fluid and changing rapidly by the hour. It's just that the reality on the ground seemed to bear no relationship to what they were looking at on the map table in GHQ in Rouen.

It was all getting a bit lively around where we were.

On a road junction between Neufchatel and Forges-les-Eaux two of us were sent to a T junction and it was kind of hilly part, the hills weren't that high, but we were put up among the bushes on the top side of a road bank where our sergeant said, "Dig in and look for Germans coming dressed as nuns and if we see any nuns coming along the road, we were to shoot them."

I said, "Really!"

We were supposed to be in this foxhole so we took the top six inches of turf off and we could not get any further. In the heat of summer, the chalk underneath was as hard as iron.

My mate said, "Can we not use our grenades to loosen the chalk?"

I said, "Don't be daft, that will only attract the attention of the nuns."

Tanks, rail parties, HQ staff of the 2nd Armoured Brigade, and one armoured regiment deployed south of the Seine and moved east with all speed to the Lyons-la-Forêt area 12km south of Forges-les-Eaux. This would place them in a position to prevent German armoured units penetrating the line of the lower Andelle towards Rouen, or from interfering with the assembly allied reinforcements.

Once back at base, life was getting very busy in the depot.

Having brought up motorised infantry divisions the Germans gained a firm hold on the Somme bridgeheads across the Somme at Amiens and Abbeville right opposite us.

GHQ cut off in the north were desperate to see the bridgeheads reduced to re-establish communications to the south west and cut off the advanced German units in the Somme valley and help to relieve the threat to the BEF, but by now this task was quite beyond the powers of the 1ˢᵗ Armoured Division, especially so as it had not yet formed and concentrated it position, its ground support group and a regiment of tanks had already been sent to Calais, and they had no artillery support.

To General Evans it was clear that such an operation crossing over the Somme without artillery their armoured infantry units was an extremely hazardous enterprise. Yet the order he had received left him no option, and he issued orders for the move forward.

It didn't help that General Georges had a different interpretation of what the 1ˢᵗ Armoured Division should do. He informed the Swayne Liaison Mission at his HQ that "While the 7ᵗʰ Army advances to the north across the Somme, the task of the 1ˢᵗ Armoured Division was to mop up enemy elements in the area south of Abbeville." (Karslake, 1979).

On this being reported to GHQ, Gort (who had no information about the position on the Somme) replied, "Consider it essential that armoured division ... should carry out its proper role and not be used to chase small packets of enemy tanks. The division should carry out the task already set it and make itself felt in the battle." (Ellis, 1953).

The right hand did not understand what the left was doing or indeed may even have wanted to do what was needed.

By now a third opinion intervened in this fog of war.

The French 7ᵗʰ Army was commanded by General Altmayer, and he was directed that the 1ˢᵗ Armoured Division was under his command and it had been given the task of covering his left flank in an attack on Amiens. This was countermanded by the

Swayne Mission who confirmed that the division was not under Altmayer's orders and would carry out the task already given.

To the ordinary soldier on the ground, we were just left scratching our heads.

The 2nd Armoured Brigade on arrival south of the Seine was moving up with all speed to join their brigade. They arrived early in the morning of the 24-May at Hornoy and Aumont, on the road between Aumale on the Bresle and Picquigny on the Somme. They had covered 120km and then prepare for battle in the twenty-four hours since they deployed south of the Seine.

At the same time General Evans ordered the Bays to move forward to the Bresle from Aumale to Blangy, and while this move was taking place, he was informed that the enemy was acting defensively on their Somme bridgeheads. As the Germans concentrated their efforts with the main German tank attack taking place north of the Somme at Arras.

It was now clear that the Germans were simply holding the line of their left on the Somme while their right flank dealt with what was left of the BEF north of the Somme.

It was probably on this basis that on 24-May, Hitler issued a halt order in the sure and certain knowledge that his own troops were exhausted having covered and gained so much ground since 10-May, and on intelligence received on the inevitability of an evacuation of BEF that did not warrant aggressive German movement. As by now German casualties had been heavy.

He wasn't wrong.

As by now the situation had deteriorated to such an extent that General Karslake landed in France on 22-May with instructions from General Ironside to save priority equipment without alarming the French. Priority was given to evacuate anti-aircraft guns that would be urgently needed for the defence of British cites should France fall.

Blimey, our lives depended on these officers!

So, the ground was seemingly being laid for a large-scale evacuation.

My pal said, "Who knew, eh?"

By 25-May Allied forces, British and French alike, were retreating on Dunkirk as Calais was hard pressed by the Germans and surrendered the next day as by now had many other channel ports of choice.

Without informing the French, the British began planning on 20-May for Operation Dynamo, the evacuation of the BEF.

Just as well we didn't take offence at this little gem of information being denied the rest of us to the south of the Somme, the French were in good company. Ships began gathering at Dover for the evacuation as early as 20-May, and it must be said, a full day before the British commenced the Battle of Arras.

And I said to my pal, "Who knew indeed?"

Meanwhile Admiral Ramsay was laying down plans at naval HQ below Dover Castle.

Immediately, Brigadier Whitfield was sent to Dunkirk to start evacuating personnel. Overwhelmed by what he later described as, "a somewhat alarming movement towards Dunkirk by both officers and men," due to a shortage of food and water, he had to send many along without thoroughly checking their credentials. Even officers ordered to stay behind to aid the evacuation disappeared onto the boats (Atkin, 1990).

Something that I witnessed first-hand during Fall Rot, but more of that later.

By now Beauman had under his command a Squadron of Royal Engineers and a light anti-aircraft and anti-tank regiment (though the anti-aircraft units were without Bofors guns) (Ellis, 1953).

A wag in our company said, "Strange to have an anti-aircraft unit without, eh, anti-aircraft guns."

By then an advance party of the 2nd Armoured Brigade had driven forward during the night and reached Airaines 6km south of the Somme and immediately lost two tanks to mines as they tried to seize the bridge near Longpré. Bridges in the sector were either mined, blocked, or guarded, while the road along the western bank was unpassable.

That said, an attack was ordered on the crossings at Dreuil, Ailly and Picquigny, an attack by such small and dispersed force was doomed to failure.

At Ailly however, the 4th Border Regiment managed to get two platoons across the river though the bridge was blown, but unsupported by tanks stuck on the other side of the river they were eventually withdrawn. Neither of the other assault parties succeeded in reaching the river, owing to the strength of the Germans holding bridgeheads.

Several tanks had been destroyed in the process, and the 4th Border Regiment suffered considerable casualties by the time the attack was abandoned.

It was a salutary lesson on the German's determination to hold onto their gains.

That night the 4th Border Regiment retired to a wood 12km south of Ferrières, while the Bays remained in observation of the country between Ferrières and Cavillion.

Late at night 24-May General Evans received orders from GHQ modifying the role of the 1st Armoured Division, emphasising the need to cooperate with the French, and ordering him to hold on to his present position.

By now the 51st was being transferred from the Saar and on arrival on the Somme Front would form a group with the 1st Armoured Division, whose first task would be to take up a covering position from Longpré east of Abbeville all the way to the channel coast in the west.

General Georges also told the commander of the 3rd Army Group that the 1st Armoured Division were to hold the line until the 51st arrived, and further, "to establish small bridgeheads and prepare all bridges for demolition."

Men in the ranks murmured, "Really?"

"Was there any intelligence worthy of the name at HQ?"

This was a quite unrealistic order as the line of the Somme was firmly in German hands, and their bridgeheads extended five or 10km south in some parts of the river in this sector. Confirmation of this from GHQ stated that the enemy was not only reliably reported to be entrenching themselves but had strong patrols, including light armoured cars between this line and the Bresle.

To us at Forges-les-Eaux, the Bresle line was looking alarmingly porous.

Again, General Georges issued orders addressed to the French 3rd Army and "la Division Evans" repeating instructions and adding that enemy bridgeheads already established were to be eliminated.

My mate Johnny laughed, "Are they working for the Germans?"

It did make me wonder.

The War Office in London endorsed the situation confirming this arrangement concluded, "...consider defensive attitude south Somme quite unsuitable role this juncture. Suggest employed both 1st Armoured Division and the 51st offensively and go all out." (Ellis, 1953).

When this suggestion was made, it was not yet known at the War Office that by now Lord Gort was being forced to send these divisions preparing for the attack on the bridgeheads southwards to fill the widening breach between the BEF in the north and in the south; as well as the French inability to stage an effective attack from either the north or the south of the gap.

Nor was it known that the Germans, now preparing for Fall Rot, regarded their hold on the Somme and on the bridgeheads which they had established as of prime importance and that day by day they had been strengthening forces north and south of the river where they could, by 25-May they already had two divisions there, facing south from Amiens to the sea, with others moving up.

As soon as it was known that the 1st Armoured Division (and the 51st when it arrived from the Saar) were to come under French orders, General Evans went to see General Altmayer and received verbal instructions that on the following day, 26-May, the 2nd Armoured Brigade would concentrate in Biencourt, 10km east of Gamaches to be ready to support a French Cavalry Division in an attack on the German positions; while the 3rd Armoured Brigade would go to Buigny, 5km east of Beauchamps and await orders.

Orders for an attack on the Abbeville bridgehead were issued at 9 o'clock on the morning 26-May.

It must have looked promising.

It was planned that the 2nd Armoured Brigade would capture high ground south of the Somme from Bray-les Mareuil to Longpré overlooking the Somme immediately southeast of Abbeville. The French would supply artillery and infantry support. The 3rd Armoured Brigade had as its objective the high ground covering the northern sector of the Somme from Rouvroy to St.-Valery-sur-Somme. There also the French were to supply support to the attack.

The extent of the German bridgehead at this time was as far west as Grébault Mesnil with patrols running between them and Eu on the Bresle with anti-tank weapons in position.

General Evans explained to the commander of the French 3rd Army, General Besson, and General Frère commanding the French 7th Army that the British tanks were designed to exploit open warfare and not to support infantry in breaking through prepared positions and that they should be compared with those of a French light mechanised division and not with those of a French armoured division. They had assumed heavy tanks.

The advice went unheeded.

On 27-May the attack was launched.

The attack was scheduled to start at 05:00hrs, but the French artillery were not ready, and the start time was delayed by one hour. The delay meant that there had been no time for careful reconnaissance and only vague information about the German strength and positions were available. The country between the Bresle and Somme is an undulating plateau with steep sided valleys carrying with small streams, mostly dry in the summer, running down to the Somme to the north or the Bresle in the south.

There were any number of small villages and hamlets in the steep wooded valleys accessed through open cultivated fields on the higher ground. The outposts of the German bridgehead covering Abbeville were in fact as far out from the river as Moyenneville, Huppy, Caumont and Bailleul, and in each they had anti-tank guns hidden in the woods and well dug in.

The German positions were well prepared and would blunt the attack to good effect, especially so without the support of infantry and artillery. And this did not seem to be forthcoming in anything like the quantity needed for such an action. Add to this the fact that cooperation with the French divisions was ineffective, and close mutual support almost non-existent.

On the right wing the tanks made little progress, and in trying to do so suffered severely from anti-tank guns in Caumont and Huppy that caught them at close quarters as they crossed ridges of open ground. On the left the 3rd Armoured Brigade found less opposition outside the enemy's Abbeville bridgehead and reached the high ground overlooking the Somme near Cambron and Saigneville and the outskirts of St.-Valery-sur-Somme at the mouth of the Somme river.

There were no supporting troops to occupy the ground with them and when it was learned in the afternoon that the French were taking up defensive positions behind them at Behen, Quesnoy-le-Montant, and Brutelles the tanks were withdrawn.

Nothing effective had been achieved.

Heavy Cruiser tanks were used, but without supporting infantry and artillery and as a result many tanks were lost in the attack against very well-prepared defences. The distance travelled since they were first deployed south of the Seine took its toll in the battle. Out of the sixty-five tanks lost fifty-five of those were due to mechanical failure because of the lack of maintenance and spare parts. The supply line logistics were no match for the requirements of the Cruisers.

This was one of many setbacks, and so, it started under the codename Operation Dynamo, the Allied evacuation of 340,000 troops from Dunkirk, began 27-May and lasted until 04-Jun attracting the ferocious attention of the Luftwaffe.

If the evacuation was making a deep impression on the minds and hearts of those back home, it was making an even bigger impression on us who were to the south of the Somme front. And as the nation gave a collective sigh of relief, the evacuation only heightened our anxiety as to what was going to happen next. And as the Germans were standing on the cliffs taking holiday pictures across the Straits of Dover, the German planners were already turning their attention to Fall Rot.

But the south coast of England now seemed vulnerable with the enemy now in sight of the cliffs of Dover and that they might attempt at any moment to invade England.

Thankfulness merged with tense anxiety, and the nation turned with new fervour and concentration to preparation for defence.

That it should come to this, comparatively little public attention was being paid to what was happening in France after Dunkirk.

Approximately 140,000 of us were still there!

Operation Fall Gelb (Operation Yellow) was more or less concluded, Operation Fall Rot was about to begin.

The Allied forces, contrary to popular belief, enjoyed a numerical advantage, and their equipment was not inferior to that of Germans. Take armour, for instance, the French and the British had 3,383 tanks, while Germany's invasion force had only 2,445.

It was the way they were used that made the difference.

The Germans did not waste those inter-war years.

The Allied tanks were not inferior, either; the French Char B1 tank was mobile and packed ample firepower, but inept tactics deployed them ineffectively, and fritted them away. Two distinct advantages the Germans had were radio and field commanders' freedom to make decisions.

All German tanks were equipped with radio to allow coordinated action on the battlefield, while only 20% of Allied tanks had them. General Kluge, commander of the German 4th Army, commented on the freedom of the German field commanders when he said, "...the most important facet of German tactics remained the mission directive, allowing subordinates the maximum freedom to accomplish their assigned task. That freedom of action provided tactical superiority over the more schematic and textbook approach employed by the French and English." (O'Neill, 2010)

In the week beginning 27-May during the mayhem and destruction in and around Dunkirk, we were by now firmly cut off south of the Somme.

By now the 51st had been taken out of the Saar line and moved to Étain between Verdan and Metz then Varennes-sur-

Seine south of Paris where they learned that the Germans had broken through the French lines separating them from the rest of the BEF.

After a period of indecision, when the next task for the division was unclear, a 500km road and rail move brought the 51st to a position overlooking the Somme at Abbeville.

As the BEF retired from Dunkirk, it was left to the 51st to fight with the French Army as part of the French IX Corps and initially to hold a line northwest of Abbeville to the coast.

The 51st was thinly stretched over 50km, holding a line of the Somme from Erondelle around Abbeville to the sea, and without any mobile reserves. While attempts were made to reduce the German bridgehead at Abbeville on the south side of the Somme this kept us busy in the supply depot back at Forges-les-Eaux.

Belgium finally surrendered to the Germans and King Leopold III was interned.

Next day, on the 28-May the German defences at Abbeville were being tested by the French who made ground on both flanks of the bridgehead and gained ground up to the Somme River, they were unable to move the centre of the German salient at Abbeville or St.-Valery-sur-Somme.

General de Gaulle's 4th Armoured Division arrived, a much more powerful formation than the French partially horsed cavalry divisions which had so far been employed, though it had suffered heavily in earlier actions.

The next day the division attacked on an axis either side of the Blangy/Abbeville Road but soon ground to a halt by well-placed anti-tank defences in the woods and on the ridge running northwest from Villers-sur-Mareuil. De Gaulle suffered the same fate as the British, he had little artillery support and there was no infantry to consolidate ground won and very soon had to give up his gains.

There was no surprise.

Nevertheless, De Gaulle attacked again on the following day this time supported two other French divisions on the ground. Again, and obstinate German resistance did not give way for the same reasons. The lessons were gradually being appreciated that against well prepared positions, mobile armour alone could achieve little. At the end of four days fighting the enemy's bridgeheads remained untaken.

While these abortive attempts were being made to recover the Somme bridgeheads and the BEF in the north was withdrawing into Dunkirk, the 51st had been arriving on the Bresle from the Saar front. Their journey was completed on 28-May, and divisional HQ opened at St. Léger, 10km south of Blangy.

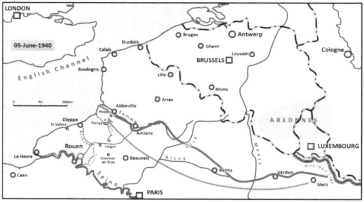

Map 4: By 05-Jun the 51st Highland Division are on the Somme Front at Abbeville.

Regarding any sense of a command structure the British generals were liable to receive fresh orders from the War Office, either directly or through the Swayne Mission based on out-of-date intelligence. A situation that was to only get worse.

For supplies, what was left of the BEF south of the Somme was dependent on the British lines of communication which, with all other troops in the area, were now under the command of General Karslake. These troops were organised into improvised formations collected by Beauman, 'Beauforce', 'Vicforce' and 'Digforce'. The latter had been formed from reservists and on 31-May these forces were formed into an improvised Beauman Division.

To us on the ground it was all as clear as mud and I for one did not have a clue as who was in my line of command and I was beginning to forget that I was supposedly still a soldier in the 1ˢᵗ Battalion of the KOSBs, which by now were back across the Channel having a nice cup of tea in Blighty.

A few of us thought, "Cheers lads!"

By now we had two British forces south of the Somme, the 51ˢᵗ and 1ˢᵗ Armoured Divisions, under French command, and Beauman Division (me?) and other lines of communication troops under the command of General Karslake (may even have been me also, who knew?). The former took over a position on and in front of the Bresle making ready for yet another attack on the Somme bridgehead in conjunction with French divisions.

Main fighting elements of the Beauman Division held a defensive line behind the Bresle, on the Andelle and Béthune rivers covering Rouen and Le Havre to their rear, from which an evacuation of non-fighting troops and surplus stores and equipment had already started.

The British Government seemed determined to rebuild the BEF as quickly as possible after Dunkirk, but to all it became obvious that this would require time. Rather cynically only a small fighting force could be sent and regarded as evidence of British intentions rather than a substantial contribution to the battles ahead.

And all the while the British were ramping up their evacuation plans looking to repatriate non-fighting troops surplus to requirements who worked on supply line logistics and other professions who had been formed for an army far greater than the one the British intended as resident in France.

The huge supply depots at Le Havre and Rouen that I was first stationed at on arrival to France at the beginning of May-1940 had already been significantly reduced by simply not resupplying.

The writing was already on the wall, but some chose to ignore it.

Much of what was in the deport had by now been dispersed to the rapidly formed improvised units that now made up the Beauman Division. These supplies had been held in reserve but were now urgently needed and as dispersal continued it became evident that moving the tons of reserve ammunitions held in the Buchy area was way beyond the capabilities of existing depot transport and manpower.

Nevertheless, on the line now occupied by the 51ˢ opposite Abbeville things were beginning to liven up.

A column of troop transporters proceeded through Rouen to Neufchatel and a rendezvous in the Forêt D'Eu. A perimeter was formed of anti-tank positions on all roads, and the forest in this area was very thick and gave good cover from air but was intersected by second class roads and rides running parallel to each other in all directions.

Orders were received that an armed reconnaissance was to proceed through Blangy across the Bresle to the village of Le Translay.

Reconnaissance of this village was to be made with a view to proceeding to that area and taking up positions to hold the village and protect the crossroads there on the main Abbeville Road.

Information on the enemy in this area was vague but they were known to be in Huppy some 10km east of Le Translay. The French were also going to attack Huppy.

No enemy was seen in the area of the village and the reconnaissance was carried out successfully. Orders were issued to move to Le Translay. While information was received, a French attack on Huppy that afternoon was completely successful.

As these abortive attempts were being made to recover ground at the Somme crossings, the BEF in the north was being evacuated to Britain, and the 51st had arrived in the Bresle area from the Saar front.

All the while the French armies south of the Somme/Aisne line were regrouping and moving up towards the southern flank of the German break-through, and divisional HQ opened at St. Léger aux Bois, 12km south of Blangy, on 28-May.

In preparation for a coming assault to reduce the German bridgehead at Abbeville, orders were received that the positions either side of Le Translay all along the 51st line would take a central position in the assault with the Seaforths right at the centre. The Seaforths carried out a recce of Grebault-Mesnil during the afternoon as troops filtered forward and were in position shortly before darkness fell.

A tank-proof perimeter for the village had been laid and an HQ established in a farmhouse near the centre of the village. Other Highland regiments of the 51st took similar position all the way to the Channel coast.

The battle would last four days.

And all the while troops were being evacuated from the beaches at Dunkirk.

The fact that the French had made little use of the 1st Armoured Division was probably due to earlier instructions issued by General Georges following representations made to him by General Evans.

As Georges' instructions made clear to French commanders the ways and means of the proper employment of the British, pointing out that the British division was a light mechanised division rather than an heavy armoured division of light tanks very lightly armoured and therefore vulnerable against enemy anti-tank guns (Karslake, 1979).

The Evans Division therefore was to be used as a unified tactical group comprising the 51st and the 1st Armoured Division limited to operations on the French left flank facing the Somme.

That simple statement does little to explain the convoluted chain of command that now existed south of the Somme.

To illustrate this point: the French 7th Army was under General Frère, as part of the 3rd Group of Armies and formed the left wing of Georges' command, which were deployed south of the Somme/Aisne line. The 7th Army, in turn, included a group of divisions commanded by General Altmayer, and the 51st like the 1st Armoured Division was included in the IX Corps (Ellis, 1953).

Thus, the chain of command in this area was as follows:
General Weygand (Supreme Commander)
- ↘ General Georges (Commander North-East Front)
- ↘ General Besson (3rd Army Group)
- ↘ General Frère (7th Army)
- ↘ General Altmayer (10th Army)
- ↘ General Ihler (IX Corps)
- ↘ General Evans (1st Armoured Division)
- ↘ General Fortune (51st)

And yet, in London Chamberlain and Halifax argued in Parliament debating continuation of the war.

We heard that Churchill won the vote. "So, I won't be going home anytime soon." I said to my mates.

It was now apparent the British government desire to rebuild the BEF as quickly as possible, after Dunkirk, became obvious that this would require time.

The decision was made that only a small fighting force could be sent in the near future. This would be regarded in the first instance as evidence of British intentions, but secondly, and secretly by the British, a much-reduced contribution to the battle that lay ahead.

One fellow commented, "Can't wait to receive the train and boat tickets."

Commanders of the 51ˢᵗ were at a conference at Huppy which had been bombed early that morning.

A French commander informed that the French were holding Moyenneville, Bienfry, and Behen.

The French were to attack with tanks from these positions that afternoon, and he wanted the Seaforths to be standing by ready to move to Behen and support the French in stemming a counterattack by the enemy should the French attack be a failure.

The 51ˢᵗ replied that they would prefer to move into position at Behen before the French attack was launched in order that they in position to support the French should the attack fail.

The Seaforths moved forward into position and existing French HQ was taken over. The French attack commenced with tanks unsupported, again, by infantry or artillery.

The progress of the attack was watched by the Seaforths in Behen, and its failure was soon evident.

German defences were strong and took heavy toll on the advance French tanks. As darkness fell, disorganised bodies of Frenchmen started to come back through the village together with the surviving French tanks.

The general information supplied by these men was that all their officers were dead and that there were no Frenchmen left in Moyenneville.

As operations were now beginning to unfold south of the Somme front the Navy developed contingency plans to mop up the relatively smaller fighting groups that remained in France. They involved the evacuation of surplus men and material from the Dieppe - Le Havre coast immediately behind the Somme front line; and at Cherbourg, Brest, St. Nazaire, and La Pallice further to the west.

Although overall the Navy's capabilities had not been impaired it had sustained losses at Dunkirk and at Lofoten as these had to be replaced it did render a complicated task more difficult. Despite the losses the Navy had inflicted on the German fleet, which left them with insufficient strength in surface ships to contest the Channel between France and England.

It was the sheer size of the task that provide the logistical problems, trying to evacuate smallish groups of fighting troops from several locations along 1,000kms of coastline required a number of simultaneous flotillas on escort duty was even beyond the capabilities of the Royal Navy.

For unexplained reasons, some seven German submarines were stationed off the west coast of France, but while these evacuations were in progress, they made no effort to intervene as had been the case in the operations off Holland. Only the Luftwaffe tried to make evacuation impossible.

By the end of 31-May all medical stores had been cleared from Dieppe and a demolition party had been landed to destroy the port installations should that become necessary.

This event did not bode well for those of us stuck behind the Somme line. In the depot we were reflecting, "That if we need a sticking plaster, we need to find a chemist shop."

As Weygand was very much intent on reducing the German bridgeheads south of the Somme, he had abandoned any hope of a successful attack north from the Somme line. His priority now was to prevent the expected German thrust south and west towards Paris.

General Georges decided after a few days' pause for reorganisation and regrouping around the Abbeville bridgehead, determined that an attack on the Abbeville/St. Valery-sur-Somme bridgehead should be renewed early on the morning of 04-Jun.

Certain structural changes in the command and Army structure were taking place in both French and British armies in the area. General Altmayer's group in the French 7th Army now became a separate 10th Army, still under his command and still including the French IX Corps, the British 1st Armoured Division, and the 51st.

General de Gaulle's division was however withdrawn (except for the divisional artillery) and in its place two new French divisions, were brought into the 10th Army.

All this going on as the by now General, Beauman had reorganised the improvised fighting units into the Beauman Division, with its own HQ, three infantry brigades, a regiment of anti-tank guns, a battery of field artillery, and other divisional services.

But to what end?

As it was at this point the British government informed General Karslake that all improvised forces should be disbanded and evacuated to England, and only sufficient lines of communication troops kept in France to continue to supply a British force of one armoured division, four infantry divisions, and an air striking force for the immediate future.

But General Georges pointed out the importance of retaining the Beauman Division on the Andelle/Béthune line.

Their withdrawal would, he said, have, "an unfortunate effect on the French Army and the French people." (Karslake, 1979).

The War Office accordingly agreed to their remaining.

By now we were openly talking about, "our fate being sealed."

Back up at Abbeville German shelling was fairly active during the morning of 02-Jun on Moyenneville and enemy mortar positions were located in front of Moyenneville, and in a valley immediately in front of the village.

Germans were also observed making defences in haystacks and on the high ground to our immediate front.

A very successful artillery barrage on these operations was arranged and the enemy were observed rapidly evacuating their haystack.

The Camerons replied to the German mortar fire with fair success. Orders had now been received that the Seaforths would be relieved by the Gordons on the night of 02-Jun.

The Gordons arrived at HQ while enemy artillery had been shelling Moyenneville and the exits from Behen periodically during the morning.

Unfortunately, a party of Gordons going up to the area was caught by an enemy concentration between Behen and Moyenneville. Their leader was killed, and the other two men were wounded. The enemy continued shelling and mortar fire at intervals during the afternoon. Enemy mortar positions were located and successfully shelled.

As it was growing dark, about 100 of the enemy were concentrating in the hollow to their front and they were expecting to be attacked. Moyenneville was again shelled while the British shelled the hollow the Germans were in.

The Gordons were now arriving to take over the Seaforths' positions and guides from companies had reported the enemy now started shelling behind Behen near British artillery positions and to the rear exits to Behen.

Things were getting a bit hot around here.

The attack on the Abbeville bridgehead was now in the planning in the opening days of June, the 51st, with some composite regiments and what remained of the Support Group of the 1st Armoured Division were relieving two French divisions in the forward positions facing the Germans' Abbeville/St.-Valery-sur-Somme bridgehead in preparation for the projected renewal of the attempt to recapture them.

Of the 51st, and brigades 152nd and 154th held forward positions, while the 153rd was place in reserve on the Bresle between Senarpont and Blangy. The 15km stretch of the Bresle on their right was held by an anti-tank battery and a company of the Kensingtons and their machine guns, with the composite regiment from the 1st Armoured Division behind them. In the 25km stretch on the 153rd Brigade's left was the 6th Royal Scots Fusiliers.

Wonder if my old RSM was with them?

The Support Group of the 1st Armoured Division held a flanking position between Aumale and Forges-les-Eaux. The Beauman Division was disposed in the 90km stretch between Pont St. Pierre southeast of Rouen near the junction of the rivers Andelle and Seine to the coast at Dieppe.

Thus, we had one territorial division (51st), one improvised division (Beauman), and a fragment of the 1st Armoured Division, distributed over an eighteen-mile-wide front, 80km of the Bresle and 90km of the Andelle/Béthune line.

In the late afternoon of 03-Jun the road from Blangy to St. Maxent was closed to the 51st to allow the French to bring forward their troops, tanks, and guns from the Bresle.

The battle would begin early the next day, but ammunition for the French Sumas was late in arriving, and the attack was postponed.

All through the short night the road from Blangy was hugely congested with refugees, but before daylight it was clear again, and the French tanks had their shells.

At 3 o'clock on 04-Jun the Allied artillery laid down a barrage on the German positions, and half an hour later Allied tanks and infantry, French and the 51st, advanced towards their first objectives.

Their goal was the scarp ground overlooking the water-meadows from Caubert on the right to the Cambron woods to the west of Abbeville. The Camerons attacked Caubert and the wooded ridge called the Hedgehog.

In the centre the French with their tanks, and the Seaforths under French command, would make for Caesar's Camp to the east of Abbeville on the north end of the Mont de Caubert, and try to clear all the country between the two main roads that lead to Abbeville,

The Gordons, on the left, would attack from Cahon and the Cambron woods and the spur overlooking Cambron. The task of the 154th Brigade, on the extreme left, was to prevent the enemy from reinforcing his bridgehead (Linklater, 2007).

Troops were rested during the morning, but a warning order was received for an attack by the 51st with the French on 04-Jun.

On that 04-Jun a low summer mist developed over the lower Somme valley, shrouding the tanks and troops from distant observation and shielding their movements.

A barrage from the artillery opened up to cover the French tank attack in the right centre and came down on the woods around Bienfay and Villers where there were known to be German outposts.

After ten minutes the barrage lifted, and though the heavy French tanks did not appear, the Seaforths set about their task of clearing enemy posts in the forward edge of the woods with their usual efficiency.

Reconnaissance parties went forward to the Camerons, south of the main Abbeville Road and opposite the Bois De Villers. The attack was carried out under difficulties as the enemy was very close and was active with mortar and machine-gun fire.

The attack was launched in five different phases:

1. A barrage opened on the Bois De Villers to cover the noise of the tanks coming forward and was lifted gradually to the other side of the Somme.
2. French heavy tanks followed the barrage and captured the high ground of the Mt. Caubert and Caesar's Camp.
3. The Seaforths attacked the Bois De Villers to clear it of enemy as far as its eastern extremities which was their final objective.
4. French light tanks followed the Seaforths advancing on each side of the Bois De Villers were to attack the Mareuil Caubert and consolidate on this objective.
5. This necessitated the northernmost Seaforths wheeling right after having cleared the northern side of the Bois de Villers, to bring them into line with the others to the south to attack the high ground of Mareuil Caubert.

French Dragoon-Portés were to advance through Seaforths and to follow the heavy tanks to the Mareuil Caubert and Caesar's Camp and hold this ground until the arrival of the slower moving infantry.

It was stated that air cooperation would be available for the attack and that the bridges over the Somme were to be bombed. The French were to be responsible for all artillery liaison and support.

The morning of 04-Jun was exceptionally quiet, and a fine June dawn was just breaking. The barrage commenced and sounded exceedingly effective.

The Seaforths attacked the Bois De Villers and encountered little resistance.

Two French heavy tanks now appeared and advanced to the right of Bois De Villers.

There was no sign of the light tanks, and the Seaforths were preparing to move forward without them, when at the last gasp they arrived on our right flank, and the Seaforths moved off with the light tanks following.

Although there was some success the late arrival of the tanks meant that they had missed the cover of the barrage and as they advanced between the Blangy/Abbeville Road and the woods near Villers they came, first, upon an undetected minefield and, shortly after, under heavy fire from field and anti-tank guns well sited and dug in.

An advantage lost.

A few tanks were lost to the minefield and subsequent casualties from gunfire were severe, but some reached the base of the Mont-de-Cambron ridge and some made it to Mesnil Trois Foetus, from which they drove the enemy.

No tanks had arrived on the front on the left, but a Frenchman reported that they had gone to the north of the Bois De Villers and would be picked up there.

The Seaforths allocated there then went forward on the north side of the Bois De Villers. They found no sign of French tanks but continued their advance.

We do not know why the French tanks were late, and the number which eventually turned up was far short of what we had been told to expect. But the result of this delay meant the loss of all protection we might have had from the barrage, and the loss of the dawn light.

It was now much lighter, and the enemy was shelling the Abbeville Road and the north side of Bois De Villers causing several casualties to the Seaforths. The advance on both sides of the wood continued.

As the Seaforths continued their advance through an orchard to the north of the Abbeville Road, two heavy French tanks had been hit by enemy artillery and were on fire and in flames.

The Seaforths were to follow up the attack supported by light tanks, but again they had to wait until three of the latter eventually turned up and then they went forward on the south-eastern side of the Villers woods.

They soon came under withering machine-gun fire from Mont de Cambron, but despite mounting casualties strove vainly to reach the heavy tanks. But they and the tanks they tried to reach had shot their bolt. The latter had suffered crippling losses, and when they were ordered to retire to the position held in the morning, six out of thirty heavy tanks returned, as did 60 out of 120 of the light tanks.

Things had gone no better in the left centre. The only regiment of the French 31st Division deployed made little progress as they were held almost from the start by enemy troops dug-in in the woods west of Mesnil Trois Foetus.

The Seaforths left the cover of the orchard and proceeded to cross the open ground in front of the Mareuil-Caubert to make their final assault but were caught by heavy machine gun fire on their right flank which caused enormous casualties in them. All officers were killed

Two more French Suma tanks arrived in the area and also a Dragoon-Portés. The officer commanding told them the situation and asked their co-operation to dislodge the machine-gun nests on the right front.

They showed very little enthusiasm and wouldn't even attempt to make a look to see where they might be able to help. After a great deal of talk and private conferences amongst themselves they re-entered their vehicles and went off in the direction of Zallieux from where they had come not long before.

The front of the wood was however being subjected to heavy machine-gun fire and the enemy seemed to have very good observation of this area.

The Seaforths were in the eastern edges of Bois De Villers. The British artillery not wishing to rely on the French, had sent forward an armoured observation vehicle that did excellent work trying to bring ground-fire onto the anti-tank guns and machine-gun posts, but his wireless was very soon jammed by the enemy.

German dive bombers commenced systematic dive bombing of our line from the Camerons area and the orchards in the Seaforths area including the front edges of the Bois De Villers at Villers Sur Mareuil. This bombing although extremely nerve racking did not produce very many casualties as the Seaforths had consolidated their position in the orchard and had a good position.

The Seaforths were told to hold their ground at all costs and were told that further orders would be issued regarding further action. When they came, they were told that the line was to be withdrawn back that night.

They would withdraw to les Alleux. Enemy shelling activity and bombing had quietened down on their positions and shells were falling on back areas and on the crossroads at le Croisette and French troops would relieve them.

The Camerons were also to withdraw from their objective south of Cambron. The whole position found the Germans well dug-in with machine guns. At one point advancing German infantry were encountered and there was hard fighting in the standing corn.

Two platoons did indeed succeed in fighting their way into Cambron but they could not be supported and were cut off. The following day the Camerons fought their way back into Cambron and retrieved the two platoons.

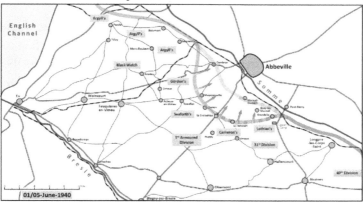

Map 5: Abbeville Bridgehead 01/05-Jun-1940

Only the 153rd Brigade's attack further on the left flank was successful. There, the Black Watch not only held their line in the Cahon Valley they then pushed forward and established themselves in the Petit Bois to cover the flank of the Gordons.

The Gordons themselves moved from Gouy and drove the enemy out of the Grand Bois, and reached the high ground at the eastern side by noon.

Objectives achieved the Gordons were keen to press on, but higher ground northwest of Cambron was still in German hands and their advance remained checked and the ground won became untenable.

To their great disappointment they were ordered to give up their gains and return to their starting point.

The desire to reduce the Abbeville bridgehead was a strong one. The Germans had been holding it and extending it slowly for a fortnight now and they continued to build their defences at an almost leisurely pace without much interruption.

The Allied troops had no opportunity for adequate preparation.

The Gordons and their supporting artillery had arranged a system of signals that was a potent factor in the reduction of German machine-gun positions.

In the rest of the battle no similarly successful cooperation was achieved, and in its absence had much to do with the failure of tanks and infantry to overcome the enemy defence in the centre and on the right flank as it did to poor communication between the French and the British.

For the rest, insufficient preparation, and consequent faults in the coordination of forces largely accounted for the failure of the action.

Chiefly it was due to bad communications between British artillery, armour and infantry, the French suffered the same affliction; a convoluted chain of command; attendant with poor intelligence regarding the true strength of the German bridgeheads had been well underestimated.

North of the Somme only pockets of resistance were left to by mopped up by the Germans outside of the British salient centred on Dunkirk.

Back on the Channel coast, by the end of the night on 04-Jun Operation Dynamo was complete and a grateful nation rejoiced in its deliverance of 224,686 British and 121,445 French and Belgian troops being evacuated to Britain.

In just 26 days the Germans had swept through to the Channel coast, and I found myself on the south side of the Somme, cut off from my battalion in the north which by now had been evacuated back to Britain on 31-May.

In a little over two weeks the Germans had shattered the armies of France and ejected the BEF and as the initial German invasion Fall Gelb drew to a close the Germans bombed Paris.

Churchill delivered his, "We shall never surrender," speech to the House of Commons.

The Battle for France was far from over for us, but back in London there was little appetite for it.

To the south of the Somme, we fought on.

Chapter 3: Fall Rot – Second Battle for France

We waited, but we did not have to wait for long.

At 9 o'clock in the morning of 4-Jun the last of the French northern armies who had not been evacuated surrendered at Dunkirk.

All depended now on the troops who barred the enemy's progress southwards.

Our attempts to reduce the German bridgeheads on the south side of the Somme did not succeed; by now the Germans were strengthening them as operation Fall Gelb came to an end.

Operation Fall Rot (Operation Red) was about to begin.

Throughout the last week of May the Germans had been busy outside of their bridgeheads at Abbeville and Amiens. German spotter planes were up in numbers carrying out reconnaissance, and as the flights grew in number, we could tell from the ground that the Germans were going to turn their attentions towards us in the south.

As early as 25-May, General Weygand had seen little hope of a successful defence of the Somme/Aisne line and had advised the French government that the desirability of asking for an armistice should be discussed with the British government. He had also told them that he did not consider possible a retreat from the Somme/Aisne line, as a breach of that long, thinly held front would make it impossible to continue useful military operations.

It was thus with a heavy heart, inadequate forces, and in a mood of inevitable defeat that the French High Command waited for the opening of the final battle.

For such defeatist talk we could easily have been shot.

All the while the Germans prepared.

The German plan for Fall Rot had been set out in an order issued by OKH on 31-May over the signature of the Commander-in-Chief General Brauchitsch.

The purpose of the German Command was to annihilate the allied forces resistance that still remained in France by means of Operation Fall Rot following Operation Fall Gelb as rapidly as possible.

They knew that operational allied reserves in considerable numbers no longer existed. Their assumptions now held that all they need to do was to break down under heavy assault the hastily constructed enemy front south of the Somme and the Aisne and then carry out rapid deep penetration to prevent the Allies from carrying out an ordered retreat or from forming a defence line in their rear areas.

My view at the time was, "Nice to know that my future lay in good hands?"

Fall Rot employed all three German Army Groups A, B and C and their reserves. In all, nine armies and 140 divisions, of which 137 were to actually be used, were available.

It was nice to know that the Germans were saving the best for last. My reputation obviously preceded me.

At a conference on 02-Jun Hitler expressed his belief that "the French and English have at most sixty to sixty-five divisions left against us" which was not far wrong. He was less accurate when he added, "doubtless Weygand will withhold an operational assault group which is to be sought in the area of Paris and eastwards. It must also be expected that the enemy will settle down and prepare resistance further south."

Given the nature of German confidence in the outcome, the reality was that there remained forty-three infantry divisions (some only in course of formation), three armoured and three cavalry divisions albeit greatly reduced in strength by the fighting;

and the equivalent of thirteen fortress divisions in the Maginot line and on the Swiss frontier.

The attack of the German right flank on the Somme, where the French 10th Army was alongside the only active front line remains of the BEF would be involved, was to be made by the German 4th Army. Their orders read, "4th Army (two armoured divisions, six infantry divisions, one motorised division, 11th Motorised Brigade and 1st Cavalry Division) will attack from Abbeville/Amiens area and defending their Paris flank will advance towards the lower Seine. The army will take early possession of Le Havre and the bridgeheads at Rouen, Les Andelys and Vernon."

Further advances across the lower Seine in a southerly or south-westerly direction was to wait for special orders.

While on the south side of the Somme, on the eve of 05-Jun General Fortune of the 51st wrote a strongly worded letter to General Marshall-Cornwall, who had been appointed by the War Office to coordinate the actions of the British divisions.

Due to the exertions of the 51st on the Abbeville bridgehead, he pointed out the condition of his men and the length of his front, he asked, "...that half my front be take over at once by someone—that I be authorised with my neighbour [the French 31st Division] to retire on the river Bresle."

But there was no one who could take over the ground on this front he wished to vacate.

The battle for Abbeville mauled the already thin British and French troops. The attacks of the 1st Armoured Division, cost the British 65 tanks, and another 55 were lost to mechanical failures. While the French lost 105 tanks and by 04-Jun Franco-British forces suffered about 1,000 casualties, fifty other tanks and assorted armoured vehicles on this Somme front.

The most that General Marshall-Cornwall gained from the French 10th Army was an agreement to retreat to the Bresle and allow the 51st to hold the new from the sea to Gamaches, shortening their front by 20km, and that the French 31st Division hold the line from Gamaches to Senarpont.

In the early morning of the 05-Jun, opposite the positions held by the British, the German divisions assembled on the Somme went over from the defensive to the offensive along a line running from Mareuil-Caubert south of Abbeville to St. Valery-sur-Somme near the sea.

When the BEF was fighting for survival at Dunkirk the decision to operate RAF sorties from Britain seemed reasonable. Fall Rot now moved the conflict south further away from the Kent airfields and the fighters would have to use airfields in France to refuel and rearm for this fresh assault.

Arrangements were made with the French for the use of three airfields northwest of Paris and two south of the Seine.

Just prior to this latest attack Air Marshal Barratt's HQ brought together an improvised collection of ground staff, servicing sections, armourers, defence units, and transport; and in the last week of May airfields were brought into use by the fighter squadrons of the Advanced Air Striking Force based in Champagne. The England-based squadrons were at that time busy over Dunkirk and for the moment had no need to use the French airfields.

So long as the Dunkirk battle in the north absorbed almost all available air strength, stronger forces could not be supplied for the fighting south of the Somme.

This small fighter force was at first retained in England. But Barratt, with good reason, questioned the practicability of such remote control, but the plan was adhered to until the German offensive southwards started on 05-Jun.

The most that can be said with certainty is that bombing of columns and communications and what patrols there were over the fighting area north of the Somme did some damage to the enemy, but not enough to stop them bringing forward their forces.

The RAF did hinder movement to weaken or interrupt Luftwaffe assaults, but they could not stop them either.

In the two days which preceded the opening of the enemy's new offensive, the German air force again designed its bombing attacks to weaken the Allied defence. They carried out attacks on sixteen French airfields, five depots, airports, and several aircraft factories near Paris.

On the ground, the night of 05-Jun passed quietly for us in the rear depot except for some sporadic artillery fire in the distance, but there had been a number of incidents indicating that the enemy was garnering itself for a new offensive, and about 4 o'clock in the morning the Germans did just that, attacking all along the 51ˢᵗ front line on the Somme.

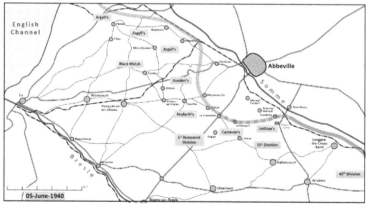

Map 6: Somme Front Line at 05:00hrs 05-Jun-1940

Their first thrust came from the bridgehead at St.-Valery-sur-Somme. In the villages of Saigneville and Pende, the Argylls came under heavy attack by German infantry who had plenty of artillery and mortar support, while more of the enemy's troops pressed forward through the open country between the two villages.

The Argylls villages were too far apart for the companies to give each other support, and although the Argylls fought with their usual dogged resistance they were forced back or gradually overwhelmed. Mounting casualties and dwindling ammunition, and the superior numbers of the enemy, were too much for the village garrisons.

The villages of Saigneville, Mons-Boubert, Catigny, Pende, and Tilloy were all lost in quick succession in the late afternoon.

The Argylls Battalion HQ at Franleu by fast moving German infantry as nearby Mons and Arrest were being attacked. The only reserve available was a Battalion of the Black Watch who were ordered to move on Franleu to relieve the pressure on the Argylls HQ, but the enemy gained momentum and continued to advance and were only held up when the Black Watch arrived.

Another company of the Argylls went to the rescue of Battalion HQ, but they were themselves cut off and surrounded in the outskirts of the village.

In the evening Col Buchanan of the Argylls had sent away four crowded truckloads of his men, including many wounded, but he, Capt. MacInnes, the padre, along with the wounded remained and were later overwhelmed (Ellis, 1953).

The last man to leave at 18:00hrs stated that the enemy mortars were still landing around the HQ and all the buildings and trucks were on fire.

The liaison officer and about 30 wounded men remained in the cellar with Capt. MacInnes and Col Buchanan. Other wounded and many dead had had to be left out in the posts where they had been hit and there may have been isolated parties of men who were unable or unwilling to leave.

Surrounded in the outskirts of the village, the company which had tried to rescue this hard-fighting HQ held out for more than twenty-four hours, as the German tide of battle swept past them and left them deep behind the enemy's new front line and they too were soon overcome.

What remained of the 51st's 154th Brigade, and they were very few, were back that night on a new front that lay between Woincourt and Eu some 15km to the southwest.

By nightfall the Argylls had been fighting hard since early morning. German Stukas, mortar, and artillery fire in coordination with their infantry were used to good effect. The Argylls were gradually driven back until they held a front which ran from Toeufles through Zoteux to Frièreille keeping in contact with the Black Watch at Feuquières-en-Vimeu.

At which point the German attack gradually came to a halt with the help of British artillery and machine-guns. In the evening, as the German infantry had drawn off, the 153rd Brigade positions were again shelled and mortared.

Further to the right the French 31st Division astride the Blangy/Abbeville Road fought doggedly, but by the evening they were forced back to the Behen/Limercourt/Limeux line, continuing thus the line held by the British 153rd and 152nd Brigade on their left and right respectively.

During the day the 152nd had been forced back between Oisemont and the Blangy/Abbeville Road.

Finally, the Lothians, doing flank guard to the 51st, met the full weight of the enemy's opening attack at Bray-les-Mareuil early in the morning, and after fighting all day fell back in line with the British 152nd Brigade to the country east of Oisemont at Fontaine-le-Sec.

The composite regiment of the 1st Armoured Brigade had several minor engagements at threatened points and had several tanks knocked out. In the evening they assembled at Beauchamps midway between Eu and Blagny-sur-Bresle.

The men of the 51st had themselves been the attackers throughout the first few days of June. They took severe casualties amid a gruelling and unsuccessful experience. They needed above all things a good night's sleep. But 05-Jun had hardly dawned when new and yet more gruelling fighting began.

Map 7: Somme Front Line at 21:00hrs 05-Jun-1940

The next day on 06-Jun there was indiscriminate shelling and dive-bombing activity by the Germans during the morning, but no casualties as yet reported although fairly heavy shelling was concentrated on the La Croisette crossroads. Very little other activity during the morning.

All ranks were extremely tired after the attack and the days preceding it and had had practically no chance of decent rest for days. During the morning Camerons passed through our frontline sections heading back to Huppy. In the early afternoon Huppy immediately to our rear was heavily bombed.

Various adjustments were made during the night and when the second day of the German offensive opened the 51ˢᵗ and the French 31ˢᵗ Division held a line which ran from Oisemont to Woincourt and from there to the Bresle just south of Eu.

I remember the weather very well.

It was high summer, and the days were long and blazing hot.

After all the exertions the soldiers on the frontline had had but little rest, and they were to get none this day. Mostly they were too busy even to eat, dive-bombers roared down on their positions, and they were shelled, mortared, and machine-gunned.

They were attacked by infantry who outnumbered them, and while they held off their immediate attackers, they saw other enemy columns bypass their strongholds and penetrate their front.

Often it was impossible to evacuate their wounded.

Sometimes it was impossible to get away themselves when retirement was ordered as troops on their flanks had fallen back and left them exposed. The villages they defended were peopled only now by disconsolate dogs whose owners had forsaken them, and cattle bellowing to be milked.

It was a doleful sight, even if it was the best of summers.

The Highlanders fought as Highlanders do, as their casualties bear witness.

In the first day of Fall Rot the Argylls lost twenty-three officers and nearly 500 others either, killed, wounded, or missing, the whole division was cruelly mauled.

The task before them in resisting their foe was beyond their powers and that of any frontline division.

They and the French 31st Division had been made responsible for the defence of a 70km front. What this meant can be illustrated by one example.

The 1st Black Watch had to defend a 70km front of broken country, dense wood and deep sided valley heading either to the Somme to the north or the Bresle to the south.

An impossible task for any battalion when the enemy had the numbers and modern weaponry of this so-far victorious German Army.

They did their best.

Heroism lay all around us in this part of the battle, the heat of high summer was scorching as small platoon, companies, and battalions held their ground for as long as they could to give others a chance to retreat or bring relief to other similarly hard-pressed groups as they themselves fell back to fight another rear-guard action in another position.

The British artillery worked their guns till they were 'red' hot to protect infantry positions and routes of retreat and hinder and harry the German advance, while they themselves became vulnerable as they maintained forward positions so long that they too were nearly engulfed, and when orders to withdraw reached them they needed all their skill to get the guns away.

We worked like beasts of burden in the depot areas loading trucks with bullets, shells, fuel, and food. I had never worked so hard in my life trying to keep the frontline supplied in the hope that they would keep the enemy at bay at some point.

The RAF give little help to the Allied troops engaged.

Indeed, since I had come up the line to Amiens and then back to Forges-les-Eaux, I don't recall seeing a single RAF plane. Plenty Jerry planes but none of the much-vaunted RAF that I was so desperate to join as a youngster.

Rare As Fairies was an increasingly used term to describe their absence.

The 51st sent urgent requests to RAF HQ at Boos asking for protection against the Luftwaffe bombers, but the three squadrons of fighters that they were supposed to have on paper were on this day reduced to a total of eighteen serviceable aircraft. They had themselves lost four in battle that morning.

Information suggested that the Germans were planning a big air attack on targets in and around Rouen itself. Important industrially it was also a focal point in road and rail communications, and a centre of military and air activity for both the French and the British. Most of our supplies at Forges-les-Eaux were coming up the line from Rouen.

I never saw any of this, but some of my mates in the evening were talking of a great show they witnessed down at Rouen that day. No. 1 RAF Squadron was on early patrol and, together with French fighters, engaged a very large formation of German bombers strongly protected by Messerschmitt's.

A bitter dogfight ensued that saw some of the enemy come down as others dispersed, whiles others managed to steal through the menagerie and bombed the military camp and airfield at Boos. In the evening another German formation went overhead to finish off the afternoon work and were met by another RAF squadron, this time enough of the enemy got through to additionally damage the main bridge across the Seine at Rouen, a power station, railways, and factories at Sotteville.

Along the Aisne front that very same day the RAF had twenty-four Blenheim's attack German transports behind the new battlefront in a determined attempt to support a hard-pressed French frontline, that night the enemy concentrations behind the front, along with their lines of communications in France, oil targets, and marshalling yards in Germany were attacked by 103 bombers, of whom three failed to return.

So, the RAF was still in the fight supporting us, apparently?

Now things were getting a bit serious.

There was a huge increase in traffic coming and going from our supply depot. Huge amounts of stores were coming up the line from Le Havre, Rouen and the main depot at St. Saens. As soon as they arrived, we were detailed to unload the trucks as quickly as possible and check stores against paperwork.

The Army loves its paperwork.

No sooner had we done that than it had to be redistributed to the ever-getting closer front line.

At the opening part of the new campaign the Wehrmacht was 60kms away to the north at Abbeville and there was little chance of us being able to see or hear anything of the activity around the Abbeville bridgehead they had established.

By the end of the first day of Fall Rot the Wehrmacht had reduced that to 50km and there was an increasing amount of activity over us and unfortunately it was not the RAF or French Airforce either.

To help cope with such a situation, a number of improvised decisions were being created. Some such as the Beauman Division had already been formed on 18-May and being provisioned and ordered into a loosely constructed defence force by a very energetic Beauman.

Men of the 4th Battalion Border Regiment were tasked to take up defensive positions as early as May 1940. This battalion was tasked with defending the BEF lines of communication and as Beauman's Division began to enlarge, they became the 'A' Brigade of the Beauman Division

By 29-May, three formations had been formed and combined to form Beauman Division and Beauman himself was promoted to acting Major-General commanding.

The use of the word 'division' caused some difficulties with the French high command as their definition led them to believe they were supported by artillery, engineers, and signals in the same way as a regular division.

We were in fact a rather motley collection of largely untrained troops armed only with light weapons.

Beauman placed these forces in defensive positions along the rivers Béthune in the north running up to the Channel at Dieppe and the Andelle that ran south and entered the Seine between Rouen and Paris. This line would defend Rouen and Dieppe from the east.

Waite's Rifles was the final group we were in, I think?

By now the situation with these improvised forces looked like this (Karslake, 1979):

'A' Brigade 'Beauforce' (tasked with Line-of-Communication defence) contained:

- 4th Battalion, The Border Regiment (detached to 1st Armoured Division by 06-Jun)
- 5th Battalion, The Sherwood Foresters
- 4th Battalion, The Royal East Kent Regiment (The Buffs)
- 6th Battalion, Duke of Wellington's Regiment (attached from 46th Division on 06-Jun)
- Brigade Carrier Platoon
- 'D' Machine Gun Company (improvised from No 5 Infantry Base Depot)

'B' Brigade 'Vicforce' (provisional battalions formed of reinforcement and depot troops) contained:

- Perowne's Rifle Battalion (disbanded and split between Rays, Davies and Meredith's Rifles by 01-Jun)
- Waite's Rifle Battalion (disbanded and split between Rays, Davies and Meredith's Rifles by 01-Jun)
- Rays Rifle Battalion (later renamed 'Newcombe's Rifles', then '1st Battalion')
- Davies Rifle Battalion (later renamed '2nd Battalion')
- Meredith's Rifle Battalion (later renamed 'Merry's Rifles', then '3rd Battalion')
- Brigade Anti-Tank Company (Two 2lbs pounder guns and two 25mm guns; later renamed 'Z' AT Company)
- Brigade Carrier Platoon

'C' Brigade 'Digforce' (provisional battalions formed of infantry reservists serving in the Auxiliary Military Pioneer Corps) contained:

- 'A' Battalion (Nos 3, 10, 18 and 28 Companies AMPC from Rennes Sub-Area)
- 'B' Battalion (Nos 5, 21 and 111 Companies AMPC from Nantes Sub-Area)
- 'C' Battalion (Nos 4, 13, 113 and 114 Companies AMPC from Nantes Sub-Area)
- 'S' (Scots) Infantry Battalion (formed from General Base Depot troops on 14 Jun; joined 'C' Brigade 15-Jun)
- Brigade Carrier Platoon

Divisional Troops

- Syme's Rifle Battalion (formed in late May)
- 'E' Anti-tank Regiment (twelve 2lbs pounder anti-tank guns (later 14) improvised from base reinforcement details and men returning from leave)
- 'X' Field Battery (twelve 18lbs pounder field guns; improvised from base reinforcement details - many guns lacked dial sights)
- Divisional Tank Company (five infantry Tank Mk I and 5 (later 6) x Infantry Tank Mk II, later also one x cruiser tank and one x armoured car; formed from 27-May)
- Divisional Engineers: 212th, 218th, 291st Army Troops Companies, 271st Field Company and 670th Artisan Works Company, Royal Engineers.

I still do not know to this day which of these formations I was in, as the chains of command were changing on a daily basis. I would not have been surprised one morning if I woke up and was detailed to report to the platoon cat for duty.

If I were to make a guess it seems most likely that I was in A-Brigade Beauforce, 'D' Machine Gun Company improvised from No 5 Infantry Base Depot, as a best stab.

Whichever it was, I just kept my head down and just did what I was told to do.

One day I was on a detail to Regimental HQ that was set up in the village chateau in Roncherolles-en-Bray. Of course, when you see or hear French chateau you have visions of grandeur and the lifestyle of the French Deuxieme état, the second estate.

Well, this wasn't it.

It was a large, square, rather austere brick-built building ranging over four floors. Needless to say, I didn't get to see la salle de bal a été décorée pour le banquet.

I was directed round the back of the chateau looking for the kitchen door (porte de la cuisine was the best I was going to achieve) and report to the cook.

The Army cook ordered me to go to a local dairy farm to buy a litre of cream with French money he gave me.

Hmm, wonder what he's going to do with that I thought?

On the way back the cream looked so good that I started drinking it and as I approached Regimental HQ it was more than half gone.

Wondering if the cook would buy the consequences of war inflation, I dug deep into my own pockets to find enough money and then set off back to the farm to make up the missing half.

By now I was wondering if in fact, there is any left at the farm, I gained a sinking feeling.

If I could not square the French money, I was given with the quantity of cream I actually had then the HQ officers were going to get poor fare that night from the cook and they would probably just hand me over to the Germans.

As I approached the farm, again, the big farmer's wife was standing at the door to the dairy with folded arms giving me that laconic look that simply said, "Spill some did we?"

Or its French equivalent.

She looked into the small cream churn, took an overly long look, shook her head as her eyes rolled at me and I just held out a bunch of notes and coin.

She muttered something like, "God help us if this is the best the British have to offer, idiots."

And came back holding a big cream jug and poured in enough to restore the balance of what I had drunk, and then dismissed me in a way that only the French can, with haughty disdain.

The British are famous for beating retreat.

I put my money back in my pocket and walked off smartly, in the finest British tradition giving her my grateful thanks.

But I think she had other things on her mind.

As I should have had as well as things were about to get worse.

After a few days at the chateau, I was detailed to drive from Forges-les-Eaux to Buchy to get petrol. It would have been fine, but I had hardly any driving experience.

But I thought, what the hell, I'll just follow orders and give it my best shot.

My passenger detailed to come with me of course knew nothing about my lack of driving experience, but did ask, "Are you all right to take the wheel?"

I said, "Aye, no problem,", and we set off.

It all went well as army vehicles had priority over everything else that was on the road that day and I was given a wide berth by men, women, children, cyclists civilian vehicles, and horses.

Which was just as well, as I said to my "navigator," "There's nothing to this driving lark".

His look was sceptical, but he seemed happy to just give directions as I murdered the gearbox as it screamed for mercy as I mangled the gear changes all the way to Buchy and back.

Perhaps this would be my gift to the Wehrmacht who would think that they had captured one of Britain's finest pieces of mechanical engineering only to find that it would probably not get them 200km.

As we were returning from Buchy with 80 gallons of petrol in jetty cans, we were spotted by a Luftwaffe ME109, probably drawn to the noise of my gearbox.

The ME109 was coming in from my right up ahead, heading diagonally across the road to the left. As I watched the bullets lifting the dirt across the field and heading to a meeting point with us on the road ahead at the last minute, I yanked the steering wheel to take a sharp right onto a track into the wood.

And the speed of the ME109 took it away to our left as we rattled down a forest track. We were well under cover by now, and I pulled the truck to a halt and we both jumped out and ran like the clappers to put some distance between the fuel on the truck and ourselves.

As we stood about 100m away we could hear the ME109 engine scream as the pilot fought to turn the fighter around and come back for another go.

And he did come back, but by now we were off the main road.

He seemed to sense that we were in the wood somewhere, but he couldn't see us.

So, we just struck up a couple of cigarettes and just stood there watching him flying backwards and forwards and started to place bets with each other on how long it would take before he lost interest.

Gradually the sound of his engine began to drift away into the distance, and we stayed there for another hour before we felt it was safe enough to venture back out onto the main road back to the depot at Forges-les-Eaux , making sure that I completed my job on that gearbox.

We were then redirected to an RAOC HQ that had been set up in Forges-les-Eaux. There was a large collection of cars there, so we unloaded the petrol cans and returned to the depot.

On the night of 05/06-Jun General Fortune wrote a strongly worded letter to General Marshall-Cornwall, who coordinated the activities of the British divisions from HQ with that of the French 10th Army.

He pointed out the condition of his men and the length of his front, and then he asked, "...that half my front be taken over at once by someone—that I by authorised with my neighbour, the French 31st Division, to retire on the Bresle."

But there was no one who could take over additional ground on this front.

By 02:00hrs in the early morning of 06-Jun units began to move back via La Croisette and Les Alleux to Limeux. Breakfasts were served at Les Alleux.

Soon after, one of our company's reported enemy activity on its front. Orders were given for withdrawal to Ramburelles between Le Translay and Oisemont.

By 23:00 hrs units had withdrawn to rendezvous at Huppy and then marched to Ramburelles. Some units had some unpleasantness on the left flank while getting out owing to well-placed enemy artillery fire. The remainder got away without any fuss.

Meanwhile the 06-Jun passed without much incident on the 51st front. As the enemy tried unsuccessfully to capture Oisemont with the help of repeated air and artillery bombardments, the Lothians and troops of the French 2nd Cavalry Division suffered considerably in beating off the attacks.

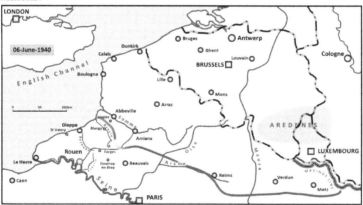

Map 8: German pivot towards Forges-les-Eaux.

German attempts to advance stalled as they came under withering British artillery and machine-gun fire. The only threat was at Eu as German pressed on Beauchamps and Pont-et-Marais.

On seeing the danger the 1st Armoured Division was ordered to this danger area early in the morning, and after clearing up enemy posts in front of the Bresle, capturing an officer and forty-three other prisoners in the process, was then moved back across the river to stop further penetration through Eu (Karslake, 1979).

During the quiet of the 06-Jun the French 40th Division moved into position in front of the Bresle between Senarpont and Aumale in the afternoon, where detachments of Royal Engineers and an anti-tank battery from the 51st had several flank guards posted.

However, the peace and the quiet of the day foretold that something else was in the air.

Reports were coming in that the German armour had broken through on the right flank further along the Bresle line to the south, away from that part of the front held by the 51st.

Many of these were false or exaggerated, but in fact the German 5th and 7th Panzer Divisions had begun to pressure the point in the front between two French armies and found the weak point.

The Germans by now could 'smell' Rouen as their leading elements were already a few kilometres south of the road between Poix and Rouen; their 2nd Motorised Division was to follow close behind; the 6th Infantry Division coming up on the left and the 32nd Division on their right just slightly less than 20kms away.

The German XV Corps Diary records, "... avoiding woods, roads and adjoining villages and favoured by the gently undulating country practically free from ditches, the Corps advanced southwards across country, deployed with tanks in front and infantry in vehicles in rear." (Ellis, 1953).

The 51st was now only a fraction of its full strength, and 'A' Brigade from 'Beauman Division' (about 900 strong) was sent up to reinforce it. This brigade consisted of the Buffs, Foresters and the Border Regiments. They took over the left or northern sector of the divisional front and the 152nd Brigade, or what remained of it, moved back into reserve at the south-eastern edge of the Haute Forêt d'Eu.

The mounting pressure to the east of Forges-les-Eaux made it clear to various British HQs in the field that any success here in favour of a German thrust towards Rouen would necessitate the retreat of the 51st and the French divisions now fighting alongside towards Le Havre before there was a repeat of what happened in the north.

All the while the British government was intent on sending out fresh forces as quickly as possible, all be it on a smaller scale and for 'political' reasons. Gort would command a new BEF as soon as it was ready and meanwhile a first corps was already forming. The Swayne Mission was notified that Brooke, who would command the corps, would proceed to France within the next week, and a brigade group of the 52nd Highland Division would sail next day, 07-Jun.

Quite frankly it was all pie in the sky as decisions being made back in London bore no relationship to the real situation we were experiencing on the ground. By the time intelligence and other situation reports got back to London they were hopelessly out of date.

The War Office tried to secure a line of retreat for the 51st, not towards Le Havre but towards the main French forces and our own base south of the Seine.

This was again a situation where only foresight and prompt action could avert calamity. But Weygand had other plans and forbade retirement; the Bresle was to be held "at all costs."

So, nothing came of the War Office decent intentions, and their fear played out when two days later the German breakthrough in the south was completed and the confounded retirement was ordered.

The decision came too late, and the full costs of procrastination were duly paid.

During the morning twelve Blenheims flying from England with fighter cover had attacked enemy columns moving towards the Somme crossings, losing five aircraft in the action.

In the afternoon another twenty-four Blenheims bombed bridges and roads in the Somme valley between Abbeville and St.-Valery-sur-Somme, and all returned safely. That night eighty-four aircraft attacked German communications and oil targets.

It was all too little too late.

The following morning the Camerons were being heavily attacked and infiltration of the enemy was taking place on our left. All defences were manned, and companies dug themselves in. Some of our light armour took positions on high ground on the left which overlooked open ground beyond the railway and across the main Abbeville Road. From here they could cover the Camerons.

Enemy aircraft were more active all day and had complete command of the sky and orders were received that we should withdraw across the river Bresle that night.

As the Camerons left Ramburelles enemy shelling was increasing along the battalion route-march through Blangy in the early hours of the morning. The crowd in Blangy of refugees, and all types of French soldiers was phenomenal, and the battalion was thankful to be through the town and across the Bresle without incident.

The Bresle line was gradually being formed.

In the early morning of 07-Jun the 51ˢᵗ were in their designated position on the Bresle with the French 31ˢᵗ Division on its right from Gamaches to Senarpont. At this point General Fortune took the advantage to be relieved of responsibility for the command of this French division and concentrate on the needs of his 51st Highland Division.

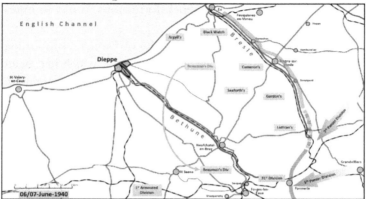

Map 9: Bresle Front Line at 06/07-Jun-1940.

The only point of concern on the Bresle line was the German probing at Eu and Pont-et-Marais. At this point where the Bresle gains the sea it affords a decent anti-tank defensive line and the breaking of manged water courses and weirs further up the valley extended this defence. Further up the valley the ground is firmer and the Bresle becomes no more than a stream and then a ditch toward Forges-les-Eaux.

It was to be at this point that the battle would pivot.

The 5th and 7th Panzer Divisions were already outflanking the Bresle Line. To prevent the breach from opening up the 1st Armoured Division should move up to Gournay-en-Bray and from there strike at the flank of the advancing German armour. The Division had forty-one cruisers and thirty-one light tanks, and six light tanks of the Bays and lorry-borne troops of the Hussars.

That evening, Weygand arrived at 10th Army HQ and saw General's Marshal-Cornwall and Evans in the presence of General Altmayer. Weygand described the 10th Army's fight as "the decisive battle of the war" and said that, as no French reserves were available, all depended on the 1ˢᵗ Armoured Division. It was to hold to the last 20km of the Andelle river line from Nolleval to Serqueux; French formations would counter-attack from the south.

Evans recounted again the state of his division, no supporting artillery, no anti-tank weapons, and no infantry which had been taken for use elsewhere. He then urged that his tanks were quite unsuited for a static, defensive role, in any case they were already on their way to counterattack the enemy flank.

Weygand would have none of it.

All he would concede was that if it became necessary to retire from the Andelle, the 1ˢᵗ Armoured Division should withdraw across the Seine where it would still be available for counterattack.

So, Evans retired to issue fresh orders and recall the units moving up to attack the German flank, some of whom were already in contact with German advance patrols 8km northwest of Gournay.

By now it was too late.

Streams of refugees added greatly to the danger and difficulty of our task, making it impossible to close roadblocks or prevent espionage.

Throughout 07-Jun, the Border Regiment and a company of Foresters made strenuous efforts to eliminate an enemy pocket on the west bank pf the Bresle, but they only succeeded in confining German troops to the north-western part of the Eu Forest, as the Lothians moved up to this danger-point to provide support.

On the rest of the 51ˢᵗ front it was a day of comparative quiet for most of the troops. Moreover 900 reinforcements of A Brigade Beauman Division arrived to make good the earlier losses sustained by the 51ˢᵗ.

While the situation on Fortune's front was relatively improved, the situation further south rapidly deteriorated. As a result of the German thrust by the 5th and 7th Panzer Divisions he now found himself separated from the French 31st Division and the 1st Armoured Division which he had posted as a flank guard between Aumale and Serqueux.

The latest intelligence was that the German Panzers were breaking through the French defences between Grandvilliers and Formerie, and this was indeed true, as leading elements of the German 5th Armoured Division had overrun a troop of anti-tank guns and a company of the Surreys in position south of Aumale.

Other elements on this Aumale/Serqueux Line had repulsed an attack, but the German Panzers then turned southwest and had attacked and roughly handled other posts near Forges-les-Eaux .

At this point we were detailed to go from Forges-les-Eaux to St. Saens and shoot any parachutists who were likely to drop in that area. For this they gave us an old long wheel-based flatbed Bedford lorry that once belonged to a fruiterer in South Shields.

I was given an old rusty Vickers machine gun that I attempted to clean and get into working condition by the time we reached our target area. Looking at the condition of the gun we would have been more effective throwing oranges at them.

When we got there the place had been flattened by the Luftwaffe, so there was nothing there for parachutists to drop for and we returned to base back at Forges-les-Eaux.

And all the while we continued to dig in constructing what defences we could, in a very unforgiving landscape along our part of the 90km Andelle/Bethune line. Being high summer the chalk had baked to concrete.

We got what was called a continental daily mail, it was just one sheet, a kind of flyer. And it was telling us how well we were doing in the war and that we had 56 Spitfires to support our superior fire power. In the years since then the mail hasn't changed much.

We never saw a Spitfire.

The RAF weren't popular with us on the ground in France, 56 Spitfires in Paris and we're well supplied?

Clearly written by some Fleet Street hack seeing the war from behind a desk in London or sitting in a Fleet Street pub more like having too many pints.

While I was reading this, I heard the drone of a plane coming over, it was a lovely, lovely sunny day, beautiful weather and you could see this plane and it was very high.

All of a sudden, I saw something reflecting from it and I shouted get down!!!

Just as well we did because it was a bomb that dropped on our cookhouse, and another landed in an orchard about a 100m away.

The Germans must have heard about our army's quality of cooking.

By now we could hear the frontline which was only a few kilometres to the east. We knew very little about what way things were going on the front. Communications were terrible. It was the difficulty of maintaining communications and control which led Beauman to issue instructions that troops would hold on, "as long as any hope of successful resistance remained" and that, "Brigade commanders will use their discretion as regards withdrawal." (Karslake, 1979).

Such conditional orders placed a heavy responsibility on local commanders who could have little knowledge of the general course of a battle and so could hardly judge what was required of them.

But judging by the fact that day as the noise of the front was getting louder and louder it began to tell its own story.

Early in the morning the Support Regiment at Haute Forêt d'Eu near Airaines was ordered to re-join the 1st Armoured Division to defend the left flank of the formations holding the Andelle line. They reached close by to where we were at Bois de l'Epinay Wood in the afternoon.

Suddenly the frontline was closer than we thought.

As they were sorting themselves out before their squadrons could deploy or any effort could be made to get into touch with the rest of the 1st Armoured Division, German tanks followed by lorry-borne troops came up the road from Serqueux.

A furious fight then took place that lasted three hours where several British tanks were put out of action as the Germans also suffered a similar loss. Only when German dismounted troops threatened complete encirclement was the engagement broken off.

This incident was followed up by a fierce firefight which in the main centred on controlling the railway junction at Serqueux, while I and the others were held to the rear in the main depot; it went on for three days until finally the Germans gained the upper hand.

Serqueux was lost, recovered by counterattack, but lost again finally.

Signy to the south of Forges-les-Eaux was heavily attacked by dismounted German mechanised infantry; after the defending troops had been subjected to dive-bombing, artillery, mortar, and machine-gun fire. Light tanks of the 1st Armoured Division in the area were armed only with machine-guns, or at best two-pounder guns, while the Beauman Division were only armed with rifles. They were completely outgunned.

Gradually we were overcome and forced back, and our positions pierced in many places.

Meanwhile, further north, Neufchatel was in flames and the enemy's armoured patrols had reached Mathonville pushing on towards the road from Neufchatel to Rouen.

The first attacks of the German Panzer Divisions were at Forges-les-Eaux and in the neighbourhood of Signy on the Andelle.

Streams of French refugees, stragglers, and vehicles had converged and passed through Forges-les-Eaux throughout the night and early morning, making it impossible for Beauman's infantry to close the roadblocks they had built.

French tanks were known to be operating in the neighbourhood, and when some arrived, they were allowed to go through. They were indeed French tanks, but they had been captured by the enemy and were being used as the leading tanks of a larger German formation (Ellis, 1953).

Once past the defences they turned on our posts from the rear as the main forces attacked frontally over a wide area.

We were eventually retired to Roncherolles-en-Bray and given brand new weapons and armed to the teeth.

This was all a bit of a surprise as up to that point I had only handled a rifle with very little training on how to use that.

My mate, Jimmy Scott, was detailed to an HQ being established in St. Saens and he went off to his new post.

I was given a Bren sub-machine gun as were most of us in the hastily brought together company of about 130, and all the ammunition I could carry and grenades by the dozen.

We looked a sorry bunch really, as we were from all manner of units. I don't think anyone of us were from the same regiment or unit and all our uniforms were different.

Quite the collection of army cap badges really.

We were also given home cards, we hastily wrote out our cards for those at home in the morning, simply just to say hi, still alive, all is going swimmingly sort of thing.

I didn't discover until I came home after five years that my father had got it and he'd kept it. He gave it to me when I came home.

It was at this point that we learned that all the HQ staff who had moved back to St. Saens were by now well on their way to crossing the Seine.

Good for them.

Sounded ominous to us!

The last orders we were given were to make for, St. Saens, and we were to keep off main roads.

And you were to avoid crossroads, keep off crossroads.

We were now also told that it was, "every man for himself."

In the strictly military context, this meant a lot more than this.

It signalled the immediate suspension of formal military discipline. We were suspended from military orders, which annuls this authority, at least for the present emergency. After this order soldiers may make their own decisions free from their superiors without being guilty of mutiny.

We were now in a very disconcerting situation because it also meant that if we were caught in difficulties then there was very little chance of calling for relief.

We were quite simply, on our own.

Once we were kitted out there was a discussion about what to do next and it was agreed with the company Sargent that we should head west keeping off the main roads, staying on side roads, small country lanes and seek the cover of woods and forests which were fairly extensive in the area.

We set off from Roncherolles-en-Bray and started down the road to Mauquenchy.

As the night closed in, we decided to seek a billet and came across an abandoned house just outside of Mauquenchy and took what rest we could for the night. There was a lot of activity in the distance that we could hear, but we couldn't see anything because by now the night was pitch black.

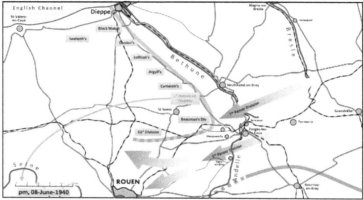

Map 10: The 'Ghost Division' Breakthrough at Forges-les-Eaux.

We could see in the distance to the north what looked like Neufchatel in flames some 10kms away.

What we didn't know was that we were full square up against Rommel's 7th Panzer Division also known as the "Ghost" division. A name earned by the ghostly speed, stealth, and surprise it consistently used to the point where both the enemy and the OKH at times lost track of its whereabouts.

It was only later that we discovered they had earned that name for good reason.

The units in our division were pushed back and the line was penetrated in many places, despite the support of 1st Armoured Division on our left.

And at dawn on 08-Jun, the 5th and 7th Panzer Divisions renewed their drive towards Rouen.

Other German units began to push on from Forges-les-Eaux heading towards Buchy and Rouen.

Picture 1: A semi-abstract landscape showing the ghostly shapes of tanks on the horizon line, just beyond the iron bridge which crosses the river on the right. Hughie O'Donoghue[1] (O'Donaghue, 1996-1999)

Eventually the battalions withdrew, fighting a rear-guard action all the way to the Seine, throughout the afternoon and during the night all that remained of the 1ᵗ Armoured Division and Beauman Division withdrew across the Seine. Of the

---

[1] The artist's father was a despatch rider with the BEF. After the collapse of the Somme front, he took part in the retreat towards the Channel ports. At Forges-les-Eaux they were attacked by German tanks. The painting depicts a scene experienced by the artist's father, Daniel O'Donoghue, attached to the 51ᵗ, he witnessed the advance of German tanks and an exchange of fire at Forges-Les-Eaux.

The looming turrets of two tanks move across a bridge at the top of the composition, the water of the river visible in the foreground.

British troops of the 51st (still on the Bresle), and a fragment of the Armoured Support group under their command, were now left north of the Seine as the bridges had been blown.

Now, when it was too late, the retirement of the French IX Corps was at last ordered. Weygand sent a personal message to the CIGS in London (Chief of the Imperial General Staff), saying, "orders were given this morning to the commander of the French IX Corps who commanded 51 British and 31 French Divisions to withdraw these divisions to area Les Andelys/ Rouen." (Karslake, 1979).

Weygand exhibited his by now characteristic refusal to face facts, with a denial through a subsequent attempt to mask the consequences of delay by the issue of orders that could not be reasonably be carried out.

The wisdom of early withdrawal from the Bresle, while still possible and retire behind the Seine, was not recognised, and when withdrawal could no longer be avoided he ordered IX Corps to retire through an area which had been open to them earlier but was now occupied by the enemy.

We cautiously exited the house we were in for the night and took our bearings to start out in the general direction heading west. And slowly it was beginning to dawn on all of us that we were by now probably in a kind of no-man's land at best, or worse, as we were behind the German frontline.

There was soon talk amongst us as we set off down a narrow deep country lane about a handful of fellow soldiers who had quietly stole away in the night probably thinking they stood a better chance of regaining allied lines on their own.

We went through Mauquenchy and as we came out the west side of the hamlet we were in a big open valley with the main Forges/Buchy road away in the distance on our left.

Above us flew a German spotter plane that seemed to take an over-keen interest in us, and we fired at it and it disappeared but very soon after that we bumped into Germans.

Suddenly we got a rattle of machine gun fire.

I immediately threw myself toward the roadside ditch and landed instead in a deep culvert, a roadside runoff for rainwater.

I lay there for a while and tried to look around without lifting my head.

There were three others with me within touching distance, one of them was killed, two of them were injured, and one fella, a fellow Scot from Bo'ness had his steel helmet on, and a bullet ripped it like a piece of paper.

The only mark on him was from the strap around his neck where the helmet was pulled back by the bullet that had left a neat red line on his neck.

Initially there was an exchange of machine gun fire.

One of our men had a position in a wheat field about 2m from the roadside ditch that I was in, to my right.

He was firing at the Germans on the main road at the other side of the field.

And as he ran out of ammunition, he shouted back to the rest of us in the roadside ditch.

I had two magazines on me, and I threw one to him which he caught and put into the Bren gun. He was lying unseen in the wheat which at this time of the year was about 1m high.

He turned around to me as I threw the second magazine to him.

Unfortunately, he rose from the prone position to his knees to catch it and he caught it in mid-flight, at that moment there was a burst of fire from the Germans that swept across his midriff and killed him instantly.

They were about a 250m away and every now and again, fired a warning burst of machine gun fire.

Our sergeant had a large white rag and he showed it to us to stand up only after it was safe to do so. He raised a rifle with a white flag on it the machine guns stopped. A couple of Germans came across the field.

It was a situation where five minutes before you were trying to kill them, and they were trying to kill you.

Tempers were raised, but none of the Germans was hurt.

After a verbal exchange they marched us back up the road to a lay-by and they took all our equipment from us.

They took the rifles and guns and caught them by the barrel and banged them on the ground and they broke off as easy as anything and left them in a pile.

They said you're allowed just one bag.

We all had our equipment, about 40kg to a man. Including a blanket, great coat, mess tin, and a change of clothing, the clothing you had on, and a water bottle.

Some wisely took their mess tin and anything personal.

Some didn't take their mess tins. So, when any food was on offer, they had nothing to put it in.

We asked if we could bury our comrade who had been firing the Bren gun.

The Germans agreed.

We dug a shallow grave by the side of the field and buried our comrade, said a few words and placed a cross on the grave with his helmet on it.

Today on a headstone in the Normandy churchyard of Mauquenchy lies:

ARNOLD, Private,
DAVID,
3192183,
1ˢᵗ Bn., King's Own Scottish Borderers.
09 June 1940.
SLEEP ON, DEAR SON AND TAKE YOUR REST WE MISS YOU MOST WHO LOVED YOU BEST.

A record in the Commonwealth War Graves Commission reads:

David was educated at Templand and Lochmaben schools. He was employed on farm work in Johnstone Parish when he enlisted in November 1939.

He was killed at Forges-les-Eaux near Rouen and is the only British soldier buried in the Mauquenchy Churchyard.

Age 21. Son of Katherine Arnold, and stepson of Thomas Lithgow, of Templand, Dumfriesshire. Grave Ref. Row 8, Grave 103.

Location notes:

Mauquenchy is a village and commune 21 miles (34 kilometres) north-east of Rouen, and 3 miles (5kms) west of Forges-les-Eaux. This is a small town on the N.15 (Dieppe to Paris) road 34 miles (54 kilometres) south-east of Dieppe. There is a bus service to and from Forges-les-Eaux. Near the south-east corner of the churchyard is the grave of a British soldier.

They took us back up the road we had just come down to a house not much bigger than a two-bedroom terrace and they packed all 130 of us into it.

We were captured around midday on the 09-Jun, and we were left there until the next morning.

At that time, we were marched off towards Forges-les-Eaux and then through the town where a few days earlier we unloaded the petrol for the RAOC.

Forges-les-Eaux was ruined, there had been refugees with horses and carts and the horses had been killed in the most gruesome fashion.

Civilians who were still in the town were laying the dead in rows on the pavements and with the rising heat of the sun during the day I'll never forget that scene.

As we were being marched through the town there were British officers who were busy stripping off the officer pips on their shoulders to try to hide their identity.

Just as quickly as they were throwing them to the ground, privates were picking them up as prized possessions in the hope that they could use them in the future to avoid POW work detail.

Thankfully I kept my Balmoral, with my cap badge on it.

As we went through the town, we entered a narrow street through an arch and on the other side of the arch was a German tank with three men standing on the tank looking at the prisoners marching past.

And as I went through, a big German warrant officer grabbed my balmoral and took it off me and of course the ones in the tank, had a smile on their faces.

As he was holding it up to show the war trophy that he had, I snatched it out of his hand and ran off.

I tried, well I tried to run off, but another Jack Boot caught me, and they took it off me and he hit me such a kick in the backside that I thought to myself, it's better that I just do as I'm told.

I was now back under military orders, only German ones this time.

It is difficult to describe the loneliness, isolation, and impotence one feels while enduring such conditions.

We had heard all the rumours of German atrocities over the past four weeks, and some were blood curdling crimes that defied human reasoning.

They were in fact war crimes and there had been many. The anxiety we had to live with was the fact that the Germans seemed to have very little regard for others who were not of their own.

As we came out of Forges-les-Eaux and into open countryside, we were halted for a while as transports took priority on the road. I glanced over the wall and the field was full of wagons with trailer units and all manner of aerials sticking out of the roofs of the trailers.

Running across the field were cables and pipes carrying electricity, water and fuel for the generators that were humming in the distance on the far side of the field.

It was a hive of activity and there was an awful lot of gold braid on display on some very immaculate uniforms. One guy stood out from all the others and seemed to be the centre of a fairly animated discussion as they were bent over a large map table pointing and sweeping gestures dancing across the maps.

It suddenly dawned on me that I was probably looking at Erwin Rommel, only to have it confirmed as he stood up straight from the map table, conference at an end, taking a curious interest in us.

Suddenly we were ordered to march, and we were off, to God knows where.

And he was off in his staff car, probably filled with the petrol I delivered a few days earlier, who knows?

On 09-Jun German armoured troops entered Rouen unopposed.

The bridges over the Seine had been blown and French and British troops were heading west ahead of the German advance.

The 51ˢᵗ (and what was left of the French IX Corps) were now finally severed from the main Allied forces with bridges over the Seine blown at Rouen.

The fate of the 51ˢᵗ had been sealed.

With a view to evacuation by sea the 51ˢᵗ moved towards St.-Valery-en-Caux and troops were ordered to jettison all non-fighting equipment to free up as much transport as possible for carrying troops, and ammunition was reduced to 100 rounds per gun.

The move proved a difficult operation.

It was very dark; the allotment of roads which had been made was not adhered to; French transport, much of it horsed, broke from every side road into the route intended to be reserved for the 51st and it became choked with a solid mass of slow-moving vehicles.

Alarmist rumours that the enemy was approaching added to the anxieties of the night.

Next morning General Fortune received a message from the War Office referring to an order the previous day to General Weygand reminding him of, "the importance of acting in strict conformity with any orders IX Corps commander may issue."

General Fortune must have been tested by these messages that bore no relationship to the reality on the ground when he replied rather tartly "the physical impossibility of corps commander's approach to the Seine. In same boat as me. (Ellis, 1953)".

Fortune then held a conference with his brigade and battalion commanders and told them to make ready for evacuation.

His directive was as follows, "the Navy will probably make an effort to take us off by boat, perhaps tonight, perhaps in two nights. I wish all ranks to realise that this can only be achieved by the full cooperation of everyone. Men may have to walk 10 or 15km. The utmost discipline must prevail. Men will board the boats with equipment and carrying arms. Vehicles will be rendered useless without giving away that this is being done. Carriers should be retained as the final rear-guard. (Ellis, 1953)"

To provide cover for the evacuation a perimeter was established both east and west of St.-Valery on the cliffs overlooking the town. And as divisional HQ moved into the town the enemy started to bombard it. The Mairie was ablaze; the post office HQ was soon untenable and the station square heavily shelled.

The German tanks broke through near Le Tot and gained the cliffs overlooking St.-Valery-en-Caux from the west.

In the afternoon and evening a number of spirited efforts were made to dislodge the Germans from the gains, but to no avail because by now they had complete artillery command from the cliffs above maintaining continuous fire on both town and beaches.

So, the night passed.

The surrounded parties on the perimeter held on. The rest waited in St.-Valery-en-Caux for the ships to take them off.

But no ships came.

And by 03:00hrs Fortune realised that with dawn nearing he could not leave his men on exposed beaches or crowded in the centre of the town.

Orders were therefore issued for all commanders to rendezvous in the station square so that the defence of a small bridgehead could be organised.

This would require the recapture of the western cliffs. His intention was to hold the town and cliffs on either side of it in the hope that his force would be taken off next night.

Meanwhile the Germans were about to play out the final actions.

As the Gordons approached the cliffs east of St.-Valery-en-Caux German tanks were moving in, at that point French troops marched across the Highlanders' front carrying white flags masking their fire.

The enemy quickly seized the chance of confusion created and the Highlanders' forward companies were quickly surrounded.

On the west there was similar difficulty, for the Black Watch, and the Camerons found their movements hampered by French troops who had surrendered or were about to do so.

At 08:15hrs a white flag fluttered from a steeple near the 51ˢᵗ HQ.

Orders were given that it should be cut down at once and whoever had hoisted it should be arrested. But the offender proved to be a French officer who said that General Ihler had indeed surrendered.

A dispatch rider then arrived with an open message informing all concerned that IX Corps would cease fire at eight o'clock.

With the message came a request that the surrender telegram be sent to French HQ.

There was now no possibility of holding off the enemy until nightfall. Moreover, Fortune was serving under French orders. Yet at 10:30hrs he notified the War Office, "I have informed corps commander that I cannot comply with his orders until I am satisfied that there is no possibility of evacuating by boat any of my division later."

But all French troops had ceased fire and white flags were being hung out, and in the end, before sending his message, he added a further note, "I have now ordered a cease fire."

At 11:00hrs he received a message from the commander-in-chief at Portsmouth, "Regret fog prevented naval forces arriving earlier off St.-Valery-en-Caux last night. SNO afloat will make every endeavour to get you off and additional ships are being sent to arrive tonight. (Saul, 2018)"

By the time this message was received the cease-fire had already been ordered.

Historians of the 1939-40 war have, notes Jean Louis Cremieux-Brilhac, "often overlooked the national awakening that was produced when French soil was invaded, and a front seemed to be re-established: The morale of the divisions that defended the Somme and Aisne was extraordinarily high; they resisted tooth and nail."

By June 1940 the resolve of French combat units had stiffened, and they were employing much more effective tactics. The battle for France after Dunkirk was a more even contest than admitted in the conventional historiography. The Wehrmacht found it could not, in June, shatter or scatter the French using their elite units, almost unaided. The much broader frontage of the June operations required the commitment of almost all the German forces.

This stretched the French and provided opportunities for German breakthroughs, as when 7th and 5th Panzer Divisions punched south-westward from Hangest-Sur-Somme, via Forges-les-Eaux to St-Valery-en-Caux.

These breakthroughs eventually unhinged successful defensive action by many French infantry divisions, sometimes blocks of two or three adjoining divisions, on the Somme and Aisne. However, to draw in the French reserves and undo the Weygand Line required the Wehrmacht to attack with all its standard rifle and reservist divisions.

German casualties rose markedly, and in many places, as noted, their assault faltered or failed.

Fall Rot was very broad-fronted, entailing the deployment of non-motorised and reservist Wehrmacht infantry of indifferent quality.

They encountered resolute British and French troops who had rapidly assimilated better methods of defensive combat.

Some of the Wehrmacht armour also endured multiple mauling in June -- especially Panzer Corps Wietersheim and Panzer Corps Hoepner, battling to break out of the Amiens and Peronne bridge heads.

These attacks, German sources acknowledge, "demonstrate that it is quite useless to throw armour against well-prepared defensive positions, manned by an enemy who expects an attack and is determined to repulse it." (von Mellenthin, 1977).

Allied troops by June were, notes Kenneth MacKay, "coming to terms with the bomber, realising that its bark was often much worse than its bite. Allied infantry, who had surrendered on call to German tanks, soon discovered that these machines were highly vulnerable, their thin armour easily penetrable by the existing anti-tank guns." (Alexander M. S., 2007)

The shock and awe of blitzkrieg would not give the Germans easy victory in June.

The strategic historians, Cohen and Gooch, harsh critics of the French in 1940, note that, "significantly, the French units performed much better in the battles on the Somme and the Aisne in early June," though they add the qualifier that this was when the French "were fighting a holding battle of the kind with which they were familiar from training and exercises." (Cohen & Gooch, 1990).

It is apparent that the Wehrmacht took heavy losses after Dunkirk and the French, even when dislodged from the Somme, Aisne, and Oise, made their withdrawals to the Seine, Loire, and Moselle in good order.

Their army did not collapse, because its divisional, regimental, and battalion commanders refused to let it. These officers, themselves often in the thick of the fight, demonstrated genuine qualities of leadership.

They rallied their troops to construct the "Weygand hedgehogs" during the respite from 25-May to 04-Jun, and then shared the danger at the "sharp end" when battle recommenced.

A German officer who took part in the assault across the Aisne in mid-June paid a handsome tribute, "this was where the Wehrmacht rediscovered fesoldat de Verdun."

No staff exercises in the 1930s had prepared French officers for the location of the battles of June 1940.

In even the most pessimistic forecasts, any German army reaching French soil would be stopped in the department of the Nord if they had not been already in Belgium.

Resistance had been configured as semi-mobile and defensive counteroffensive. It was supposed to stop an attack by manoeuvres anchored on field obstacles erected by the army engineers to augment pre-war "obstacle-bastions" (moles de resistance) just inside France.

A fighting defence had never been war-gamed so deep inside France as the Somme, Aisne, Oise, or lower Seine.

Weygand and the Army Council had, in 1932, deliberated whether to declare Lille an open city. Its location in the departments adjoining Belgium put a future German incursion there in the realm of the possible. A deeper break through, however, was unthinkable and so the question of a fighting defence of Reims, Beauvais, Rouen, or Paris was not considered.

Doubtless aghast at having to demolish the properties of their compatriots to form new defences, the French troops nonetheless accomplished the distasteful task. They did not lay down their arms just because it was now their homes and hearths being smashed by German bombs or shells or, more often, by the demolition work of the French army's corps of engineers.

They had not planned or trained for war here. All the same, in the "hedgehogs" of northern and north-central France, they fought it. 'There were pockets of resistance', noted one German, "where they held out when our infantry were already thirty kilometres in their rear [...] the French regiments fought as if they felt they were defending the last street in France in a battle that would decide the very existence of their country."

The fighting in 1940 cost the French armies 123,000 dead and another 250,000 wounded (the Germans losing around 49,000 killed and missing, and 111,000 more wounded.

Disaggregating these statistics reveals that most French combat deaths, about 92,000 (and about 100,000 of the wounded), occurred in the first 15 days (10/24-May).

The fighting on the Meuse, in central and western Belgium, was fiercer than many accounts allow. And the French death toll in this opening phase of operations was also disproportionately high because French defensive techniques were poor. Further lives were then lost in the last-ditch defence at Dunkirk, to enable the evacuation of 338,226 Allied troops (of whom between 102,560 and 123,090 were French).

In contrast during June, while opposing Fall Rot, the French army's death toll was only 24,000. The far lighter losses occurred despite a more determined fight, despite no wholesale surrenders, no positions quickly overrun, no entire units put to flight. Terrain, tactics, firepower, artillery support, and divisional, regimental, and battalion leadership -- all were markedly better than in May.

The French fought their battles in June more skilfully and more economically. About 1.6 million troops became prisoners of war. But the bulk was bagged from 22-Jun onwards. The armistice put them into German captivity; it was emphatically not that their capture caused the armistice.

What the documentary record leaves beyond a doubt is the disintegration of command, control, and communications above the divisional level (Forczyk, 2017).

Too often divisional commanders were left to their own devices. They went hours, sometimes several days, without instructions, unaware of developments unfolding 20 or 30 km to left or right, blind to the bigger picture. Yet the *raison d'etre* of corps was to co-ordinate manoeuvre and battle by groups of divisions to ensure connected and synchronised operations.

According to (Alexander M. S., 2007) French communications were hugely problematic in the battles of

May/June 1940 at intermediate command level, army/corps, and corps/division interfaces, as technology, systems were in the main incompatible.

To illustrate the point an instruction to Baudouin of 13th Infantry Division, fighting west of Amiens late on 05-Jun, transferred him with immediate effect to Ihler's IX Corps; right in the middle of the process of being decapitated by a rampant 7th Panzer Division's advance sweeping past his HQ;, forcing staff to pack and hastily retreat 14km to the rear of the German spearhead by nightfall on 07-Jun).

Another example affected Jeannel's 23rd Infantry Division in General Fougere's XXIV Corps. On 12-Jun the divisional war diary records how "an order was received during the morning to put ourselves at the disposition of I Corps (General Sciard). Just a few hours later the order was rescinded."

Disorganisation and disorientation on this scale in the French higher-intermediate command and control echelons meant that the patriotism and even death of French soldiers were not enough (Alexander M. S., 2007).

Failure in 1940 was not, then, down to the divisional and regimental commanders and field officers. And rarely was it down to the men, Captain Barlone of 2nd North African Infantry Division recording that his troops fought with, "morale and courage [that] were equal to that of the last war's army."

The fatal flaws lay with the senior military hierarchy and with insufficiently supple command, control, and communications procedures together with an overly rigid conception of how to mount a successful defence.

Cohen and Gooch noted, "everything was being extemporised," "for the pace of war no longer allowed for the preparation, writing, and transmission of orders. This disoriented French commanders (at all levels), who had expected to receive, and to offer, continual written guidance during the conduct of battle."

It was not the French soldier's readiness to fight that the Germans were sure they could expose. Rather, it was the inflexibility of the French senior leaders and their fragile, unwieldy command, control, and communications arrangements if forced, "to react to changing situations by rapid decisions'" (Cohen & Gooch, 1990).

In war "knowing your enemy" is always crucial. In 1940 the Germans had evaluated theirs more accurately than vice-versa.

In the French higher and intermediate HQs and staffs, military radicalism, thinking the unthinkable and working out responses to it, was kept out by locked mental doors.

Gamelin, the French army commander-in-chief, had preached the ultimately fatal orthodoxy well before fighting began, "Manoeuvre always ends up resulting in fronts," he said, lecturing to the Centre for Higher Military Studies, France's senior officer school in 1937 (Forczyk, 2017), "And more than ever, in the face of the progress of motorisation and mechanisation, any deployment must allow rapid establishment of a front."

This displayed complacency and disastrously limited imagination. The French high command was "so accustomed to the idea of a continuous front line, like that of the last war," noted one infantry captain on 15-Jun, as the Germans breached the Loire, "that it seems difficult to conceive how to organise resistance without it."

By contrast the German spearhead generals were improvising new rules of war, albeit giving the Wehrmacht high command many qualms as they did so.

Their methods, boldness, and dash instituted a disruptive change that the inflexibility of the French command and control could not accommodate. Hence the rapid and unpredictable movements of German spearheads subverted and progressively destroyed the French operational management systems that relied on a campaign unfolding conventionally, and at their preferred pace.

The French higher and intermediate command's reaction times and communications technologies (telephones, motorcycle dispatch riders, liaison officers travelling by car on congested roads) were consequently overwhelmed.

But underlying this was a more profound impact, the German innovation in warfare overwhelmed the French higher and intermediate commands mind-set. The fast-paced and alien German style of warfare forced disjointed and isolated decision-taking at divisional and subordinate levels by individual commanders, unprepared and untrained for the eventuality.

As a result, the French army was denied a capacity for effective army and corps-level command and control as battles ranged in depth, on some days in May and June, not across 3 or 4km of terrain but across 30/40kms.

The French had subordinate generals and colonels with energy, men who displayed decisiveness, fortitude, and physical courage. These commanders had the strength of mind to ditch pre-war mantras that did not work. And since they themselves were willing to apply disruptive tactics in warfare, they were able sooner than hidebound commanders to recognise and fulfil the need to adapt.

The evidence shows that they did adapt, with Captain Barlone of 2nd North African Infantry Division spotting glimmers of success and hope, "It seems," he noted, "that during the Somme battle certain generals showed a better understanding... which, for reasons I still ignore, did not develop, perhaps... because the right tactics were employed only by certain units."

However, Barlone also noticed a loss of respect for army officers among French civilians, in the campaign's final week.

This was understandable.

With Paris gone and the Loire breached, the perplexed populations of central France felt the army had let them down, had not done its job.

Inevitably growing numbers of people, bitter and bemused, just wanted the fighting to end immediately, like the angry and tearful woman who harangued Georges Sadoul of Baudouin's 13th Infantry Division at Sully-sur-Loire on 16-Jun.

Others, recorded Barlone, "do not distinguish between those officers who, on the whole, have fought admirably, sustaining grievous losses, and the High Command, which as I see it, has not been able to fulfil its task."

True, the army was beaten, "but it had been an honourable defeat and not a rout." The best commanders were not just highly patriotic and competent, but willing to adapt and innovate, for example "experimenting with patchy success in the tactics of defence by means of strong points in depth, recommended by Weygand."

They included de Lattre, Mast and Juin, Gerodias, Baudouin and Jeannel, Arlabosse, Mendras, Perre and de Gaulle.

Some of them passed the test of war in 1940 but unfortunately spent the next five years in captivity. While others inspired the French army's resurrection from 1943 onwards.

Yet the central problem during the battle of France was that these officers were insufficiently senior to override the slow-witted ideas about defensive modes of war retained and disseminated by too many of their superiors.

German spearhead generals possessed and acted on ideas for deep penetration and exploitation inconceivable to Gamelin, Weygand, and most of their army group, army, and corps commanders.

The campaign in France-Belgium in 1940, just like the campaign of 1939, was not a "war of fronts" (though Russia from winter 1941 onwards would be, with catastrophic results for the Wehrmacht).

Ironically, the less doctrinaire and more pragmatic British were less vulnerable. They were more accustomed to muddling through, to some extent making this a national virtue. They were less likely, therefore, to be paralysed than were the over-methodical French.

On this point, of all the many contemporaries trying to forecast how a war might unfold, it was the US military attaché in London who identified the danger. He mused in 1939 that, "the British, hardly had plans worth the name from which to be derailed," and from the French viewpoint, he noted, "it is maddeningly muddled. Just meander along, doing one thing after another. It certainly isn't the most efficient way of doing business."

"Or isn't it?"

Certainly, the British will not likely be confronted with that greatest of demoralisers, the plan-gone-wrong.

As a comment on 1940, this offers a piercing insight.

For it is in this precise sense that we can see how Marc Bloch, the great Sorbonne medievalist and reservist captain in 1940, correctly diagnosed the French army's defeat as a defeat of military conception, military imagination, and military intellect.

"I think," reflected another, Captain Daniel Barlone, "that perhaps we may have had arms in sufficient quantity and quality to resist and beat the enemy and that our disaster could have been avoided, if our High Command had been equal to its task."

The approach of the French senior military leadership to their loss of the battle of France, although not before the French army's impressive recovery of resolve and rediscovery of a spirit of adaptation in mid-campaign, and infliction of considerable losses on the Germans.

As the shooting stopped on 25-Jun, the Wehrmacht and Luftwaffe were convinced they could now rely on operational and tactical flair, improvisation, and the ad hoc. France's swift and stunning defeat hid from most of the victors, as well as from many of the vanquished, that this would not suffice to win a global war.

On 22-Jun negotiations took place at Compiegne and the armistice was put into practice on 25-Jun-1940 effectively ending the Battle of France.

By the end of Fall Rot the Royal Navy rescued 558,032 people, including 368 491 British troops but the BEF in the second campaign lost 66,426 men of whom 11,014 were killed or died of wounds, 14,074 wounded and 41,338 men missing or captured (Forczyk, 2017).

I was one of them.

We were marched across northern France heading towards the Belgian border to an uncertain future.

It should be remembered that some of us were front line infantry, so when we prepared for action, we were in battle dress. For some this meant no greatcoats or blankets, only what was deemed necessary to do battle.

Consequently, we "froze" at night and "baked" in the daytime.

"And we marched."

Chapter 4: Fall Überleben – Survival

"And we marched..."

Initially there were about 200 of us in the column as more captured troops joined in Forges-les-Eaux.

We were ordered to march off to who knows where. With the direction and altitude of the sun we kind of worked out that we were heading in a northeast direction, which only meant one thing, the Belgian border and eventually Germany.

We looked a sorry bunch. There was very little in the way of chatter or even banter between us as we were uncertain about our future and many of us were thrown together at the last moment before we were captured so there wasn't much in the way of having things we shared in common.

It was by now nearing mid-June and high summer as we marched out of Normandy. The days were long and very, very hot, and the growing thirst was crushing.

As we passed along the roads past houses in hamlets and villages the locals put out buckets of water by their front doors, but just as we got to it, a Jack Boot came along and kicked the bucket, over, so we just carried on with a growing burning resentment that matched our growing preoccupation to slake a thirst in the growing heat.

Slowly adjusting to the reality of our new situation we marched on until we came to just outside of Doullens. We were herded into a field and warned that if any of us tried to escape, they would shoot ten of us. We had heard rumours that the Germans weren't taking any black prisoners but many thought that was just propaganda, I never saw any of that happening. But we knew that Hitler didn't like black people.

This hatred of black soldiers went back to the presence of French colonial troops on the Western Front during the First World War. The Germans use them as propaganda to accuse the Allies of savagery on the battlefield takes an unfortunate account of this hatred. The German army had itself been rightly accused of atrocities against civilians, especially in Belgium.

Consequently, in response they used the image of the African sharpshooter as a propaganda weapon.

The peace settlement signed in the Treaty of Versailles meant that the Ruhr and Rhineland, along Germany's western border, were occupied by France. Many troops from French colonies were stationed there and only served to aggravate this growing perception (Trouillard, 2020).

In Germany at the time there was a very intensive, mendacious propaganda campaign accusing African soldiers of mass rape and kidnapping. German propaganda called this the "black horror on the Rhine"; a slander which the Nazis would reuse 20 years later.

When the Wehrmacht entered France in May 1940, they had memories of this propaganda to fuel their revanchist mood.

African soldiers were abused by the invaders throughout the country. These troops often fought very well, while the Germans sustained many losses, this produced anger, fuelled by a revanchist belief that further fuelled pent-up resentment already stored up.

This revanchist philosophy also resulted in several war crimes committed against the British and white French soldiers. In particular, the soldiers in Waffen-SS divisions were recruited from Hitler Youth and were heavily indoctrinated by Nazi exceptionalism.

It was in this state of mind that 97 soldiers of the Norfolk Regiment were murdered in a French field at Le Paradis on the 27-May, and the Wormhoudt massacre where 80 British and French POWs, having surrendered after a fierce firefight, were murdered by soldiers from the Leibstandarte SS Adolf Hitler Division during.

That day we marched 60km to Amiens and had nothing to eat; the following day we reached Doullens some 30km north of Amiens and still nothing to eat.

By the evening of the following day, we reached a place called Bethune, another 50km, and we were put into a school there for the night where I passed some time thinking about an uncle who fell in the First World War.

My mother's brother was only 20 when he was killed serving in the Seaforth Highlanders and is buried at Mailly-Mallet Wood Cemetery, just a few kilometres away from where I now was.

And still nothing to eat, a familiar pattern was forming here.

We learned that Paris had fallen, and the battle continued to the west and south of the city.

Two days later Pétain became prime minister on Reynaud's resignation, as de Gaulle formed the Comité Français de la Libération Nationale, effectively a French government in exile.

Map 11 : Forges-les-Eaux to Duisburg

We reached a place called Tournai, after yet another 50km; we were put into an evacuated Belgian barracks there.

We still had nothing to eat and we're starving by this time.

Wandering around the place outside, on some of the windows were some crusts of bread which were turning mouldy. Around the corner of the building were some Belgian prisoners and they had the field kitchen with them, and we asked them did they have any dripping.

We asked them for some of their fat.

I went and collected the crusts in the mess tin, and we lit a fire.

We fried the bread and ate that.

From Tournai we reached a place called Aalst in Belgium, another 50km.

We stayed in an old school with bunks in dormitories that were eight high. Other POWs had been there before us and it was in a filthy state. So, I went outside and found a pigsty that was spotlessly clean, so I put my head down there for the night and had a great sleep.

The Battle for France was now lost, and Britain embarked on an evacuation of remaining troops on French soil from ports in western France through Operation Aerial.

Some 191,870 Allied soldiers, airmen and civilians escaped from France, but the sting in the tail was the sinking of the liner Lancastria off St. Nazaire while being used as a British troopship — at least 3,000 were killed in Britain's worst maritime disaster.

From Aalst we arrived on the Rhine near Rotterdam on 18-Jun at a place called Willemstad where we would be loaded onto barges.

In the eastern European theatre, developments were taking place that would prepare the way for my life over the next five years, although I did not know that at the time.

The Soviets had implemented a total military blockade on the Baltic States with their Baltic Fleet.

Soviet troops were arraigned along the Baltic borders ready to organise communist coups and Soviet bombers shot down a

Finnish passenger airplane Kaleva flying from Tallinn to Helsinki carrying three diplomatic pouches from the U.S. legations in Tallinn, Riga and Helsinki. And on the 15-Jun Lithuania was given an eight-hour ultimatum to surrender. President Smetona escaped from the country, so the takeover was not possible to do in a formally legal way. Soviet troops entered Lithuania and attacked Latvian border guards.

At this point the Soviet Union gave an eight-hour ultimatum to Latvia and Estonia to surrender. Soviet troops entered Latvia and Estonia. Estonia, Latvia, and Lithuania were occupied by the Soviet Union by the 21-Jun.

On the 22-Jun France signed the armistice with Germany in the same railway carriage near Compiègne that the Germans signed the armistice that had ended the First World War.

Three days later the armistice site was destroyed on Hitler's orders.

We stood on the banks of the Rhine at Willemstad, and didn't know what was coming next.

There were dozens of barges with huge ship holds in them covered by a big tarpaulin.

By now the reality of our situation was beginning to take hold. We were POW's and we could end up anywhere.

We knew that there were certain rights that were enshrined in articles of war at a convention of the League of Nations in Geneva. Sixty-one nations attended and there were only two countries that I know that didn't attend that and weren't party too it, the Soviet Union, and Japan.

But who knew what they are going to do to us?

Eventually we were loaded into the hold on each of the barges. No water, no food, and a bucket in the corner of the hold that was the latrine for 300 men. At the height of summer, we suffered the heat for three days as we were moved upriver.

We eventually arrived at Duisburg on the Rhine where we disembarked in a pretty sorry and filthy state.

That evening, we were given bread, which was supposed to be black, but was in fact green with mould. This piece of bread, about 200g had to last each of us two days.

We were then put on an overnight train to Dortmund and we spent the night in an indoor stadium at Schutzenhof sports centre.

It was a huge, cavernous space, a big high place, seats all round and a running track around the bottom and that's where we spent the night so leave it at that. Looks like the place was built for the build-up to the 1936 Berlin summer Olympics on which Hitler had spent millions to demonstrate the invincibility of German sporting prowess and the supremacy of the Aryan Race.

But then Jessie Owens spoiled the party, and we all remembered him.

There were no beds, no blankets, no nothing. It was a stadium seated on both sides, that was in the dry and it was in the warm. We spent the night in there and next day we were put on a train, a civilian train this time.

We boarded the train at 12 o'clock.

At about 10 o'clock that night the train stopped, and we were told to get out. It was out in the country in what looked like the middle of nowhere. I didn't know where it was.

Later we found out that we were just outside the little town of Gardelegen, and it was in the middle of a thunderstorm.

We were marched off into the night and deep into a forest for about 10km. Out in the moors you couldn't see anywhere because it was midnight and we were soaked, but we got to the camp, and we were put into tents.

We were in fact in a large Wehrmacht camp at Altmark in the Colbitz-Letzlinger Heide between Gardelegen and Haldensleben just to the north of Magdeburg.

Next day we were taken individually to say who we were, name, rank, number, regiment.

Or rather they told you who you were, all you had to do was confirm it. No use trying to hide anything because they knew all about you, which was a bit strange.

On the 30-Jun-1940 I became a number: 5710 Stalag XXIB. The shiny new dog tag was telling me where I would end up, but God knows where that was.

Then the Germans did their best to photograph my best side and took my fingerprints should I get lost.

Which was very nice of them!

Picture 2: My POW Dog Tag.

We were at the Altmark camp for three days and thankfully we got to eat. They gave us a litre of ersatz coffee, which was made of a roasted barley.

Good to see the Royal Navy was doing its job blockading German ports.

There was a loaf of rye bread about 30cm long and 15cm high, and that was to be the ration. For now, we were beginning to get used to the ration.

For each of the six days of the week you got a loaf, on the seventh day you got a quarter of a loaf with just one slice extra, you got a cube, an oxo size of butter and a teaspoon full of jam and a pint of barley soup, that was your ration.

After three days we marched out of the camp back down to the railway and there were three goods wagons (cattle trucks) there. This time we were loaded into goods wagons -- 75 of us in a wagon.

A goods wagon was about the size of the average sitting room, imagine 75 people in one.

The doors were shut and locked. The only window was at the back of the wagon in the corner and one on the side diagonally opposite. The windows were 18 inches long by nine inches wide and with metal bars. There was no sanitation, nothing.

We were in there in the railway sidings for three days before there was any movement. The train started moving, and we were in this wagon until I think it was 12 o'clock the next day and we landed in a place called Schubin in Poland.

Whilst we travelled on the train to a POW camp in Poland, the journey was a hellish nightmare, with many of the men suffering from dysentery caused by eating the mouldy bread.

We we're taken out of the wagons and marched to a camp with nothing there apart from a big building and a chapel. It turned out it was an ex-Polish agricultural college that had been taken over by the Germans with barbed wire running around it.

The building was for the students in the college before the war; however other POWs had been there before us, so we were put into the chapel, and we were housed in there for a week before we were moved into big canvas tents. The tents had straw on the floor of the ground and that's where we lived and slept.

Welcome to Stalag XXIB.

Map 12 : Duisburg to Grunfeld

It took us 19 days to go from France to where we were in Poland. As soon as we got up the Rhine and arrived at Duisburg, we were told there that if we worked, we would get something to eat.

By the time we got to Schubin of course, everybody volunteered for work.

The work turned out to be driving fence posts into the ground with tube handles, to a height for them to build huts on; they were making barracks.

We worked away for about a day driving these fence posts into ground but by now we and our uniforms were a bit ripe to say the least and the Germans decided that they were going to give us a bath and to disinfect clothes.

I think the Germans were getting fed up with lice jumping from us onto them.

The way to get rid of lice is to disinfect your clothes in a heat room and they put our clothes in there and drove the heat up until they were nearly burning and that killed all the lice and the eggs.

Of course, by now we knew how to kill lice, but their eggs were a different matter. No matter how many lice you managed to squeeze and kill between your thumb nails, by tomorrow their offspring were back feasting on your body.

The water in the washrooms was delivered by pipes with holes drilled in them and it acted as a shower, and it was cold!

Then you were sprayed with lice dust. I don't believe for a minute that the Germans did it for our health. What they were really scared of was contracting the lice themselves and the possibility of typhus from them.

I had a gold wristwatch, I got from a girlfriend, and when we arrived in Schubin we had all our gear that we'd taken with us from the day we were captured taken from us.

And of course, watches were worth money and some of the boys were selling their watches and I wasn't going to sell it. So, I opened a seam in the lining of my cuff, and I put it in my small pack.

All your small packs were piled outside the washroom.

When I came out of there, my small pack was the only one that was missing. I lost everything, all my personal photographs, all the little trinkets, all the letters from home, the watch was gone.

Somebody must have been watching me.

I knew it was hopeless trying to get it back. But anyway, it taught me a lesson.

By now the Red Cross knew more or less where we were and we were given the first opportunity to write home, but there were only certain things you could write about. You couldn't tell them how you were or, or anything that could remotely be regarded as military sensitive. I'd also seen letters coming from Britain and at the top would be the name and it would be Dear John, or Dear Peter, yours sincerely.

It was all blacked out.

So, censorship cut both ways.

We did learn that the only way we could beat the redacting excesses of the censor was to press hard on the paper and imprint the paper with your writing, and you could turn the paper over and with a light pencil rub you could highlight in reverse what had been redacted.

All the signs seemed to suggest that the tide of war was against us, turning in the favour of the Germans, Italians, and the Soviets. By now the Channel Islands had been occupied, and Hitler had his plans for invading Britain.

By mid-July the Battle of Britain had started and went on well into August as the Luftwaffe started to bomb Channel shipping; military and infrastructure targets all over Britain, even as far afield as Wales, Northern Ireland, and Scotland; and then inadvertently the Germans bombed the church at Cripple Gate in London; to which Churchill's response was to bomb Berlin.

However, on 13-Aug Göring declared his Adler Tag (Eagle Day) and started a two-week assault on British airfields in preparation for invasion. Five days later Göring accused his fighter pilots of cowardice, an accusation that did not sit easily on the shoulders of those who given so much already, and ordered them to stay close to the bombers, further restricting their capabilities.

On the 26-Aug both Berlin and London were being bombed and then we had the start of the London Blitz. By the end of the month the Germans had turned their bombing attention to airfields and radar all along the south coast of England.

The Battle of Britain grew in intensity and German losses on both bomber and fighter formations began to mount, as RAF victories over the Luftwaffe continued, in a wide-ranging fight along the East coast. British fighter aircraft production began to accelerate. And eventually Churchill's speech, "Never was so much owed by so many to so few" delivered the nation's gratitude to "the few" in a speech delivered to the House of Commons.

Effectively the Battle of Britain had been won as the Luftwaffe's failure to achieve air supremacy forced Hitler to postpone his plans to invade Britain (Operation Sealion) indefinitely.

The operation was never formally cancelled.

Meanwhile the Soviets were not exactly being idle taking every opportunity to push the boundaries of the Soviet Union to match that of the old Tsars.

Soviet Foreign Minister Molotov reaffirmed the Molotov-Ribbentrop pact in the Soviet Supreme Council while he also asserted that the boundaries of the Soviet Union were moved to the shores of the Baltic Sea with the annexation of Lithuania, Latvia, and Estonia, and in the south Bessarabia and Northern Bukovina.

As POWs, Britain's "darkest hour" matched that of our own languishing in the middle of Europe as a guest of the Germans.

Food was becoming a major preoccupation due to our now being put on work detail. We were constantly hungry. And I was getting bored.

Red Cross parcels were not arriving in anything like the quantity needed to make up for the deprivation we were suffering under the Germans. Some guards played on this and were teasing us with crusts of bread and other assorted scraps. It was very difficult to hold onto your dignity in such circumstance.

The situation began to slowly improve with more frequent Red Cross parcels arriving with nourishing food, clothing, and cigarettes. At that point the German guards started to lose interest in baiting us but seemed awfully keen to get hold of the cigarettes and chocolate we were being sent.

Their eagerness to do business was somewhat dulled by the effect of severe punishments for those caught in such a transaction.

Work parties, I suppose did break the routine, but the lack of food made you constantly tired. Work included shovelling coal at the railway station, but for the first week rations were minimal. Then the Germans started increasing the ration, but it was hardly Miss Cranston's Tearooms!!!

One of the first additions we got were hard tac biscuits and they were like dog biscuits.

God knows what they were made from.

We got a pint of ersatz coffee in the morning and extra bread but basically the loaves were just a crust. For dinner it was a litre of barley soup or two boiled potatoes.

We were only at Schubin for about three or four weeks, and then we were transferred.

So it was back to the railway station and put onto a train, and we seemed to go back along the track whence we came and quite shortly we arrived at Gnesen (Gniezno) 70km down track.

During the invasion of Poland Gnesen was captured by Germans troops on 11-Sep-1939, by 26-Oct it was annexed into Nazi Germany as part of Reichsgau Wartheland.

During the German occupation, local Poles were subjected to arrests, expulsions, and mass executions. The Germans murdered several hundred inhabitants, and more than 10,000 inhabitants of the city and county were expelled to the general government area in Poland proper or imprisoned in Nazi concentration camps.

In late 1940 at the Tiegenhof psychiatric institute near Gnesen, 1,172 patients were evacuated and then killed.

Again, in late 1940 hundreds of patients were gassed in gas vans by the Lange Commando, a sub-unit of Einsatzkommando.

Despite this, Gniezno remained a centre of Polish resistance. The history of the place was dire.

At Gnesen we got off the train, and we were marched 8km south of the town to Grunfeld and we spent some time there in old Polish army barracks. While we were there, we organised a football match and two teams were picked so that it could be Scotland versus England and we won 3:1!!!

I'm still waiting for my cap and jersey from the SFA.

We were given a job there digging drains way out in the countryside. There is a lot of flat land out there and they had to have these drains to take the water away in large volume. These drains were 3m deep, but on the sloping banks there would be maybe 6m across sloping inward to about 1m for the waterway, we were cleaning the banks.

We didn't mind the work because it was out in the country and the lanes ran through a lot of small holdings and the people that had the small holdings were mostly a mixture of Polish and Germans and friendly enough. We were given a break in the morning about 10 o'clock and another one at about 3 o'clock, and the people from the smallholdings used to bring out coffee, cakes and apple tarts and things like that.

Back at the camp there was a strange episode at Grunfeld where the Germans asked for all our boots as they said they were going to repair them, and they gave us wooden clogs to wear.

If you were lucky to get a Dutch type, they were quite comfortable but as we headed from autumn into the winter, they became even less so.

A few weeks earlier a German army truck arrived loaded with boots and great coats that were neither British nor German, but clearly army issue so we assumed Polish.

Keeping an eye out to get our boots back we watched closely where they put the boots. They were stored in the loft of the building we were billeted in and then locked up. Once they had gone, I climbed up onto a wall and the roof of a lean-to on our billet and squeezed in through a window in the hayloft and started to hand out boots.

To avoid getting caught on parade with them I always stood in the third row back from the front because of the way the Germans counted attendance at rollcall.

With the boots I picked up some great coats for some of us who needed them and took them back to our hut.

We then noticed dried blood stains down the back of the coats but there were no bullet holes in the coats themselves.

Speculation was rife on how the stains might actually have got there.

It was more than just rumour however, there was a widely held belief that in some theatres of the war in Poland that there had been activities that suggest that the Polish officer class were indeed disappearing as we certainly did not see much evidence of camps containing Polish POWs. Something that was confirmed to me by my own eyes in a few months' time.

When we were in Gnesen we learned about the Hood, which had been sunk by the Bismarck on 24-May-1941, we renamed each truck after a battleship as it was sunk.

Some Germans tried to goad us whenever they enjoyed a success against the British Navy. All we would say was give it five years and we will be back and win the war.

At the time this seemed a pretty hollow claim, and I don't know where it originated from, but we all used to say it to the Germans, which seemed to bemuse them as all the evidence to date suggested otherwise.

But our confidence in our claim always used to make them uneasy. Perhaps this was being compounded by the increased

RAF activity in attacking military targets in the Ruhr and repeatedly bombing in and around Berlin.

There was always a doctor. That was one thing that if you asked to see a doctor, you got to see the doctor. In the winter of 40/41, some of us caught diphtheria, and we were all injected with quinine. As I was on night patrol looking after the camp carbide lamps, I used to collect icicles from the overhanging eves of the huts for those who were ill to keep them cool.

I got the job of looking after the carbide lamps as more or less a full-time job as the rest of the gang had to walk seven kilometres to work on a building site and then the same back at night again, while I got to stay in the camp.

I and another fellow POW took the lamps down and opened them up and although only half the carbide was burned, we did our bit for the war effort and emptied them into a hole in the campground and then completely refilled them with fresh carbide, but not really thinking of the potential consequences, we had been doing this for over a week.

One day the rain came on and all the unused carbide in the hole began to emit a foggy haze. Standing over it I lit a cigarette, and I tossed a lighted match into the haze, and it went boom!

Camp guards were running all over the place like headless chickens wondering what the hell had happened. Once they figured what had happened and who it was, I got my own personal protection guard every morning after that.

Our little camp at Grunfeld was out in the countryside and the ground was flat for miles around all the way to the horizon.

Outside the barbed wire there was a small gauge railway that ran all the way to Gnesen. Every morning there was a girl on the train, and we used to go up to the wire and as she was passing, she would throw food parcels over the wire fence into the camp.

It was a small camp, about 120 of us and the locals used to come up like tourist to look at us.

Once we were digging trenches for electric cables for a half-track factory manufacturing vehicles for the Afrika Corps. As we backfilled the trench, we would put our pickaxe through the cable and then carry on filling the trench in.

Our little contribution for the British war effort.

Needless to say, after that we were on the next train to Schebin.

Meanwhile the Germans and the Soviets were busy dividing the spoils of war as they conducted broad talks regarding spheres of influence between Russia, Germany, Italy and Japan.

Molotov met Hitler and Ribbentrop in Berlin.

The New World order was under discussion.

Molotov expressed Soviet interest again asking for acceptance to liquidate Finland.

However, Hitler now resisted every attempt to allow the expansion of Soviet influence in Europe.

He saw Britain as defeated and offered India to the Soviet Union.

The Soviets were invited to join the Tripartite Axis Pact and to share in the spoils of British Empire.

And a few weeks later the Soviet Union gave its terms to join the Pact including substantial new territorial gains for Russia.

But Molotov met German Ambassador Schulenburg in Moscow a few weeks later and the Soviets were surprised that they had not received any answer from Germany to their offer to join the Axis.

The German Ambassador to Moscow, Schulenburg replied that it must be first discussed with Italy and Japan.

A portent of the future?

Sometimes when you ruminate as you do repetitive tasks, you just get a feeling that there is something going on and you are not quite sure what it is.

We all got this feeling as we headed into the spring and summer of 1941.

There was something in the air.

We could see and hear a lot of activity going on even in the vast expanse of countryside we were camped in.

Increased road traffic, railways getting very noisy; very busy skies as we began to feel that things seemed to be moving east.

Even our German guards were beginning to notice it.

The hum of movement was even more pronounced in the evenings as sound travelled louder and across greater distances in the vast expanse where we were.

What was it?

In the west the war was also increasing in tempo as a massive overnight bombing raid on Liverpool and on Southampton in southern England; the city was hit again the next night, followed by Bristol, and Birmingham.

However, in the most unlikely of theatres the Axis fortunes were put into reverse as British and Indian troops of the Western Desert Force launched Operation Compass, an offensive against Italian forces in Egypt.

The Italians had seven infantry divisions and the Maletti Group in fortified defensive positions. Initial attacks were launched against the five Italian camps around and south of Sidi Barrani.

The camps were overrun, Italian General Pietro Maletti was killed, and the Maletti Group, the 1st Libyan Division, the 2nd Libyan Division, and the 4th Blackshirt Division were all but destroyed. The Italians were forced to withdraw towards Libya.

Initially more than 39,000 Italians were lost or captured in Egypt.

This was followed up as Australian troops captured Italian-held Bardia and 45,000 Italian prisoners were taken and they then went on to capture Italian-held Tobruk.

Some Italian POWs ended up at Glenbranter on the West Coast of Scotland. As British forces in North Africa took Derna; 160km west of Tobruk and the Indian 4th Division flanked and then captured Agordat, Eritrea, Italian East Africa. More than 1,000 Italian troops and 43 field guns were captured.

The thing we didn't know was that Hitler issued a directive to begin planning for Operation Barbarossa, the German invasion of the Soviet Union.

After the carbide incident we were moved back up to Schubin, in transit to Thorn on the Vistula by the 01-Jun. We were there only a few months when things really kicked off as the Germans launched their Operation Barbarossa to expand their Lebensraum.

The genesis of Lebensraum was deeply rooted in the German psyche since renowned German geographer Friedrich Ratzel coined the term in 1901. He and many others at the turn of the century believed that a nation had to be self-sufficient in terms of resources and territory (a concept known as autarky) to protect itself from external threats.

Ratzel and others were also deeply influenced by the new work of Charles Darwin and his theory of natural selection.

However, they mistakenly applied the concept to nation states, contending that, like the species Darwin studied, nations too struggled over resources for survival where only the fittest would win.

Ratzel argued that the development of a people was influenced by their geographic situation, and that a society who effectively adapted to one geographic territory would logically expand the borders of their country into other territories.

Pointing to the British and French Empires and to American "Manifest Destiny," Ratzel contended that Germany required overseas colonies to relieve German over-population.

The East presented another logical outlet for growth.

Long before the Nazi period, many Germans looked to eastern Europe as the natural source of their Lebensraum.

Beginning in the Middle Ages, the social and economic pressures of over-population in the German states had led to a steady colonisation of Germanic peoples in eastern Europe.

Increasingly by the twentieth century, however, scholars and the public alike began to view the East as a region whose vast natural resources were wasted on racially "inferior" peoples like Slavs and Jews.

A biological view of Lebensraum resonated with an inaccurate historical view of the German role in the East during the ancient and medieval periods.

Expansionists clung to this mythic German "history" in eastern Europe, arguing that these regions were lost German lands. As one German publication stated in 1916, "we Germanic people build up—create—the Slav broods and dreams—like his earth."

Ironically, during World War I, the German state achieved its goal of conquering Lebensraum in the East, extending German dominance as far east as Minsk and constructing a military dictatorship dedicated to exploiting and altering the landscape.

The eventual German defeat in World War I resulted in not only the loss of all its overseas colonies but also the eastern military "kingdom" known as Ober Ost.

The war and accompanying deep sense of loss heightened the German conviction that its salvation lay in the East.

Hitler, himself a World War I veteran, recognised the effect that the British naval blockade and material shortages at home had had on the home front, weakening morale, and increasing civilian suffering.

This contributed, in many conservative Germans' minds, to the "Stab-in-the-back" explanation for Germany's defeat which blamed the loss not on military failures but on Jews, liberals, war profiteers, and others on the home front who had compromised the war effort.

Hitler vowed that Germany would never again be defeated by a lack of resources. In his unpublished second book, he lamented that "the German people is today even less in a position than in the years of peace to feed itself from its own land and territory."

In 1936, he glowingly spoke of the "incalculable raw materials" in the Urals, the "rich forests" of Siberia, and the "incalculable farmlands" of the Ukraine.

In the Nazi state, Lebensraum became not just a romantic yearning for a return of Ober Ost but a vital strategic component of its imperial and racist visions.

For the Germans, eastern Europe represented their "Manifest Destiny." Hitler and other Nazi thinkers drew direct comparisons to American expansion in the West.

During one of his famous "table talks," Hitler decreed that "there's only one duty, to Germanize this country [Russia] by the immigration of Germans and to look upon the natives as Redskins."

The concrete measures taken by the Nazis to secure their Lebensraum (Holocaust Encyclopedia, 2020) demonstrate the very real power of ideas. Again, in his second book, Hitler wrote that Germany should "[concentrate] all of its strength on marking out a way of life for our people through the allocation of adequate Lebensraum for the next one hundred years."

Naturally, the inferior races that occupied this region must be removed, both Slavs and Jews.

The drive to clear the East of inferior populations in preparation for German colonisation1 led to intensive planning for the mass starvation of more than 30 million people there.

Policy guidelines issued before the invasion of the Soviet Union stated unequivocally that "many tens of millions of people in this territory will become superfluous and will have to die or migrate to Siberia... With regard to this, absolute clarity must reign." Known as the Generalplan Ost, this set of economic and demographic plans placed the necessity for Lebensraum and the colonisation of the East at the centre of the invasion.

By blaming Jews and Bolshevists for the "backwardness" of the region, the plans also reinforced other forms of Nazi antisemitism demanding the removal of Jews from the territory and eventually their physical destruction.

The concept of Lebensraum was not solely responsible for the Holocaust, but powerfully connected a variety of imperialist, nationalist, and racist currents that would contribute to the murder of the Jews of Europe (Holocaust Encyclopedia, 2020).

While at Schubin as Operation Barbarossa started, we were in new barracks they were using to build half-track vehicles. So, they gave us a corner of it.

But then, when the invasion of Russia started, we were all shipped up the railway line to a medieval fort at Thorn in underground barracks, or forts as they called them.

Now I was in Poland proper.

The walls of the moats to the Forts were about 6m thick, made of a polished brick that you couldn't climb up. And inside that was hallowed out compartments. Above ground on the roof, they had turrets that were made of steel or iron, and they could wind them up and down and they were like mushrooms (cupolas) but when they were retracted, they just looked like a closed mushroom

At full extension they had a good field of view of the whole of the area around them.

We were in Fort Eleven where I fell ill.

I took a sore arm, and I have the mark on my arm to this day, that was the result of a bite from something.

I don't know whether it was a flea or louse, but it turned septic, I didn't do anything about that.

We doctored it ourselves and it came to a head. We got the top of it, and it left a yellow centre and we wanted to pick that yellow centre out.

We had no tweezers or anything like that, so we sharpened 2 matches. One of my mates was picking at the centre and who walked in but our medical orderly.

I hadn't a clue who he was, I never seen him before.

He came over and had a look.

We didn't even know he was a medical orderly, and then he disappeared.

Five minutes later he came back down and said, "that the Colonel wanted to see me upstairs."

So, I did.

Well, of course I could do nothing but show him what was wrong.

I got a week in the nick for it, in the bunker.

They thought it was deliberate, they must have done.

But anyway, I was put into the bunker, it was more or less a jail and when I got in there was three other fellows also there.

I don't know what they'd been up to, but we spent about four or five days in there.

The orderly kept dressing it every day until it healed.

It was bad enough being a guest of the Germans, but to be thrown into jail by your own, well!

Then things got a bit lively in the eats.

The German Army Group Centre had crossed their start line on 22-Jun and by 16-Jul old adversaries Hoth, Guderian, and Kluge, from Fall Rot, had taken Bialystok, Minsk, and

Smolensk in turn, encircling the Soviet 3rd, 10th, 16th, and 20th armies over some 700kms.

About a week later after launch of Barbarossa, they started forming working parties together, and the first one I went on was taken out of the camp by about 2km up the road, into a cemetery.

From what little we could gather they had started building a prisoner of war camp to hold 250,000 Russians from the Guderian campaigns in the first phase of Operation Barbarossa.

When we got to the cemetery there were more than the usual number of German soldiers, officers, who turned out to be Gestapo and a handful of SS officers.

And we thought, what the hell is going on here?

There were a number of vehicles and two big 3-ton trucks.

As we arrived the first thing the Germans did was to hand out huge rubber gloves that went all the way up to your armpit.

And with hands on the butts of revolvers the SS officers motioned with their heads for us to get into the holes in the ground that were already being dug by German medics.

We soon found out what the gloves were for as the Germans began to uncover corpses in various states of decay.

Carefully we had to lift the bodies out of the ground and place them in long square boxes by the side of the grave and then carry them to the trucks.

Each truck had a trailer full of cabinet slots into which the boxes slid neatly.

Some of the corpses came out in one piece while others came out in bits and pieces.

There was one chap in a grave there and he was the crouch position. They must have just made a hole and put him in it and made him crouch down.

There was a hole on top of his skull with a broken bottle in it.

Some Germans who were prepared to pass the time talking to us gave us an insight into what had happened.

Were they German bodies or Polish?

Who killed them?

Well, they said no, it wasn't them that had done that.

They said it was the Poles.

The next set of graves we worked on had 22 bodies in it.

There were working parties all over the place doing similar work. We did this for two days and couldn't stomach it anymore and refused to do so.

Gradually we managed to put the story together from different conversations the working parties had with the Germans we were working with.

The genesis of these events had their roots in the creation of a new Poland after WW1, which had the considerable task of bringing together a new sense of Polish identity that had been torn asunder during the partitions of Poland in the nineteenth century.

From the start, the Polish authorities embarked on policies of "Polishification" that exacerbated national demands and stored up disputes for the future (Yves, 2010).

Ethnic tensions began to rise and Poland ratified the Treaty on Minorities, part to the Versailles Treaty. However, the minority populations (Germans, Ukrainians, Byelorussians, Jews, etc.) complained of numerous forms of discrimination.

With the pressure and tensions this raised eventually the inevitable happened on 01-Sept-1939 when the Bloody Sunday riots broke out as Polish patriotism and nationalism (like the situation in most other contemporary European countries).

The German minority of western Poland, maintaining its separate identity and close ties with Germany, was increasingly seen as a fifth column.

The rise of the Nazi Party only complicated matters. Adolf Hitler revitalised the Völkisch movement, making an appeal to the Germans living outside of Germany's post-World War I border.

Also, it was Hitler's explicit goal to reverse the work of the Treaty of Versailles and create a Greater German State.

By March 1939, these ambitions, charges of atrocities on both sides of the border, distrust, and rising nationalist sentiment led to the complete deterioration of Polish-German relations. Hitler's demands for the Polish Corridor, Polish opposition to appease him, fuelled this vicious cycle.

We discovered that those we were taking out of the ground to make way for the Russian POW camp were in fact the victims of these pre-war ethnic tensions.

By now, our own accommodations consisted of several long, black wooden huts. We slept on wooden bunks; three tiers high. We had straw-filled palliasses. Unless you were on the top bunk, you had a small cloud of fine straw particles descend on you every time that the person above you moved on his palliasse. The lower berths were also very gloomy as the gangways between the bunks were narrow.

Top beds had unrestricted light from electric light bulbs, and this was very beneficial when you were examining your underwear for lice. This was a regular routine, with many of the men sitting on their beds and cracking the lice between their thumbnails in the evening.

Every now and again some of the prisoners were sent off in groups to various locations for a variety of work. I think most of the men looked forward to getting away from the dismal camp atmosphere. These jobs could be farming, or road making, some went down mines, others worked in sawmills etc.

Thankfully I received a Red Cross parcel on 06-Jun, quickly followed by another on 07-Jun having received very little up to that point.

As the war went on, sanitation and, thanks to Red Cross parcels, nutrition improved, reducing the death toll. The Red Cross parcels may well have saved more lives than any medical treatment.

I was very pleased I was able to get rid of the old boots and the Polish Army great coat that we lifted during the boot heist at Grunfeld. I was now the happy recipient of a brand spanking new British Army issue greatcoat and full battle dress.

Just before I left Thorn we arranged another football match this time with the Germans .

Some of the Germans had heard about the result in Gnesen and were quite keen to have a match.

We started playing football and it was a keenly played contest.

Some distance from the field there was this guy peddling like mad on his bicycle coming hell for leather up the road, a German soldier.

It turned out to be an officer and when he got level with us on the field, he half fell off the bike, but his weight was still going, and he stayed on his feet.

He drew his revolver, and he chased us off the field firing into the air several times.

Hauptmann Rumman was not a happy chappie; he was the officer in charge of the camp.

We had a good 30 minutes of football before we got chased for our lives.

The Germans we were playing against were not that happy either, because we well understood the swear words being exchanged between themselves out of earshot of the Hauptmann.

So instead of a final whistle we got six shots cracked from his Luger.

I often wondered what happened to the German soldiers who had arranged the football match. They probably got hauled over the coals or they would get sent to the Russian front.

That was always their threat.

Chapter 5: Falls the Blossom

With our sporting achievements on hold for the moment there was a frisson of excitement, expectation, and indeed a little foreboding amongst the German population, and more closely the German soldiers we were with on a day-to-day basis.

The Eastern Front was expanding rapidly and moving faster and further into the Soviet Union at astonishing speed. As the Russians were being encircled by the Germans whole armies were being marched back behind the frontline into Poland, internment, and a very uncertain future.

With Army Group North it took just 33 days for the Germans to view the citadel of Leningrad, 650km from the start position on the East Prussian border. In Army Group Centre the Germans drove 650km to just east of Smolensk, with Moscow less than 160km further to the east; and with Army Group South the Germans drove deep into the Ukraine to Odessa on the Black Sea and Kherson on the Dnieper River, some 800km from their start position in Poland.

By any standards these were astonishing achievements.

By now our exhumation detail and construction of the internment camp at Thorn began to make sense.

We were not exactly leading the life of Riley and for us hunger was always a constant companion. But by comparison, the Germans made little effort to even supply the basic human necessities for survival to the Soviet troops they captured. The ground we had been ordered to 'clear' was turned into a makeshift camp for the Russians almost overnight and very quickly the Russian camp was overrun by malnutrition and disease for want of basic food, clothing, and shelter.

We even heard stories that the Russians were digging holes in the ground for shelter from the elements.

By mid-June we were hearing rumours that we were about to be moved and by then typhoid and dysentery was endemic in the Russian camp and thousands were dying daily. And with the onset of autumn and winter approaching the Germans did nothing to alleviate their pitiable state.

By the autumn of 1941 the German army were taking huge amounts Russian soldiers' captive and the camp infrastructure was wholly inadequate for their needs. The whole system by which the Germans 'processed' the Russian POWs was beginning to look like a deliberate act of extermination.

When Soviet POWs were transported by train, the Armed Forces High Command (OKW) permitted only open freight cars to be used (Shelton, 2005). Many died in transit; others died in the camps, while those that were left died as slave labour in occupied Poland or the German Reich. Most of the prisoners captured in 1941 had to march to the rear across hundreds of kilometres and those who were too exhausted to continue were shot to death on the spot.

The conditions were so inhumane that army reports suggest that between 25 and 70 percent of the prisoners on these transports from the occupied Baltic countries died en route to Germany. Once incarcerated in camps they were often left for months to vegetate in trenches, dugouts, or sod houses. In the occupied eastern territories conditions were even worse. In Belorussia only pavilions (structures with roofs but no walls) were available to house Soviet POWs. By the winter of 1941, starvation and disease resulted in mass death of unimaginable proportions (Anon, The Treatment of Soviet POWs: Starvation, Disease, and Shootings, June 1941–January 1942, n.d.).

On 06-Jun-1941 OKW issued an instruction from Hitler that political officers (NKVD) in the Red Army were to be shot on capture, and by extension German troops also shot Russian soldiers, alleged Jews, so called Asians, women in the Red Army and in some cases Soviet Officers.

Throughout 1941 and 1942 100,000 unfortunates who fell into those categories were handed over to the SS and very few survived. A similar number were also shot by guards marching long columns of prisoner away to the west from the front line who were fatigued and exhausted by the privations of those long marches.

While the German capture of large numbers of French and British prisoners in similarly short time periods had not led to mass deaths during Fall Gelb and Fall Rot in France. The majority of Soviet POWs died because of the deliberate undersupply of food, consequent starvation, frost, and hunger-related diseases.

Indeed, prior to the launch of Operation Barbarossa German authorities had planned the killing of tens of millions of Soviet citizens through starvation and a policy of brutal occupation. Racist and anti-communist, that scheme was to make good the overall German food deficit and the very act of Lebensraum; and to relieve the critical shortage of supplies for troops at the Eastern Front, perceived as crucial for the success of the giant military campaign. The plan was clearly backed and co-initiated by the military.

Those considered unfit for manual labour were specifically targeted with reduced rations to hasten their end. On 13-Nov the German Quartermaster-General, Eduard Wagner, stated, "Soviet POWs unfit for labour in the camps have to die of starvation." (Streit, 2000). In many camps those "fit for labour" were separated from those deemed unfit. Yet as guards often mistreated both groups, it scarcely made any difference and initially fit prisoners perished, too. Death figures shot up to

2 percent daily, especially in the German-occupied Soviet and Polish territories.

The orchestrated production line of deliberate extinction was hard to contemplate, and shocking to behold. Nearly two out of three million Soviet POWs had died by the end of 1941.

Map 13 : Marienburg and the Vistula Delta

This sudden change of events and the impact on military infrastructure on Poland compelled the Germans to move us from Thorn to Marienburg in East Prussia.

Our new home from the end of June was to be Stalag XX1B Willenberg, just 3km south from the centre of Marienburg on the east bank of the Nogat River. Initially there were some 8,000 POWs in 1941 in the camps and this grew steadily to three times that number by Dec-1945.

We arrived in the centre of Marienburg after a train journey of 15km, and then we were marched south through the town to the camp at Willenberg. The town was a very prosperous rural German town with a good solidly built commercial centre around the banhof where we alighted from the train. On the way to the camp, we marched by probably one of the biggest castles I have ever seen, so I took the opportunity to count the number of steps I took as we marched past.

600 steps, that would make the east curtain wall of the castle some 500m long.

It was impressive.

Eventually we arrived at **XXIB** which was the usual depressing sight of wire fencing, goon towers, floodlights and barking German guards. It was a huge camp with wooden barracks in an open flat plain beside the Nogat river. The camp was mainly British POWs, but there were others of various nationalities.

My heart sank, again.

We were assigned to a long hut with three tiers of bunks and an earth floor. We soon realised it was overrun with rats.

The camp Commandant was a Unteroffizier Poznasky and as expected for someone responsible for thousands of POWs wanted to make things easier for himself by running a strict regime.

Although I was only in the camp for about three months, my memories are of "Appels" (roll calls) that seemed to last forever, day and night, where we made things worse for ourselves, moving about as the Germans tried to count us, and of course, when the count did not tally, the Germans would start all over again.

To me it seemed a futile gesture.

On occasions, they would set up a machine guns in front of us and clearly the threat was to mow us down if we moved again. There were regular searches by military police, who turfed us out of the huts looking for contraband and various items we were banned from being in procession of. As they got busy kicking our worldly possessions around inside the hut it was amusing to watch our men dropping German money or other things forbidden onto the earth of the parade ground and digging it in with their heels prior to the inevitable pat down by the guards. It was even funnier afterwards, watching them try to retrieve it.

Whilst at this camp, we were offered a variety of manual jobs, loading barges, and building wooden huts, or working at the local hospital (not at all "tradesmen's" jobs). But with my gardening background and being born and brought up in the countryside with large open spaces, not a townie, working on farms seemed an attractive proposition from the drudgery of camp routine.

Within medieval Poland, Marienburg flourished thanks to the Polish grain and wood trade and craft development (Wyatt, 1876). New suburbs were created due to a lack of space within the defensive walls. In the 17th century, Swedish invasions took place. And during the Great Northern War in 1710, half of the population died of a cholera epidemic. After these wars, new inhabitants, including immigrants from Scotland, settled in the town; in 1740 Marienburg ceased to be a fortress.

It was annexed by East Prussia in the Partition of Poland in 1772 and became part of the newly established Province of West Prussia the following year. Prussians disbanded the municipal government and replaced it with a new Prussian-appointed administration. In the early 19th century, Prussian authorities acknowledged the town's Polish-speaking community, ensuring that priests could deliver the sermon in Polish. During the Napoleonic Wars, the French entered the town in 1807, and in 1812 the Grande Armée marched through the town heading for Russia. Napoleon visited the town on the route march to Moscow.

Although the town did not directly suffer from the conflict in WWI, the town felt the war's negative effects: the influx of refugees, inflation, unemployment, and food supply shortages.

Under the terms of the Treaty of Versailles eventually the citizens of Marienburg were asked in a plebiscite whether they wanted to remain in Germany or join the newly re-established Poland.

In the town of Marienburg, 17,805 votes were cast for Germany, 191 votes for Poland (Butler & Bury, 1960). As a result, Marienburg was included within the German Province of East Prussia. During the Weimar era, Marienburg was located at the cross-over point between Poland, Germany and the Free City State of Danzig.

The town was hit by an economic crisis following the end of WWI. After a brief recovery in the mid-1920s, the Great Depression was particularly severe in East Prussia.

In January 1933, Hitler and the Nazi Party came to power and immediately began eliminating political opponents, so that in the last semi-free elections of March 1933, 54% of Marienburg's votes went to the Nazis (Deutsche Verwaltungsgeschichte Westpreußen, 2020). After the German invasion of Poland in September 1939, leaders of the Polish minority in Marienburg were arrested and sent to concentration camps.

In time for the summer harvest, we were tasked with lifting sugar beets from the fields around Marienburg. Four of us were detailed to a farm at Schadwalde some 15km from the camp.

There were 12 of us POWs spread across 4 farms with one guard who went from farm to farm.

Four of us were assigned to the farm in Schadwalde; John MacLeod from Stornaway; Calum (Mick) MacLean from the Butt of Lewis); Darkie Leech was from Plymouth for a while; and Wilf Cummings from Durham.

There was a German (Swiss) family who were new to the area. They had come in from the German-speaking part of Switzerland and they were the Hans Eichenberger family. His brother owned the neighbouring farm and his mother lived with his family. While the mother had a dairy farm that made cheese, his father had died some time before we got there.

On our farm the Eichenberger family consisted of the farmer's wife; two sons around 10 to 12 and in 1943 a daughter who was born there with Hans Eichenberger, the head of the family: Elisabeth Eichenberger (wife) 32yr; Gunter Eichenberger 10yr; Walter Eichenberger 5yr; Marie Eichenberger.

Schadwalde was established as a farming village in 1352 by the Teutonic Knights. In 1367, the village had 86ha of land. The village had a Lutheran church and the scattered community extended from Marienburg on the Nogat to the south all the way up to the small rural town of Neuteich in the middle of the Vistula delta.

The partition of Poland in 1772 created the kingdom of West Prussia and included the area around Schadwalde. This remained the case until under the terms of Versailles it was administratively placed in the Kreis (district) of Marienburg until the establishment of the Free City State of Danzig (Craenen, 2012).

The village came under the control of Nazi East Prussia after the invasion of Poland; and Danzig becoming part of Germany proper.

As the village came under the control of Nazi East Prussia, in the wake came the German Ministry of Agriculture's farming policies that controlled the whole food industry as a planned economy.

In 1933 German agriculture was in the throes of a serious depression. The same could be said of all segments of the German economy and of the economies of most nations. In the late 20s and early 30s the anti-capitalist mutterings of the Nazis were gaining ground across the farming communities and the failure of the open market convinced many that they offered a route to their former preeminent social standing.

The Nazis were of a mindset that moved them towards agricultural self-sufficiency as a result of what happened after

WW1. The Treaty of Versailles didn't help as it transferred huge areas of agricultural land to Poland as part of the settlement. The German Ministry of Agriculture believed in a controlled market economy that would not only plan the whole agricultural program, but it would put price mechanisms in place to raise farmers income to a sustainable level. This was done through the Food Corporation that regulated the production and sale of agricultural produce.

Ostensibly, the Corporation was set up as a nongovernmental organisation but as the head of this body reported directly only to the Minister of Agriculture it was in effect under the direct control of the Nazi Party and wielded considerable power over food production. The structure of this organisation was deliberately set up as a command-and-control structure where membership was 'granted' to owners, occupiers, lessors, tenants and their family members and employees. It was through this structure that real control was exercised:

1) Whether the farmer can cultivate his own property or whether he has to join an association.
2) What and how much he has to cultivate.
3) What and when he must sell.
4) To whom and at what price he must sell.
5) The price at which the buyer resells it.

More particularly, in the sugar industry, the Nazis cautiously prevailed in their policies where the sugar industry was concerned. Trade Unionism was abolished, and Jewish owners forced out, to the applause of those left. The Nazis abolished the Sugar Association and replaced it with Reichswirtschaftsverein Zucker under the control of Nazi Peasant Leader Richard Darre as part of the Food Corporation program of reform. In the end the Nazis showed as little concern for the opinions of the beet farmers and sugar mill owners as their democratic predecessors. Nazi economic planners had two goals: to garner public approval by maximizing sugar consumption and to prepare for war. To that end, the government set both prices and production levels. Producers had to be satisfied with their sector's restored profitability.

Non-compliance meant that membership was withdrawn, making it almost impossible to modernise and mechanise the farm; buy seed and livestock; and sell produce. In a very heavily regulated industry, the bureaucrat wielded considerable power at a local and more or less dictated in line with Nazi policy. To do otherwise invited accusation of non-compliance with the Nazi philosophy and the party apparatchik (Lovin, 1969).

A dangerous place to be.

It was farming by political dogma for the Fatherland.

As a direct result of power and planning of the Food Corporation gross farming income rose 35% in the first three years.

The Eichenbergers were a very friendly family. For a while their old Granny stayed there. She also was a very friendly old soul and quite inquisitive.

One of the first jobs on the farm I had was to scare the birds away from the cherry trees.

There were three big cherry trees in the farmhouse garden and the birds loved them when they started to ripen. So, I was put on guard duty.

I went rummaging around one of the lofts where I found a winter snow sledge that would be dragged by two horses. In the winter the sledge and horses would be dressed up like Santa Klaus. On the bridles for the horses there were these fancy bells that tinkled and chimed as the horses trotted along pulling the sledge.

I found three of them.

Not much use in the summer I thought.

I climbed the trees and tied the bells to upper branches and linked them with twine to each other so that I only had to pull once, and all three bells would ring at the same time. I then went off and got myself a good book, one of the many cowboy books I read sent to us by the Red Cross, and I sat for days underneath the trees reading books and pulling string.

On the farm I got the books from the camp library that the Red Cross sent us. Red Shannon was my hero, he was a great cowboy who shot everybody. Once I got a book with a different title and a different front cover, but the inside it was word for word to the last one I had read!!!

Sitting under the trees as I was guarding from what were no doubt communist sympathisers, seemed to attract the curiosity of Old Granny who came out followed by three house girls who brought another chair a small garden table and laid down coffee, cake and biscuits and we sat their talking about anything and everything.

I could get used to this, but it was a false sense of security. Impressed though the Old Granny's son was he had other plans for me.

Map 14 : Schadwalde and the farming area north of the Nogat.

After a while we started to settle down to our rural way of life. We were billeted in one of the small barns that was made secure with thick iron bars placed over the unglazed shuttered window and a large latch and padlock on the barn door all used by our guard to ensure we remained "safe" at nights.

Inside we had our own little luxuries such as a wooden bed each with a sack filled with straw for a mattress and smaller sacks similarly stuffed for pillows. There was also a small pot-bellied stove, in which we could burn anything we could get, legally. In the winter the farmer gave us access to the farmhouse coal stack which we were allowed to use, within reason. We acquired some small pots and pans and a kettle on the stove to brew tea from our Red Cross parcels. And we had a plentiful supply of milk from the farm cows.

The tea and the chocolate always attracted the attention of the farm foreman and guards, which we used judiciously to gain favours. But we were more interested in the favours the

Ukrainian girls had to offer, such as sewing, knitting, herbal medicines, etc. and of course lots of fun and laughter.

The Polish girls in the farmhouse kitchen supplied us with food that we could reheat and eat when the working day was complete including a litre of coffee and bread daily; maybe a bowl full of chips, and the best pea soup I'd ever tasted.

You could stand your spoon up in it.

We came to depend on the pot-bellied stove as the winter crept in. Oh my God, the cold was something to behold as the lagoon geese began to migrate south as the first frost arrived.

And so, the blossom falls.

Three times I watched the cherry blossoms come and go as spring gave way to the birth of summer, and eventually the autumn when I stood guard again.

Around Schadwalde the Vistula and the Nogat Rivers flow south to north in a broad north-easterly loop that extends from the Carpathian Mountains in the south to its mouth on the Baltic Sea near Danzig and Elbing.

The Eichenbergers were Mennonites and had strong familial connections with the Mennonite community in the German Kanton of Freiburg in Switzerland. The movement stood in direct relationships with Anabaptists in that part of Switzerland and their doctrinal philosophy is Protestant oriented towards the Lutheran and Reformed church.

Over the centuries Mennonites were invited in by the nobility (Junkers) in the area and while most settled in cities and large towns, often governed under a form judiciary known as German town law. Anabaptists, who came from the Netherlands and Switzerland settled around Danzig and in West Prussia, where they mixed with German Mennonites from different regions. By 1940 there were 350 Mennonites in Marienburg; 133,182 in the wider Danzig district; scattered across 257 Mennonite villages.

The Mennonite Germans mostly settled on abandoned or empty land in the delta as the Junker landowners sought to re-populate their lands after the losses of the Great Northern War (1700–1721). Migration up the Vistula River, to Thorn, and beyond, continued through the period of the Partitions of Poland by Prussia, Austria, and Russia. Much of the Vistula River delta region came under Prussian rule in 1793 and became the provinces of South Prussia and then East Prussia.

The Duchy of Warsaw enjoyed a brief form of liberation thanks to Napoleon before it disappeared again following the Treaty of Paris (1815) that placed it under Russian rule again.

Despite this German migration continued into the region throughout the 19th century. They often settled in the by now existing communities but also established many new ones. By WWI, there were well more than 3,000 villages where German inhabitants were documented in the census returns, mostly German Lutheran. While they retained a clear Germanic ethnicity, traditions, and language, they often adapted or adopted Polish culture and food and sometimes their surnames (Anon, 1939: Key Dates, 2013).

Mennonites had migrated across Europe over the past 200 years, particularly towards the east mainly to avoid persecution and even regional program where they had lived. There were also sizable communities in North America in both Canada and the United States.

Original National Socialists were wary of the Mennonite communities, but those of German origin, wherever they lived were eventually recognised by National Socialists as "racial comrades" (Volkesgenossen) in the main, but for ulterior motives.

The German invasion of the Soviet Union gave direct German access to the Volkesgenossen and the prospect of repatriation from persecution under the rule of the Bolsheviks in the Soviet Union. National Socialist policy makers began to argue that settling them in occupied controlled territory would help to "Germanise" the land previously occupied by Slavic populations, particularly Polish speakers. The "Home to the Reich" program eventually repatriated more than 1 million Germans from across Europe and the Soviet Union.

In the late '20s and early '30s Mennonites were regarded as rejecting Nationalist Socialist racial ideology and their pacifist intentions caused them to be viewed with suspicion. Church leaders in the wider christian community, fearing a lowering of status under Nationalist Socialism advocated a Nazi-orientated philosophy they sought a more inclusive approach for the Mennonites.

Over the four centuries of their Prussian domicile, Mennonites continually struggled for acceptance, a struggle that revealed their proclivity to work toward a synthesis of their time-honoured religious traditions of passivity with a prevailing national ethos in the new Nazi era. By the 1930s, Prussian Mennonites had come to prioritise the latter, contrary to the inherent incompatibility between Mennonite and Nazi ideology, the Danziger Mennonites were able to maintain their community during the Third Reich.

Although aware of the Nazi brutality and genocide that was occurring in nearby concentration and extermination camps such as Stutthof, Soldau, and Treblinka just over the southern border of East Prussia, many Mennonites anticipated an eventual German war victory as the will of God.

It was against this backdrop that the Mennonites adopted a fluid national identity. When their formerly favoured characteristics of nationality, ethnicity, and language became the very things that brought the wrath of others to bear upon them. However, many Mennonites struggled to reconcile their religious beliefs with Nazi ideology and sought to remodel their existing identity to distance themselves from the product of National Socialism.

That didn't stop Mennonites from becoming Nazi Party members, particularly those from Ukraine, motivated to avenge the deaths of loved ones under Soviet rule. Many had served in the Waffen SS and the Wehrmacht. Consequently, Ukrainian Mennonites received German citizenship in 1943.

Mennonites have a long history of seeking the wide empty plains in the pursuit of their new Canaan, that country waiting for their peaceful labour, usually at the point of persecution from homelands from which they migrated. While they collaborated with the Nazis and served in the German armed forces, they had remained "Wehrlos" (pacifist) in their hearts

Mennonites were eventually portrayed as good Germans and desirable resettlers for the Wartheland (Poland) because they modelled "exemplary community life" including "highly developed forms of education and pedagogy, industry, commerce and agriculture." Such credentials as these were understood by the National Socialists as being good Ayrian qualities.

For decades German nationalists had characterised hard work as a key trait of German identity, and that partially accounts for the exclusion, expropriation, and execution of Jews and other non-Aryans in order to transfer ownership to supposidly more efficient and hardworking Germans.

My understanding is that it was under this scheme that the Eichenbergers arrived in the Vistula/Nogat delta in the late 1920s early '30s.

I was there about three and a half years and never once did Hans Eichenberger mention politics or where he came from or anything like that, and he never actually talked to us about the current situation or the war.

Maybe out of fear of local Nazi officials.

THE FALLS

Or more likely to do with the Mennonite beliefs and old mutually held suspicions between the Mennonites; and local party officials who were always on the lookout for any opportunity to pull a neighbour down to gain some form of political, career, property, or pecuniary advantage.

It did make us think who was holding whom prisoner here.

It seemed we were not the only prisoners of war.

I turned to Wilf one night and said, "We were all prisoners of war," it seemed.

Some years later I read a quote:

"Ein Mensch ist ein räumlich und zeitlich beschränktes Stück des Ganzen, was wir Universum" nennen. Er erlebt sich und sein Fühlen als abgetrennt gegenüber dem Rest, eine optische Täuschung seines Bewusstseins. Das Streben nach Befreiung von dieser Fesselung [or Täuschung] ist der einzige Gegenstand wirklicher Religion. Nicht das Nähren der Illusion sondern nur ihre Überwindung gibt uns das erreichbare Maß inneren Friedens." (Sullivan, 1972).

Einstein penned his famous words in 1950 to Robert Marcus, a man who was distraught over the death of his young son from polio.

This passage has been variously translated broadly as:

"A human being is a part of the whole, called by us "Universe," a part limited in time and space. He experiences himself, his thoughts, and feelings as something separated from the rest — a kind of optical delusion of his consciousness.

This delusion is a kind of prison for us, restricting us to our personal desires and to affection for a few persons nearest to us.

Our task must be to free ourselves from this prison by widening our circle of compassion to embrace all living creatures and the whole of nature in its beauty. Nobody is able to achieve this completely, but the striving for such achievement is in itself a part of the liberation and a foundation for inner security." **The Einstein Papers. A Man of Many Parts"** *in The New York Times (29 March 1972), p. 1*

Essentially, we were eating mostly what the Eichenbergers were eating, but there was no goose for Sunday lunch. Nonetheless we were faring far better than if we had stayed in the camp, both emotionally and physically even if the work was hard.

Eichenberger was a big practical man. Over six feet tall and quite an authority, but he knew that to get the best out of us, we had to be fed good food for energy, just like the farm horses that pulled sleds and ploughs I suppose.

The family was very private and kept to themselves, we seldom saw the children or the farmer's wife at all. Nonetheless, the farmer did introduce me to his wife one day.

They both came out to speak to me as I looked over their garden, and she was introduced to me. She was a very striking and beautiful women.

Having heard of my profession before the war they both wanted me to take over the kitchen and farmhouse garden, which would more or less be a full-time job, I hoped.

Might even get me out of lifting sugar beet in the future.

One of the first jobs she wanted me to do was plant a walnut tree in the kitchen garden.

I often wonder, is it still there?

We passed through the second winter that took us into the spring of 1942 and then spring gave way to the summer where we tended the crops ready for harvest.

We couldn't have been luckier with the farmer we were detailed to. His was a very mechanised farm and he himself was industrious and inventive, willing to try anything new. It was a land where you could grow anything. I once checked over the number of crops that we grew and there were about 13 or 14 crops that we were growing there. We were in an area known as the Polish corridor, between West Prussia to the west of Danzig and East Prussia; it was land prized by the Germans because it was so fertile, and it was land that stretched all the way south down into the Ukraine and the Black Sea.

In the spring horses were being tethered and hooked up to ploughs and other farm machinery. Our farmer had about a dozen horses of various ages. The farm foreman was working the field one day with a team of two horses pulling a plough, but he was having difficulty with the lead horse who was a bit of a cantankerous bugger. I was working near the entrance to the farmyard and close by the horses simply stopped and the foreman was trying to work the lead horse to start pulling again and the stubborn beast was having none of it.

The foreman was standing in front of the horse trying to coax it to pull when suddenly it shot forward and the foreman disappeared between the two horses and under the plough and then suddenly stopped. I ran across the field and some of the Ukrainian girls close by were wailing and screaming at what they saw.

As I approached the team of horses and the plough, I could see that the foreman was half buried in the soft earth with the plough on top of him. Instinct kicked in and somehow, I found the strength to lift and tilt the plough above the foreman and suddenly the horses moved forward a few paces to clear the plough from the foreman.

I thought he was dead.

By this time others had arrived, and we pulled him out of the earth. He was in quite a state, mostly semi-conscious. He was taken back to his house and laid on the kitchen table where he came to, but I could see that one of the horse's shoes had caught the back of his head and had peeled his scalp back like the peel of an orange. It was the soft earth that had saved him; otherwise, he would have been dead.

Some weeks later he and his wife both came to see me and thank me for what I had done. I was told much later that the foreman had deposited 100 Reichsmarks into a bank account in my name, but with the fortunes of war, I never ever saw it.

Wonder how much that is worth now?

One day the farmer sent us to his brother's farm adjacent to the one we were on. His brother had a steam-driven machine that was hooked up to a threshing machine. So, we set off early to look after the steam boiler at 6 o'clock in the morning and we stood around for a while waiting for the machine to fire up.

His brother grew a lot of peas and as we were nearing the end of the threshing when a German guard came up the road with two other POWs. As we were bagging the peas these two guys were to take them into the farmhouse for storing. There were stairs up into the loft, but the peas had to be carried up the stairs first to the bedroom floor.

There was a lot of camaraderie amongst the POWs and yet at the same time, there were all sorts, all different types and some were absolutely against the Germans and anything that they could do to hinder the Germans, they did it. While others just wanted to endure the whole situation and just get through it.

The one thing that sticks in my mind, right from the very start, when we'd be talking to the German guards about the war; maybe they were baiting us in some way or other. We would say to them wait until 1945. There retort was, "You'll get sent to Stutthof if you do not shut up!" And sure, enough on one occasion, they did.

Anyway, the peas did not make it into the loft. The guard was a lazy sod, and he was lying on his back on a hay cart smoking a cigarette waiting for his two charges to finish carrying the peas up to the loft in the house. But this pair of wide boys had other ideas. We saw what they were up to, but we had finished our job and departed the scene quickly.

We had just got back to our farm, and we were in the yard talking to the farmer when we heard the German guard shouting, "Schneller! Schneller!" As he frog marched the two heroes down the road back to the camp. We just smiled to ourselves, but the farmer's curiosity got the better of him and he went over to the guard to ask what had happened.

The two "saboteurs" had put small holes into the sacks and as they carried the sacks the peas gradually fell out and left a trail from the barn all the way up the stair into the loft.

Peas everywhere.

They then went to the guard to say they were finished, and the guard was escorting them out of the farmyard when the farmer's wife came running after them, furious.

The two heroes did a week each in the bunker for that.

One day we were told to take some cows to the cattle market in Marienburg, which was something we looked forward to because this would be more or less an all-day job. So, we set off from the farm at Schadwalde and moved the six cows along the narrow country lane to the main road into Marienburg.

To get into Marienburg we had to take the cows over a large railway bridge over the Nogat River. It was one of those bridges where the train was on a track on the bottom deck and the top deck carried foot and light vehicle traffic.

As we were crossing the bridge there was a gaping hole in the top deck and railway workers were working underneath and one of our cows fell into it and caused a lot of confusion with the workers underneath. As we tried to work out what to do, I knew we had to catch the cow first and that was going to take a bit of time to work out once caught how do we get it back onto the upper road deck.

We agreed that my mate would take the rest of the cows to the market as they were getting very restless and wait for me there. He disappeared off the bridge and into town when suddenly another two railway workers appeared, big burly guys, and all four of them suddenly lifted the cow up through the gap onto the road deck.

Never seen anything like it nor did I think that such a thing would be possible.

Once the cow had gathered its thoughts and settled down, we carried on towards the town and by now it's hearing its mates at the market but It couldn't see them and the beast was getting very skittish, and I really had no means of controlling it. Suddenly it ran off in the confusion of sound, people and traffic and ran into a dairy shop.

Windows were smashed, counters splintered; milk churns turned over spilling their contents, it was utter chaos as the cow exited the diary shop back onto the street and ran along it straight into the cattle market by the railway sidings relieved to see her mates as she re-joined them.

Me and my mate made a very quick exit from Marienburg back across the bridge before a baying mob had gathered looking for our blood. We got back to the farm and reassured him everything went fine.

Over the succeeding days we were getting that look from the farmer that made us more than aware that he knew.

He never mentioned it though.

Early in 1942, Ukrainians arrived and were billeted in an empty cottage on the brother's farm. The group included men, women, children, even a baby. We were usually segregated at work, and we were relieved when they were given the job of hoeing the sugar beets. But, unlike us, working in sullen silence, they sang all day long, beautiful, haunting melodies of Russian folk songs, the women rhythmically hoeing, dressed in multi-coloured layers of long dresses. They could be heard far away in the still air of summer. How they managed to keep all those beautiful clothes so spotlessly clean was a mystery to me.

One summer Sunday afternoon the Ukrainians come out on to the road between our farms and sang and danced their hearts out. The men doing those incredibly athletic dances and the women swirling round in their long flowing dresses, singing to Russian folk songs and music. Incredible people, taking every hardship without complaint and always seemingly happy.

They were not covered by the Geneva Convention, which Russia had not signed anyway; therefore, they had the status of slave labour. Not that they would have known the difference from working under the Soviet regime.

Although mostly Ukrainians, they included a Cossack boy, Ivan; a Tartar and even a Mongol from far away Siberia among them. I was, on one occasion working on taking sacks of corn off the threshing machine in the barn and was joined by a lovely young woman who was a science student at Kiev University. She could lift a 70kg sack of corn and toss it on the wagon as effortlessly as any farm labourer. I started to draw a diagram of the Pythagoras theory with chalk on our notice board; she took the chalk and completed my effort. I remembered most scientific words came from the Greeks, and they are almost identical in Russian.

The farmer found out that the Ukrainians knew how to tease wool, so he bought six sheep and I was asked to clip them, but the cow hair cutters kept clogging up, so we ended up pulling the wool off them, we tried knives and God knows what, but the Ukrainian's knew what to do with it by washing and teasing it and then it went into the house as spun wool. The Ukrainians could sew, crochet and spin anything.

I taught one of the sheep to rear up and box with its front legs to the amusement of everybody. That sheep used to follow me everywhere.

We used to socialise with the Ukrainians a lot. One of our POWs on the brother's farm had a guitar and there would be lively music coming from their barn. They were lovely people, very friendly and great at sewing. Anything we wanted mended or altered they would do a great job.

They could make syrup and treacle from pilfered sugar beet, and they willingly shared it with us. And they were pretty good at making various types of alcohol, not just vodka. The Ukrainians used to make beer from the sugar beet. Tasted hellish but it got you very drunk.

The reason we liked the farm was because we were in small groups, with relative freedom, and good access to better food. And the Ukrainians!

On the farm we were given all sorts of jobs. Just whatever was coming up. They grew a lot of sugar beets and the harvest started in the first week of October when the frosts began.

Across the farms POWs were assigned jobs according to their former employment in civilian life. I became the gardener, another worked different hours milking the cows in the early morning and again in mid-afternoon, and a third was assistant to the groom in the stables. Another became a pig-man. A former truck driver worked in the forge and drove whichever of the tractors they managed to keep in working order. As time went by, he and the forge master had to vandalise the tractors in turn to enable at least one to be available, as long as petrol was available.

During the summer months, from spring to autumn we worked from 6:30 a.m. to 7:30 p.m., with a twenty-minute break for what was called "second breakfast" and again in the afternoon. We also had 1½ hours for lunch at mid-day, mainly because it often took twenty minutes or more to trudge back from some distant location. Effectively we worked for eleven hours a day from April to October. During the rest of the year, we worked from dawn to dusk as the days got shorter. So, in mid-winter we only worked from 9:00 a.m. to 3:00 p.m. Even then we set out in the dark and returned in the dark. Only when the temperature fell below -20°c were we allowed to stay indoors, because of the danger of frostbite, followed by gangrene setting in, which becomes fatal.

One day the farm foreman suddenly launched an attack on one of the prisoners; he was about to slap him hard on the face. We dragged him off, but then saw the cause of the assault. The prisoner's cheeks and nose, not covered by his balaclava had turned yellow. After massaging his face for a while his colour returned to normal. Had it not been for the prompt action of the foreman the POW was on the verge of severe frostbite followed by a fatal dose of gangrene, which would have spread all over.

As the months went by, we went through all the usual farm activities. In April covering the fields in manure, ploughing, and sowing after we had removed every stone that had come to the surface and using them to fill in any potholes in the farm roads. The worst job was hoeing and singling out the sugar beets to a few inches apart in the blazing heat of June. The strain on various parts of the body was agonising, especially in the lumbar region. All you wanted to do at the end of the day was to lie down on your straw palliasse and go to sleep.

Thankfully the weeding task we gave over to the Ukrainians.

Then followed the corn harvest of rye, wheat and barley, and a crop of a combined mixture of oats, barley, and peas. Some of the crops were threshed out in the fields, some put in stacks, but most put under cover in the barns. The straw was stacked to the rafters in the roofs of the cattle sheds for the winter feed and bedding.

Following the corn harvest there were hundreds of hectares of potatoes and sugar beets to dig up. Nothing was wasted. The potatoes went through a machine with three riddles. Those that stayed on top were put in long clumps, covered with a thick layer of straw and then with a very thick layer of earth, to keep out the frost. During the winter we went out regularly to bring in a wagonload for everyone's consumption.

The potatoes that stuck on the middle griddle were similarly put in clumps for the next year's seed. The small ones at the bottom were fed to the pigs. The sugar beets were dug up in November. We chopped off the leafy tops and they were stored in a silo for winter feed for the cows, which caused the milk to turn a pale shade of green and taste sweet.

Every farm that grew sugar beets had a narrow-gauge railway running up to it from the sugar beet factory that was about 10km away in a place called Neuteich. This was where the sugar beets went. The engine would come with empty wagons, the wagons were loaded, they went back to the sugar beet factory.

When the wagons returned, they were full of chalk.

They used a lot of chalk in the factory in the sugar-making process where they extracted the sugar. The sugar comes mainly from the bottom end of the roots. The agreement was, the farmer would supply the beet, and the factory the chalk to fertilise the fields. You had to unload the chalk and fill them up again with sugar beet and send them until all the beets had gone. The main body of the beet was chopped into schnitzel and returned to the farm for cattle feed.

The tool that they gave us to dig the sugar beets was shaped with two prongs at the head of a very long shaft. The prongs started from the shaft and formed an open circle and then the prongs came together and ran parallel for 10cm to the end of the tips. You dug the prongs into the ground under the beet on the surface, the beet sat in the cradle of the open-ended circle, and you used the long shaft to lever the beet and its roots out of the ground. Within a week we had hacks on both hands between the thumb and forefinger that proved painful for a couple of weeks even after the harvest.

Towards the end of the harvest in 1942 a load of Russian POWs, about 30 of them, came onto the farms and they made short work of the sugar beet.

In terms of who did and who didn't do this work, a sergeant could work if they wanted to. A warrant officer could work if he wanted to, but if he didn't, they had no need to work, and a lot of the fellows that were supposed to work didn't like farm work, so they would be out for a week on the farm but do something wrong. The farmer would chase them back to the camp and get another two out.

They discovered the best way of punishing them was to them back to the camp, give them a week in the bunker and then send them straight back to the farm again.

One farmer that bordered our farm took a group of wide boys from the camp to plant winter cabbage. Not happy at the prospect they proceeded to plant the whole field with the leaves down and the roots sticking up.

Bunker, one week each.

When the German cow herdsmen on our farm was called up to the Eastern Front, my mate, Donald MacLeod, got the job, so now we had access to the milk, cream and butter. We had about 35 milk cows and a lot of young beasts; 10 or 11 young horses that they brought on from foals.

I also used to kill pigs for the farmer. He then took the skin to the tannery in Marienburg, who in turn gave him a cured hide that he then took to the shoemaker for his fancy knee length boots

I was on cherry tree patrol again sitting under the cherry tress tugging the string that tinkled the sleigh bells and scared the birds away as the fruit started to ripen. So, I spent a few lazy days under the tress passing the time reading cowboy books and the girls from the kitchen passed by with coffee cakes and biscuits.

But the demands of the farm meant I had to give up the string to one of them as I was sent out into the fields.

Out in the field one day, one of the Ukrainian girls had an accident as we were gathering in the last of the hay. A hay cart was fully loaded with the last load of hay for the day and a couple of the girls were up on top of the hay cart laying down the hay.

A hay fork had been left resting up against the wagon when one of the girls slid down the side of the hay from the top and the prongs went into her arm and chest. I was some distance away across the field when I heard this piercing scream as the other girls were standing around wondering what to do as the poor girl was still off her feet and couldn't unpin herself.

I ran hell for leather across the field and grabbed her around the legs and lifted her weight off the fork prongs while the other girls supported her in that position, I could slide the prongs out without making the wounds any worse.

She was back at work the next day.

And I was very popular, which was useful.

But that would lead me into trouble.

After a year on the farm the Red Cross parcels came with better regularity. A Cameroonian sergeant major who was with us on one of the neighbouring farms would take a couple of us with the guard to the main camp once a month to collect mail and Red Cross parcels.

Cigarettes were sent to us, but the Germans confiscated a lot of our rations, and we only got 50 a week. The German guards would stand over us while everything had to be emptied to show the guard that there was nothing in it, including the cigarettes. Cigarettes split in two; tins of prunes opened; packets of tea emptied etc. The label on Colman's little tins of mustard had messages in the inside of the label that had code to tell us how many made it home.

All prisoners of war that worked had to be paid.

They wouldn't pay us in Reichsmarks. We were paid in token money, two marks a week and you could only spend them in what they called, the camp canteen. Where we bought the likes of razor blades, toothpaste, toothbrushes, things like that.

Civilian shops were out of bounds to us

There was a thriving black market.

Red Cross parcels, letters and individual parcels were arriving regularly. But at the same time, you could acquire German Reichsmarks if you sold soap from a Red Cross parcel. German soap was a wee square the size of a matchbox and it floated in the water. It didn't sink and it wouldn't lather. So, our soap was valuable. You could sell that for a two or three marks whatever it was. Cigarettes, you were allowed fifty cigarettes a week.

We had all stopped smoking. There was four of us who had stopped. And we all individually saved up the cigarette money. It was another means of finance because the Jerries loved British cigarettes. The guards were buying them, although in a lot of cases if you had a bad guard, you sold them a bar of soap, or 50 cigarettes nine times out of ten you could get them get sent to the Eastern Front.

We were also allowed to buy beer, 2% strength in hogsheads barrels, but the Ukrainian girls sorted that out for us.

Through our black-market free trading spirit, we bought a powerful three wave band radio with which we received the BBC 9 o'clock news regularly. There were fixed prices for various articles:

- 5 cigarettes would buy any of the following 1 egg, ½kg sugar or 1 kg flour.
- A bar of soap or 25g bar of chocolate had the same value.
- 1 white loaf was 10 cigarettes,
- 1 rabbit or chicken was 20 cigarettes.
- A bag of tomatoes or grapes were ours for a handful of cigarette ends.

During mid-morning break we got out our thin slices of bread liberally coated with Canadian butter and cheddar cheese or salmon. The Germans got out their thick slices of bread with a scrape of margarine and a minute piece of sausage. Afterwards we got out our full packets of tailor-made cigarettes. The Germans got out their home-grown or rough tobacco and rolled a very thin cigarette. We did more in those half hours to undermine local German morale than Monty did in the whole of the North Africa campaign.

One day Hans asked me to carry out a very strange task that even to this day I find a bit odd. He gave me a bicycle and on the back of the bike was a cardboard box that had been tied down on the back rack above the rear wheel. He gave me very precise instructions as to where I was to ride the bike to and exactly where to leave it.

So, off I set.

I cycled along the side of the Nogat River on top of the levee bank that had a wide unmade path on it. At the designated spot I dropped the bike but couldn't resist a look in the box. I couldn't see anything apart from a hole in the bottom of the box that looked like it had been chewed and whatever was in there was long gone.

I just did as I was told and left the bike there and walked back to the farm.

Later that day Hans asked me, "Did everything go as asked." I just said, "Yes."

But I couldn't resist asking him, "What was in the box?"

Surprised at my asking he blurted out a couple of ferrets.

"In a carboard box! You stupid bugger, they've chewed their way through the bottom and escaped."

I found out later that they were for a local poacher, who had recovered the ferrets and used them to catch eels in the river

Nogat, but it must have been a risky business due to fishing rights and land ownership.

Otherwise, why all the secrecy?

Christ, he could have got me sent to Stutthof!!!

I got my own back on him though.

He had bought some fancy electric fencing gear and asked me one day to go out into the field with him to lay out and set it up.

We spent most of the morning trying to make sense of the kit to get it working, making sure that everything was as per the instructions.

He then connected the battery to get it working.

So, we stood there looking at the fence and then each other and then the fence again wondering if it was actually working.

I could hear a low-pitched buzz and very faint clicks, but I didn't know what to expect and remained none the wiser.

So, my idiot curiosity kicked in and I touched it.

Nothing.

He looked at me, I looked at him, we both looked at the wire and I wrapped my hand around it.

Nothing.

He then put his hand around it and got one almighty belter of a shock from it that threw him back a couple of feet.

He and I then both looked down at my feet and realised I was wearing rubber boots.

And as he looked down at my feet all I could hear was a whole new range of German vocabulary I had never heard before as he strode off back to the farm.

And there was me thinking he was a pacifist.

You just can't tell with these Germans.

At the beginning of 1942 the Red Army defence of Moscow under Zhukov went over onto the offensive and slowly begins to relieve the pressure as it pushed an exhausted and freezing

German Army front line back some 150km. By the spring the Germans were seizing the initiative again in the Army Group South area as Fall Blau (Operation Blue) encircled several Soviet armies around Kharkov in Ukraine and then advanced all the way to Stalingrad and the Caucuses. The battle proper for Stalingrad began in early September, but by late December the battle for Stalingrad was in trouble and the Germans were retreating from the Caucuses.

America had by now entered the war after the attack on Pearl Harbour that began to awaken a sleeping military giant, not before they had to give up the Philippines on 06-May; but by June America had turned the tide at the Battle of Midway.

In the spring the "Baedeker raids" took place over Britain as the Germans took revenge for similar raids on the medieval historic cities of Lubeck and Hamburg. Rommel captured Tobruk from the British in the late spring along with 35,000 British troops. He was eventually stopped at the first Battle of El Alamein in July and on 23-Oct the British went on the offensive and retook Tobruk on 13-Nov and by 12-Dec Rommel was holed up in Tripoli in Tunisia.

The second Christmas on the farm, 1942, was celebrated with a day off; the locals went to church. On New Year's Day the local gentry had a shoot over the farming estates and through local forests. The snow was several feet deep, but we had opened the roads. We were driven in an open horse-drawn wagon to the perimeters of the shoot and formed an extensive circle. We spread out and beat our way slowly towards the centre and the guns. Clustered in the middle was wildlife we did not even know existed — deer, wild boar, hares, and rabbit, and all were duly shot for a banquet, no doubt.

During the following three years we followed much the same routine. Our guards treated us as well as they could, but we were in a rut that seemed never ending. One day a recent arrival ollapsed with galloping consumption, which comes without warning because of tuberculosis. A doctor came, but the man died within a few minutes. When a van came to take his body away, we and the guards stood together outside and gave our military salutes.

The year ended on a very sour note for us.

"If you don't behave yourself, you will be sent to Stutthof!!!"

It was no idle boast and loaded with malicious intent.

We had one window in our billet in the barn; there was a thick wooden oak baton at the bottom and the same at the top. There were two iron bars, and the window was only about 80cm wide. I found that if I could get my head through between the bars and get it back without hurting my ears, I could get the rest of my body through.

At night when the door to the billet was locked by our guard, we were in and out the window like rabbits.

We were out one night with Wilf on the wrong side of curfew with the Ukrainian girls across the fields, and when we came back there was something going on, as I pulled the shutter back.

I could hear the door being unlocked.

I'm halfway in the window.

When Wilf behind me said, "Hurry up, hurry up he's coming."

The guard was opening the door and he caught me halfway in the window. It seems that somebody must have told the guard that this was going on.

A possible punishment was reported to us.

We had to face a trial to decide our punishment.

About three weeks after we were caught, we were eventually picked up by our guard and taken for trial.

The guard knocked on the door and told the two of us to get dressed, as he was to escort us to the trial.

The court was at Stutthof.

It sounded threatening and a little unusual as we had expected to be taken back to the camp at Willenberg.

Why Stutthof?

That seemed to us well out of military jurisdiction.

To get to Stutthof from the farm we had to walk about 10km to the railway station at Neuteich, taking us up the road around our fields. The guard decided that we were walking too slowly. We were going to miss the train to Stutthof. So, he decided to take a shortcut through the fields. The fields were fenced with two strands of barbed wires. One at the top nearly 2m high, another half way down.

So, he put us through first.

He had his rifle on his back and he tried to get through, but the rifle was catching on the top wire.

When he turned to go back his coat caught on the button wire and tore a strip in his overcoat.

He needed to step back and take his rifle off his shoulder. And I held out my hand to take the rifle, and he was just about to do that, but he decided he'd better not as he stood back to indicate to us to step back three yards so that he could get through the fence.

We caught the train at Neuteich and travelled up through Tiegenhof to Steegen on the Baltic coast, changed trains for Stutthof, and we weren't there 10 minutes until I was called in. There were seven German civilians and what looked a girl who was the court clerk, and they were firing questions at me.

The two of us had already made up a story between us that we were out that night pinching some apples, but we didn't get there because the guard caught us.

We bumped up the guard at how good he was as a guard at catching us.

They had me in there for an hour and a half firing questions at me left, right and centre. All in German and this young teenage girl is writing it all down.

When they finished, they asked me to sign the transcript she had written out and I said, "No way."

"I'm not signing that," and they asked, "Why?"

I replied, "I don't understand it."

And I refused to sign it, so they couldn't get me out quick enough.

Then they took my mate into the courtroom, and he was only in there about five minutes.

On the way through my mate had to pass me.

Out the corner of my mouth I said, "Just stick to the story."

And he did.

We knew Stutthof was a punishment/concentration camp.

We knew it was notorious but not as notorious as it turned out to be.

We caught the train from Stutthof back to Neuteich.

German guards always threatened us with being sent to Stutthof. What was unusual is that we were taken to Stutthof for trial and not back to Stalag. We were tried and convicted by a panel of 7 who were civilians and Gestapo.

We knew about Stutthof, but we didn't really know what that meant. There was no direct evidence that I could see of the level of extermination taking place because the camp was vast across several different compounds, and we were escorted into the administrative compound to face the court trial.

But there was this sense that "the birds don't sing in these parts"; it was all quite eerie and certainly the way the German guards themselves used to talk about it you were left in no illusion that evil was done in that place.

So, after a while as we joined up the dots, we were becoming more aware of what was happening.

It was many years later that I read a newspaper article that the stenographer in court was quite possibly Irmgard Dirksen (Furchner) (born 1925), where she worked for camp commandant Paul-Werner Hoppe. In 2021, at the age of 96, she was charged with 11,412 counts of accessory to murder and 18 additional counts of accessory to attempted murder. All relating to her period working at the camp.

Stutthof originally was a civilian internment camp under the Danzig police chief. At the end of World War 1 a number of paramilitary units formed in fringe German territories as a means of protecting minority German populations. These gradually acquired a 'security' status in pursuit of returning territories lost under the treaty of Versailles. Even before the war began, the German 'Selbstschutz' (self-protection) in Pomerania created lists of people to be arrested, and the Nazi authorities were secretly reviewing suitable places to set up concentration camps in their area (Smith, 1981).

Stutthof was a concentration camp established by Nazi Germany in a secluded, marshy, and wooded area near the small town of Stutthof, 35 km east of the city of Danzig in the territory of the Danzig Free State. Stutthof, was the first death camp to be built outside Germany and was constructed in 1939.

Over the six years it operated, until it was liberated by the Russians in May 1945, it is thought some 110,000 people were sent there, of which as many as 65,000 died in the concentration camp and its sub-camps as a result of murder, starvation, epidemics, extreme labour conditions, brutal and forced evacuations, and a lack of medical attention. Originally built to house Polish intelligence officers and intellectuals, the camp later expanded to include significant numbers of Jews, and Soviet prisoners, many of whom were transferred there from Auschwitz or camps in the Baltic countries.

The camp had gas chambers where many of the inmates were put to death, but tens of thousands died due to starvation, disease epidemics, overwork and forced death marches. Of those who died, around 28,000 were Jews. The camp staff consisted of German SS guards and after 1943 Ukrainian auxiliaries were brought in by SS-Gruppenführer Fritz Katzmann. In 1942 the first German female SS Aufseherinnen guards arrived at Stutthof along with female prisoners.

A total of 295 women guards worked as staff in the Stutthof complex. On 31-May-1946 eleven were sentenced to death for the part they played in the crimes committed at Stutthof.

Anyway, we landed back in the farm waiting on our sentence.

We waited nine months before a guard came to tell us, "You're going to the bunker; you're going back to Marienburg tomorrow."

The bunker was full, and we hung around in the camp for three weeks waiting.

We got three weeks solitary in the bunker.

Of course, we got in there and I had to go and complain to the camp commandant, who was a fellow out of the Camerons, Charlie McDowell. My complaint was the condition of the cell, particularly the condition of the lice ridden bed.

You had to have your creature comforts.

The German officer in charge would only liaise with one "Man of Confidence" (the Vertraunsmann) who represented all POWs in the camp. There were no commissioned officers in the camp, and warrant officers and sergeant majors, would take a camp commandant's job. The camp leader was elected by the rest of the POWs in the camp, but he needed strong trusted wingmen to look after his back. So, Charlie McDowell, a corporal in the Cameron Highlanders took it. He was mates with a Harry Gibbs who was a professional boxer before the war and that was Charlie's protection.

He chose well.

We went into the bunker and the jail was just a building with a door at one end and a passageway with a row of doors leading into each cell and the cells were divided by a single brick wall.

The cells had been fumigated with lice dust and furnished with a cleaned paillasse, a pile of straw, two sacks (one small for a mattress and a smaller one for the pillow. Very nice, but room service was lousy, and the chambermaids need sacking.

We were warned before we went in to wear wooden clogs, and the clogs had to be doctored before you went in. We hammered flints into the clogs and were given a celluloid toothbrush and a piece of glass by the camp "management." The glass was to scrape the celluloid to light by flint so that you could light a cigarette.

You had to flick the flint onto the celluloid. And that gave you a light for a cigarette. We were not supposed to smoke so we had to choose carefully the smoke times.

The bunker brickwork was very poorly put together. The bricks didn't go halfway along the brick joint. The sand and cement that was used for putting them together was powdery, and we bored holes in the mortar beads and headers. We could then push a cigarette through to whoever had the lighter. If you didn't have the lighter, you had to push your cigarette through and by the time it came back to you. It was just stub anyway.

There was a fella in the next cell to me out of the Seaforths, Clicks (Malcolm) Mackenzie, came from Stornaway. Clicks was one of these chaps that couldn't keep his mouth shut. He had to be on at the Germans at every chance he got, and he was always getting the clink.

He was out a week before me.

He was then sent to hard labour camp to continue his punishment. In the main camp it was one guard to 10 men and in a punishment camp it was one guard to three men. He was put on a job building a small gauge railway for extracting timber. And of course, Clicks again, was having a go at the Jerry guards. It seems they were part of a group of prisoners engaged in felling timber under the supervision of German guards. The guards were harassing a young English soldier who was not fit to work due to a bad leg injury.

Some of us could take it while others wouldn't and Clicks got worked up one day, calling the Germans all the names of the day. He stepped forward to remonstrate and with an axe in his hand held above his head he said,

I'll cut your so and so head off with this

He turned to walk away, and he was shot dead.

Among this group, Malcolm Mackenzie was a mature soldier of some 20 years, physically tough and someone who must have seemed a father-figure to some. He was the life and soul of the camp, always popular and willing to help. There were many young soldiers in the camp and Mackenzie always set them a good example. In the early days in France when these lads were first under fire, Mackenzie's courage and coolness were an inspiration to them.

He was laid to rest in the War Camp Cemetery in Marienburg on 14-Sep-1944.

We were let out for exercise every morning at 7 o'clock for one hour. The exercise yard was 4m square and all you could do was walk round, and round, and round and then you were banged up till seven the next morning.

One day, 7 o'clock came, no doors opened; 8 o'clock, nine o'clock, 10 o'clock, at 11 o'clock they let us out to exercise.

There was a bloke who was in the air force who was in one of the cells beside us.

Each cell had one small window and it was 30cm square, but this day the window was laying on the ground. The bunker block was itself surrounded by a 3m high barbed wire fence and "goon boxes" on each corner.

He had managed to get out, and it is a mystery to me to this day as to how he managed to do it.

The Camp Commandant told us later that he got home.

He must have had help both inside and outside.

While we were waiting to get into the bunker, we heard another story of how resourceful POWs could be in achieving a home run.

Under the Geneva convention POWs were given the right to repatriation should they fall victim to a disease that could not be cured.

One pal of ours contracted a kidney condition called nephritis. And as a result, was going to be repatriated.

A pal of his decided that he would get some of the same and get repatriated as well.

It was put to the escape committee who approved the escape plan.

So, a prosthetic penis was made in the camp and a urine sample was passed to the "patient" and at the examination he was given a jar to provide a urine sample which he duly did.

In the most unlikely circumstances, they were both repatriated.

While waiting to do bunker duty, blokes we're trying to escape left, right and centre.

There was always a camp roll call every morning.

If there's one missing, I've seen us standing there from 10 o'clock in the morning on the parade ground and still there at 2 o'clock the next morning because they were trying to find out who had escaped.

To bring some order to this chaos each escape plan had to form an escape committee.

As it wasn't fair on the rest of the camp, if one tried to escape why must the rest of the camp suffer. As it was no joke standing from 10 o'clock until 2 o'clock the next morning with nothing to eat, nothing to drink, no toilet, nothing.

So, they had to form these escape committees and if you wanted to escape you had to work out your plan and then you took it to the committee. If they thought it was viable, they would help you in every way they could. But if it wasn't, they would tell you straight.

Having done my time in the bunker, I was sent back to the farm.

Wilf was there looking rather pleased with himself.

When I got back to the billet there were a couple of parcels personally addressed to me, but they had already been opened by the Germans looking for contraband. I used to get lots of presents from Scottish charities in the same way other Scottish soldiers did.

However, in the parcels there were references to items that were not in the parcel, in the case pairs of thick woolly socks that were very much needed for the coming winter.

The following day I discovered a pair of socks stuffed down the toilet.

We used to visit fellow POWs on neighbouring farms and one day a couple came to visit us, and they walked straight by us and gave Wilf a good kicking.

We never found out why.

It was the German Feldwebel who discovered that Wilf had stolen the socks, wearing them until dirty then stuffing them into the midden and down the toilet hoping they wouldn't be found.

Clearly a little bit of a shit.

Every time we got lice they came from Wilf.

But with Wilf we kept each other going right up to the day of liberation.

Things were not going great on the Eastern Front by late 1943. One day in early Dec-1943 Hans Eichenberger asked me to get the horses out and dress the sleigh as by now there was a good covering of snow on the ground.

His wife's brother had been seriously injured on the Eastern Front and was in a hospital in Vienna recovering, but he was in a bad way. Hans was going to see him on behalf of his wife to see how he was and see if there was anything that he needed.

Hans made it clear that I was to wrap up warm and go with him to the station in Marienburg and then bring the sleigh back to the farm.

Sounds interesting I thought, I'll give this a go.

I jumped up onto the sleigh and we set off through the countryside and over the big bridge over the Nogat into Marienburg and through the town to the big railway station.

Hans was unusually quiet all the way, but I just put that down to the circumstance of the journey ahead of him.

We arrived at the front entrance to the station, and he jumped down from the sleigh handing the reins over to me. He was a very tall straight man, and he was wearing a huge bearskin coat, the fur on it glistened. He also had a huge fur ushanka hat on his head made from fine black rabbit fur.

He stood there for a few moments puffing on his cigar and suddenly he took his coat and hat off and passed them to me and told me to put them on. The coat looked a bit ridiculous on me as I was a good 50cm shorter than he was.

But I sat down on the sleigh, and it looked fine and boy was it warm.

He put the ushanka on my head and took one last puff of his big cigar which he had only half smoked and passed the cigar to me as well then turned and strode into the station.

I then turned the horse and sleigh around and cantered back to the farm puffing the cigar.

Every German officer I met on the way back to the farm saluted me with a Heil Hitler and I had to respond in kind.

Otherwise, it could have been Stutthof and then the bunker, again.

For the first couple of years, we knew very little of what was happening with the war outside of where we were in the Danzig/Marienburg area. But as the war went on, we became more aware of what the situation was. Dozens of radio sets were being dropped across the area by the RAF, and most were picked up by the Germans, but some sets found their way back into the camp. Gradually we were being brought up to date regarding the latest situation from the various fronts.

But that all changed when we saw first-hand how the contest had changed in 1943.

Around 1929 an airfield had been established at Konigsdorf that lay 6km due east of Marienburg on the south side of the Nogat. Early in the war the Germans had moved their Focke-Wulf aircraft product from Bremen to Marienburg to take the production plant out of reach of allied bombing raids. A 40ha site was constructed beside the airfield as a production facility. The FW 190 was the most effective of Germany's fighters at that time. More than 20,000 were built throughout the war.

We were posted only 6km away due north of the plant on the north side of the Nogat, and as we worked on the farm, we could hear the plant drone all day long as engines were run-in on huge benches at the plant before being put into the airframes.

The farmer quite often went to the local pub in Schadwalde where a lot of local Wehrmacht and Luftwaffe officers from the airfield would carouse the night away.

One day we were in the field with the farmer, and I was watching an FW-190 overhead. One FW-109 flew by and behind the farmer who continued talking to us and I saw the plane turn and dive straight for us, it then turned and came back to wave at us close enough for the farmer to recognise the pilot as one of his drouthy cronies from the pub.

Thought the farmer was going to have a heart attack, he wasn't happy.

There were many test pilots at the plant who took the aircraft up into the air to test their air worthiness and on many occasions, they used to buzz us as we worked in the fields, flying literally just a few feet off the ground, much to the annoyance of the farmer because they spooked the horses and the cows. The Focke-Wulf plant produced approximately half of all FW-190s.

Not long after that event we were out in the fields lifting sugar beets and loading them onto the bogeys on the narrow-gauge railway that took the beet from the farmyard to the sugar factory at Neuteich.

It was around midday the sky was crystal clear and up in the air we could see a number of vapour trails being formed more or less right over our heads and we just looked and watched as an aircraft began to circle above us and then it was joined by others coming in from the west. They then passed over us and just as suddenly we saw them the vapour trails form, they began to disappear.

They were the biggest aircraft I had ever seen, and we speculated as to who they belonged to and what they were doing.

Not for one minute did we think that they were American.

About 20 minutes later there was this almighty rumble coming from the south of us and then there was a series of terrific explosions some 6km away.

We watched as dozens of planes then flew right over us and reformed and turned west.

On the 09-Oct-1943, VIII Bomber Command Mission Number 113 was carried out by nearly 100 American B-17 Flying Fortress aircraft on the Focke-Wulf plant. During the mission, 4 returned to base with mechanical problems; and two B-17s were lost with 13 more damaged.

The bomb group arrived at a height of between 11,000 and 13,000 feet above the target area.

Between 12:53 hours and 13:02 hours, the B-17s arrived over the target in five waves. The air raid dropped 200 tons of explosive in very tight formation onto the production plant. Casualties among the factory work force were high. Of 669 workers, 114 were killed and 76 injured; 8 French POWs also lost their lives.

Picture 3: 09-Oct-1943 Allied raid on Marienburg Focke-Wulf plant.

Air Chief Marshal Sir Charles Portal, KCB, DSO, MC, Royal Air Force, described the Marienburg attack as the "most perfect example in history of the accurate distribution of bombs over a target."

The war was getting closer, and it made the Marienburgers very uneasy.

In the late autumn of 1943 Grandmother Eichenberger left for Switzerland, probably to take all her valuables and money back to Switzerland. And we wondered was it to resurrect familial ties that the Eisenbergers could take advantage of should the need arise.

We never thought much about it at the time, but after a while we began to speculate on the reasons for the sudden departure. The year 1943 was a year of military catastrophes one after the other for the Germans and the omens for the outcome of the war were not looking good for them.

As the new year dawned in 1944 The Germans didn't appreciate that as far as the war was concerned, they had reached their high-water mark while suffering a second freezing cold winter on the Russian steppes, particularly in and around Stalingrad. Stalingrad had become a cauldron, a meat grinder as the troops on the ground coined it. The Soviets went on the offensive to try to encircle and trap the German 6th Army.

Elsewhere on the eastern front the Germans were trying to shorten the frontline, a euphemism for large retreats in some sectors.

By mid-January the Soviets had seized the only airfield the Germans had for resupplying the Stalingrad pocket and by the last week in January the German forces in Stalingrad were in the last phases of collapse. On the tenth anniversary of his rise to power, Hitler made a speech in which he promoted General Paulus to field marshal. This included a reminder that no German field marshal has ever surrendered or been captured.

The very next day Generalfeldmarschall Paulus and his staff and troops surrendered to the Soviets, Stalingrad had fallen. The German public was, for the first time, informed of a defeat of German arms in conflict. The disaster could not be hidden.

Even Goebbels' skills in the dark arts of propaganda could not hide the magnitude of this military disaster.

Elsewhere the news was equally bad for German arms in the field. The British and Americans cornered Rommel's Afrika

Corp in Tunisia as they completed the retaking of Libya in the North African campaign. North Africa was all but lost, but the real psychological blow was the loss of Stalingrad. It was a shock the Germans were never really to recover from, and it showed on the faces of those we worked with daily.

Their bravado had gone.

By now several cities across Germany were suffering from increasingly potent allied air raids day and night. Hamburg, the Ruhr cities, Munich, Berlin had all suffered grievously and continued to do so night after night.

Back on the Eastern Front the Soviets entered Kharkov but were later driven out in the 3rd Battle of Kharkov. On the 11-Mar-1943 the Germans entered Kharkov and the fierce struggle with the Red Army continued.

In mid-May the remaining German Afrika Korps and Italian troops in North Africa surrendered to Allied forces. More than 250,000 prisoners are taken.

However, something was brewing in the centre of the Eastern Front line.

The Battle of Kursk began.

Operation Citadel is still the largest tank battle in history and was the Germans' attempt to reduce the Russian salient around Kursk and wrest the initiative in the centre of the Eastern Front. The battle proper started on 05-Jul and by 13-Jul Hitler had called off the Kursk offensive, but the Soviets continued the battle.

Initial confidence turned yet again into another military catastrophe.

The Eastern Front would never be the same again for the Germans; it was now a fighting retreat.

In September the Red Army retook Smolensk.

In Italy German troops started pouring in to take over Italy's defences as the Italians signed a secret armistice with the Allies and Italy dropped out of the war.

Mainland Italy was invaded when the British landed at Reggio Calabria. By 17-Sep Sicily was now in the control of the Allies. Neapolitans completed their uprising and freed Naples from German military occupation. Italy then declaresd war on Germany.

Up until the spring of 1944 Hungary had been an ally of Nazi German, but there was always a strong undercurrent of resistance.

The then government had resisted the deportation of Jews, despite the range of brutal antisemitic laws they had enacted. When the reality of the outcome of the war became apparent that the Nazis were heading towards defeat, the Hungarian government attempted to pull out of the axis powers alliance with Germany and made overtures towards a separate settlement with the Allies. In response, in March 1944, Germany invaded and occupied Hungary. The Nazis set up a new government loyal to Germany (Moore, 2020).

Miklós Horthy did not resign under the German occupation of Hungary, but instead helped to appoint a new government which was more submissive to the Nazis' demands.

Adolf Eichmann was sent to Hungary on the 19-Mar-1944 to realign Hungary towards the Wannsee Conference agenda of the Final Solution of its Jewish population. This would involve the deportation more than 800,000 people to the camps in the east. Despite the likelihood of defeat in the war by this stage, genocide was still a priority for the Nazis. Arriving with just a few German staff, Eichmann was reliant on the collaboration of the Hungarian authorities to achieve this aim. The Hungarian authorities now in power cooperated enthusiastically with Eichmann's plans.

In little more than two months, more than 200 camps and ghettos were created and filled with the Jewish prisoners.

Some 437,402 Hungarian Jews were deported in 56 days between May and July 1944, primarily to Auschwitz, where almost all of them were murdered (Moore, 2020).

It was during the summer of 1944 that some of these Jews were brought onto the farms to work alongside ourselves and the Ukrainian girls. They were a pitiful sight; they were evacuated firstly into ghettos and then transported to camps that were overflowing across Poland.

They worked in the usual striped suits made of rough cloth with a big yellow star on them. Initially their language was strange to us, but it didn't take us long to work out who they were. They were basically in transit because of the Jewish pogrom that was taking place in Hungary. They only stayed working on the fields with us for about three or four weeks and then they were taken away.

Did we know what happened to them?

By then we had a good idea as rumour laid on rumour and gradually a picture emerged as more evidence suggested that there was in fact an extermination program taking place. We did manage to talk to some and gradually we pieced together what was happening. First, they were dispossessed of career, work, and property ownership; and as the restrictions grew, they were then made to migrate to ghettoes from where they were systematically sent on trains with the offer of a better community life in the east.

It was at that point they arrived on the fields where we were working.

Because of what we knew about Stutthof, when they disappeared, we could then guess the rest.

When the attempt was made on Hitler on 20-Jul-1944 we were ordered to leave all our clothes outside the door at night in a pile for the guard to take away and then return in the morning should we try to escape in the night however, the German guards were as much in the dark as we were, and they didn't know what was happening with the attempt on Hitler, they didn't know how wide the conspiracy was.   We were also moved out of our little stable and we were put into a hen house with two fellows from the neighbouring farm who came to join us

This lasted about three weeks.

It didn't really matter, because if we wanted to go out the Polish and Ukrainian girls would bring us clothing and hand it to us through the bars in the window that we then removed and climbed out through.

We didn't mind that they were women's clothing of course.

One night I got caught up an apple tree shaking apples to the ground as a dog started barking the Ukrainians ran off and left me in my skirt up the tree.

It was a fetching little number, but the shoes were hell to wear.

Then, early one morning in the spring April sunshine we saw the vapour trails again.

This time there were 40 B-17s over the target area variously between 15,000 and 17,000 feet.   It had taken six months for the Germans to re-equip and get the Focke-Wulf plant back to anything like full production.   What made this raid unique was that the Americans were not just carrying bombs, they were also tasked with dropping propaganda leaflets across the Marienburg area.

On 18-Feb-1943, a few weeks after the catastrophe of Stalingrad, Goebbels put the question to a mass meeting at the Berlin Sportpalast.

Goebbels called for *totaler Krieg* and exhorted the German people to continue the war even though it would be long and difficult because, as he asserted, both Germany's survival and the survival of a non-Bolshevist Europe were at stake.

Ominously he started his speech "inadvertently" mentioning "Ausrotten" (extermination) a reference to the Holocaust.

Because of events the Nazi government closed restaurants, clubs, bars, theatres, and luxury stores throughout the country so that the civilian population could contribute more to the war.

Damn!

We had made plans for Friday night.

Literal Translation:

"DO YOU WANT TOTAL WAR?"
An enthusiastic YES was the answer of the Nazi meeting. Today Germany knows what total war means, better than Goebbels and his yes-shouters foresaw. The total war, wanted by the Nazis, will be continued with ever increasing weight and effectiveness, until Germany capitulates unconditionally.
(Beneath Picture)
THE GERMAN PEOPLE MUST CHOOSE FOR THEMSELVES:
EITHER continuation of the total Nazi-war until final destruction of German manpower and industry.

Picture 4: 09-Apr-1944 Allied raid on Marienburg Focke-Wulf plant and leaflet drop (United States Department of State, 2022).

The bombing was every bit as accurate as the last raid, only this time louder. The payload carried by the B-17s included 250kg bombs that made the ground shake 6km away from the target.

This raid more or less put to an end meaningful production for the rest of the war of the Focke-Wulf at the Marienburg plant.

As the four of us had given up smoking we used our additional 'currency' to buy stuff. At one point I had 15,000 cigarettes saved, and I spent 10,000 of them to buy a gramophone from the Ukrainians and some records for cigarettes that had been made in the Soviet Union. All the metal and springs were chromed steel, it was a lovely machine.

And then we made a cabinet out of the boxes that our Red Cross parcels came in. We acquired three records, all Russian music, singing drama and opera. Every night we took it in turn each evening to do the winding.

The three records were eventually played to death.

We used to stuff a sock in the speaker part so that it muffled the sound, but it didn't stop them from sleeping. About 12 o'clock one night I was on gramophone duty, and I was lying listening to the music.

I heard something, and I said to the other ones, "Did you hear anything?"

"I heard something, but what was it?"

So, we got a candle lit to take a look and there was a slip of paper on the floor that had been put in through the window, and that was the sound that I heard, it must've been the paper just fluttering down to the floor.

The paper was asking us to join the German army with instructions on how to do so. Along with how we would we treated after the war and suitably rewarded?

Others had received the same paper on the neighbouring farms, so we all got together, there was one fella on the next farm who had been studying to be a lawyer, before he was called up, and we selected him to represent us as they asked for volunteers to go to a meeting.

Our "lawyer" went there and listened to what they had to say and came back and told us all about it. We could volunteer to join the British Friekorps.

No one did.

By now we had a fair idea of which way the war was going.

All the Irish soldiers were called to a separate meeting.

It has to be remembered that in the British Army there were Irish soldiers from both north and south of the Irish border.

They were treated like lords and not one of them joined either.

A lot of Poles joined the German army.

We had one fellow on a neighbouring farm who was a milkman and looked after the cows; he was a communist and he used to come and visit us in our billet.

He told us that he would be called up eventually. And when he went, he said he would go.

But whenever he went, whichever front line, he went to the first opportunity he got, he would give himself up to the British or allied forces and of course he was, and we never saw him again.

He was called up right enough and that is when Donald MacLeod from Stornoway was tasked to look after the cows.

There was another man there and his son was working on the farm and when he became 18, he was called up and he was put onto the Western Front in France.

As we progressed through the war our guards on the farm were getting older and older as the younger soldiers were being posted to the various fronts.

We were always being turned over by the SS and Gestapo, but the guard we had at the time always gave us a nod and a wink. Occasionally we had visits from them, but they were more or less ignored by us, much to their annoyance.

On this occasion a higher-ranking German officer looked in and gave us a pep talk, on probably the last occasion, near the end when the Russians were advancing fast.

He looked at a map of the Eastern Front I had taken from a discarded newspaper found blowing around in the road.

I had stuck it on the wall with little flags to show where the front was supposed to be.

I expected trouble.

But he roared with laughter and moved the flags another 150km further forward and said that I was behind the times.

He then went on to warn us that trying to escape was no longer the sporting activity that it had previously been regarded. There were so many paratroopers being dropped to confuse the matter and therefore they had orders to shoot on sight, which was nice of him.

27-Apr-1944, I'm 25 now and I'm in the kitchen garden looking up at the cherry trees I stand guard over every autumn thinking of home and the passing of my youth.

The blossom falls on another spring, how will it all end?

News from the east did not look good, but the locals dare not speak of it, their growing expectation, their dawning reality, their recurring consciousness of entrapment, their growing fear and anxiety of trying to plan for a very uncertain future as all around no longer seems certain or real.

Those who hold us prisoner have long lost their certainty to a growing realisation that they too are now prisoners to an inevitable consequence of their hubris, ambitions, and exceptionalism. But they were in denial.

That spring their world changed.

For the Soviet army the whole of the second half of 1944 was taken up by Operation Bagration, the code name for the 1944 Belorussian Strategic Offensive Operation, which would clear German forces from Belorussia between 22-Jun and 19-Aug

1944. The offensive was named after Prince Bagration who fought and died from fatal wounds at the battle of Borodino as a general in the Imperial Russian Army (Anon, 1939: Key Dates, 2013).

The operation resulted in the almost complete destruction of the German Army Group Centre and three of its component armies the 4th and 9th Army, and the 3rd Panzer Army.

It was the most calamitous defeat for the Wehrmacht. By the end of the operation most of the western Soviet Union had been retaken and the Red Army had achieved footholds in Romania and Poland. German losses soared from 48,000 in May to 169,000 in July and 277,000 in August. German casualties eventually numbered well over half a million killed and wounded.

The primary target of the Soviet offensive was a bridgehead on the Vistula in central Poland, and Operation Bagration was designed to create a crisis in Belorussia to divert German mobile reserves to the central sectors, removing them from the Lublin, and Lvov area where the Soviets intended to undertake the Lvov and Lublin offensive.

This allowed the Red Army to reach the outskirts of Warsaw on the banks of the Vistula by December and put Soviet forces within striking distance of Berlin.

German Army Group Centre had previously proved a tough nut for the Soviets to crack. By Jun-1944, despite shortening its front line, it had been exposed following defeats of Army Group South in the aftermath of the Battle of Kursk, the Second Battle of Kiev, and the Crimean Offensive in the late latter half of 1943.

The Soviets were initially surprised at the success of the Belorussian operation which itself had nearly reached Warsaw. The Soviet advance encouraged the Warsaw uprising against the German occupation forces.

The Soviet Stavka had committed approximately 1.7m soldiers, 24,000 artillery pieces and mortars, 4,080 tanks, and 6,500 aircraft. German strength was approximately 800,000 troops, 9,500 artillery, but only 553 tanks, and 839 aircraft. Army Group Centre was seriously short of mobile reserves and had only semi-formed reserve formations.

In the centre of the front, within 11 days, the Soviets had moved the frontline 80km from the start line and entered Minsk on 03-Jul, and by 28-Jul a staggering 700km had been covered from the start line to Brest-Litovsk. In the middle of these advances Hitler rejected Field Marshal Model's proposal to withdraw the German forces from Estonia and Northern Latvia and retreat to the Daugava River to shorten the line and bolster Army reserves.

In the south the Soviets had entered Hungary on 05-Oct, while in the North the Soviets had launched an offensive to capture Riga, Latvia, and by 10-Oct the Red Army had reached the Niemen River in East Prussia and started to probe German defences all along the East Prussia border. On 20-Nov Hitler left his wartime HQ at the Wolf's Layer at Rastenberg, East Prussia, never to return; he went to Berlin, where he would soon establish himself at the bunker under the Reich Chancellery.

Over the years I had managed to get used to manning the machine used for sowing the crops. The machine had a huge span of 26 spouts at the rear, which were lowered into the ground as it moved forward.

My job was to stand on a platform at the back and keep the spouts clear of soil or mud, to allow the free flow of the seed. On a high seat at the front was the operator of the steering wheel; and the whole contraption was drawn by four horses with a driver in the saddle of the rear left-hand horse.

In spring and autumn, for several seasons, I plodded along the rear platform; the man steering the machine was a tough, strong, middle-aged German labourer named Hans Weiss.

By the last autumn the horseman was a small Russian Cossack boy, Ivan, of course, who coped easily with the four reins in his hand and who enjoyed cracking his long whip above the heads of the leading pair of horses.

On the very long, last day, we worked until late at night to finish the job, by the light of a full moon when the last seed had been sown, Hans fell into a long, silent reverie, motionless on his seat.

Ivan and I did not disturb him in his thoughts and waited patiently for him to come back to life.

Then he suddenly straightened up and said words I will never forget.

He told us he had just been called up to join the Volksstrum, and that we would probably never meet again (which was why we had worked long into the night to finish the job before he left).

He said that most people would laugh at us in scorn for sowing crops we would never reap. He said he would probably be killed, Ivan would go home to Russia, and I to Scotland.

He ended by saying that someone, the next summer, would gather in the crops we had sown, and thank God for what we had done.

It was a sad end to a long friendship; I have always hoped that he survived.

The 30 or so Ukrainian and Polish girls were easy to get on with. They always seemed so happy and were always chattering and singing through the day and into the night. They had about as much German as we knew by that time and that was the medium through which we could converse.

One day the four of us were out strolling along the lane and were walking by and they were all busy reading each other's cards.

"So, you want your cards read," they called out to me.

"No thanks, a lot of nonsense you're not reading my cards, it's a lot of tripe."

However, they were persistent kept it up until they got to read my mate's cards.

All right they said, "Let's read the cards."

So, they got their cards read.

They kept on at me.

"No, away you go."

But anyway, in the end I relented, and they asked me to mention certain numbers, like five, ten, twelve, something like that.

After that we went and visited our mates on the other farms.

Eventually we were making our way back and as we got to where the girls were billeted, my mates said, "We better go in and see what our fortunes are."

"Away you go I'm not going in there, it's a lot of nonsense."

The others went in, and when they came back out, they said to me, "Your cards are not good."

In the end I picked 3 cards.

A couple of days later I was walking by their billet, and they came out wailing and crying.

My cards read that I was going, "on a long journey by foot," the card reader said.

And that I, "would suffer great hardships."

And I would be very lucky if I survived.

I said, "Away you go, a lot of nonsense, a lot of tripe."

Little did I know.

We often spoke about that on the march and my mates would repeatedly say, "Do you believe your cards now?"

A couple of weeks later I was in a field with some labourers pushing a couple of bogeys along the narrow-gauge railway towards the farm filled with the last of the sugar beets.

I stopped to have a pee in the hedge and the others just carried on.

About 100m back down the track a German officer suddenly appeared and stood there looking up and down the track and as soon as he saw me, he came striding down the track towards me.

I was kind of rooted to the spot not really knowing who he was; why he was there; and what did he want.

As he was getting level with me, he suddenly flipped open his leather pistol holster. And levelled the point of the barrel literally on the point of my nose.

His uniform was immaculate, epaulets with two gold studs.

A captain, with skull and crossbones on the middle of his dress cap.

SS!!!

By now he was screaming at me in German, and he was so enraged I really didn't understand anything he was saying, or rather screaming at me.

Suddenly he looked past me, and the anger seemed to subside, but the pistol was still on my nose.

What I didn't know was that a couple of the Ukrainian girls who watched this unfold ran to the farmhouse shouting for the farmer to come and save Peter!!!

Then I heard this big booming voice carry down the field to where we were both standing, and the SS officer smartly holstered his pistol and swung round on his heels and went striding off back down the track to where I first saw him and disappeared through the gap in the hedge.

At that point I turned round to see Hans Eichenberger standing at the barn door looking and watching as the two

Ukrainian girls came running across the field to hurry me back to the farmyard.

By the time I got to the farmyard Hans had gone.

I don't know what he said that could persuade an SS officer from shooting me on the spot, but whatever it was it worked.

I'm pretty convinced that Hans saved my life that day.

There was a growing expectation amongst us as news was filtering through to us on events on the Eastern as well as the Western Front. We knew of the growing intensity of the bombing raids, and we witnessed it on the airfield raid at Marienburg. We learned of the allied landings in Normandy a couple of weeks after the event in Jun-1944, and by the end of the year France and Belgium had been mostly freed from Nazi occupation.

For the Germans things were by now in a parlous state on the Eastern Front. The Russians now sat on the East Prussian border some 150km to the east of us, exhausted and resupplying themselves after Operation Bagration.

Map 15 : Situation Map pf the Easter Front After Operation Bagration 19-Aug-1944.

The Bagration campaign was a huge success for the Soviets on the Eastern Front. Vast amounts of home territory were retaken as the Red Army swept westward to the Polish border and those of the Baltic states. The Russians advanced through a landscape subjected to a scorched earth policy where cities lay in ruins, villages depopulate, and soviet citizens deported west to work for the German war effort. Tens of thousands of German troops were encircled and surrendered during the battles for Minsk and were taken to Moscow and paraded before the world press as part of Operation "Great Waltz" (Anon, Operation Bagration: Soviet Offensive Of 1944, 2006).

Russian black humour there.

The Wehrmacht never recovered from the material and casualty losses sustained, having lost about a quarter of its Eastern Front soldier capability, the losses exceeding that of Stalingrad. They included many experienced soldiers, NCOs, and commissioned officers, which at this stage of the war the Wehrmacht could not replace.

Army Group Centre ceased to exist as an effective fighting force with around 400,000 casualties. Losses on the Soviet side were also considerable, with 180,000 killed and missing, 600,000 wounded and sick, together with 3.000 tanks, 2,500 artillery pieces and 800 aircraft lost.

Bagration drove a deep penetrating wedge between Army Group North and Army Group South in the Ukraine and subsequently weakened them as military assets were diverted to the central sector. This had a debilitating affect on both Army Groups ensuring the need to withdraw from territory much more quickly when faced with the following Red Army offensives in their sectors (Anon, Operation Bagration, 2022).

The end of Operation Bagration coincided with the destruction of many of the strongest units of the Wehrmacht engaged against the Allies on the Western Front in the Falaise Pocket in Normandy, during Operation Overlord. After these stunning victories, supply problems rather than German resistance slowed the Allies' exploitation, and advance eventually came to a halt in both the Western and Eastern Fronts. The Wehrmacht were able to transfer armoured units from the Italian front, where they could afford to give ground, to resist the Soviet advance near Warsaw.

Witnessing the alarm and resignation amongst the German population was depressing as there was a growing expectation of a seismic shift with each day the Russians advanced towards the Fatherland. Any illusions the East Prussians held regarding their future way of life had been brutally exposed with events at Nemmersdorf.

The blossom fell in the spring and the cherries were picked in the autumn after I again stood guard with my sleigh bells over the cherry trees. The harvests were in from the fields.

And we waited.

A rural idyll was about to be shattered.

In the same way as that that we had witnessed in those now far off days in Jun-1940 south of the Somme.

It was their innocence of the occasion that was about to envelope them that was the hardest to observe. We were about to witness a descent into an inferno.

We spent the intervening period preparing ourselves and the family for the flight to the West. News filtering through from the east was less than comforting and despite the prospect of liberation, news of the awful events committed on the civilian population in the Nemmersdorf massacre also included French and Belgian POWs being shot by Soviet troops.

We POWs had experience of this before but under very different circumstances. That was more than four years ago in a hot summer in northeast France.

January 1945 brought one of the coldest winters in northern Europe for fifty years. Snow was deep, drifting off the large flat fields and filling up roads and tracks between roadside hedges.

Night-time temperatures were regularly below -20°c.

The family was leaving together with the Ukrainian girls, all 34 of them, but Gauleiter Eric Koch refused to allow the civilian population to leave their homes until the last minute. For many that was a disaster as the new Soviet offensive simply outpaced and overran hundreds of thousands of civilians in refugee columns fleeing west, with disastrous consequences.

East Prussian civilians died by the thousands, needlessly.

The dressed spring wagon and three wagons were taken out of the sheds and readied for the journey.

I worked with the lads fixing large metal loops over the wagons over which we stretched large tarpaulins that made the wagons look like those used in the Oklahoma Land Rush of 1889 in the US West, that I had read so much about from my cowboy books.

The Ukrainians were all very anxious to leave and go west, only too aware of what would likely await them if "liberated" by Soviet troops.

I was particularly close to one of the girls who pleaded with me to take her with me, but in all good conscience I was well aware of what lay ahead of us all in our migration west, and I had to answer to a different command now.

The horses were brought out bridled, collars put on and four hitched to each of the wagons.

It was gut wrenching to see such a sight as the family left with their goods and chattels; the older Ukrainians were given wagon space on the wagon carrying the horse-feed; and the younger girls wrapped and booted up walked out into a winter wilderness to who knows what kind of fate.

They were great fun, but that would be a meagre ration for us all to feast upon on, on our diverging journeys.

The family, wife and three children, and the Ukrainians left the farm on 23-Jan-1945. The youngest of the children was Marie who was only two years old.

One could only wonder if they would actually make it to safety.

Eichenberger left the farm towards the end of Dec-1944 and the story was that he went into the Volksstrum working on the defences of East Prussia, building tank traps, although he was in his mid-40s. It always seemed unlikely that he would be called up to the Russian front as farming was a reserved occupation.

But these were now desperate times.

There was always a suspicion that if he was from the German part of Switzerland, as we believed him to be, then as a Swiss national he might have gone back to Switzerland to prepare the way for the rest of the family to follow.

Wehrmacht soldiers turned up one day and placed a Spandau sub-machine gun and other equipment in one of the barns with loads of ammunition.

None of that stuff was of any use to us as anybody caught in the area who couldn't account for why they were there would be shot on the spot.

The Wehrmacht came back to the farm after the Eichenbergers had left.

We were confined to our billet as the soldiers started to kill the beasts in the stables, until all were dead.

Hitler's scorched earth policy.

And then they left us to a very eerie quietness we had not heard before.

We were the only ones left on the farm.

After a while we ventured into the house, and we had a good look around.

Feeling somewhat strange to be in the farmer's house we felt really quite uncomfortable.   It was all in order and very clean and tidy as if they had gone out for the day and would return any minute with all the familiar family noises and the kitchen girls chattering and laughing at each other as they went about their chores.

Nothing.

Just a deadly eerie quiet.

We moved down into the basement, and it was full of familiar items of foodstuffs.   Much of which we had actually picked from the fields, gardens, and gained from livestock. There were two tons of coal, two tons of potatoes, there was barrels of pickled pork, sauerkraut, and a white enamel bucket full of pickled eggs. So, we started to help ourselves to some of what had been left.   But it did not taste good, it did not taste right; it was like eating forbidden fruit.

Our guard had warned us before he left that we would be on the move any day and that we should not stray from the farmyard.   He pointed to the incident with the SS officer as a case in point as to just how vulnerable we were if caught at large.

We were not the only ones at risk.

The civilian population at large were under strict orders not to move from their homes as they were all now under military jurisdiction. If they could not account for themselves being in a place where they shouldn't be then they too ran the risk of being summarily shot.

We gathered together a few provisions for the journey ahead to wherever it would take us.

The next morning guards came from the Stalag, and we were marched off the farm to join a column of POWs from Willenberg Camp.   A column that would eventually grow to some 800 men.

We left on the 24-Jan.

Two days later the Russians attacked Marienburg.

The rural idyll was shattered.

The collapse of East Prussia began to gather pace as its citizens began to suffer from the dreadful fate of total war familiar to those who had already suffered from allied aerial bombardment.

1.5 million people who either birth, choice, or compulsion now found themselves caught in the oncoming onslaught of a military juggernaut that seemed omnipotent and irresistible to suffer experiences far removed from those in other theatres of war in the west.

Refugees came from widely dispersed farming communities that occupied a fertile and verdant land that stretched from Memel in the north to Danzig in the east.

These people had suffered the shifting tides of war and were ruled variously over the centuries by Prussians, Poles, Swedes, and now the German Reich.

In the invasion of Sep-1939 the East Prussians rejoiced at the unification of their homeland with that of the Greater German Reich as it dismantled terms of the Treaty of Versailles and the Polish corridor created by it was no more.

By 1945 the population had risen to 2.1 million mostly ethnic Germans and additional some 200,000 Allied POWs, forced labourers, and thousands of German refugees from the Baltic states to the north.

This ripple of shifting populations was soon to become a tidal wave.

The social character of the state leant heavily towards the archetypal East Prussian Junker class, and additionally a great aristocratic family class. Underneath this elite ruling class of gentry, Junker and aristocrat were the ordinary citizens who were dependent on the ruling class as more or less peasants, who possessed barely enough food to live. Theirs was a semi-feudal relationship with this veneer of ruling classes as they scratched a living tilling the fields of their betters.

The ruling class had a peculiar relationship with the Nazis who seemed to take second place in East Prussia. The belted knights still held the power while the merchant middle class lived mostly in and around the provincial towns and city capital of Königsberg, while the ruling classes lived in gilded cages in their beautiful country houses.

Before the Nazis rise to power this ruling class regarded themselves as civilising missionaries upholding the principals of Christendom in a sea of East European barbarism.

Since 1939, East Prussia had been a backwater, largely sheltered from the impact of world conflict.

Whoever lived through those who were sensitive to change the last few months of 1944 must have felt that never before had the light been so intense, the sky so lofty, or the distances so vast.

Heimat is homeland in German and is an important word of significance for the people of East Prussia.

"It was incredibly quiet," said Ursula Salzer, daughter of a Königsberg railway manager (Hastings, 2004). "We had no sense of the war going on, and plenty to eat."

Nonetheless the sky was closing in as summer slipped into a familiar autumn that was beginning to witness a new sense of urgency in military activity and a rising expectation that the citizens di not want to speak of. As some desultory air rads were carried out by the Soviets on Königsberg the RAF came along to do a proper job on the medieval city.

Towards the end of Aug-1944 the RAF carried out two air raids on the city. The first raid largely missed its target, but the second raid struck with devastating effect, suffering considerable loss of nearly 10% of the Lancaster bombers on the mission due to a very effective fighter defence of the city. Bomber Command estimated that 41% of all housing and 20% of local industry were destroyed (Hastings, 2004).

Yet the people of Königsberg cared only about the destruction which the RAF's aircraft left behind. When a bailed-out Lancaster crewman was being led through the ruined streets by his escort, a young woman shouted bitterly at him in English, "I hope you're satisfied!"

Her name was Elfride Kowitz. Her family's dairy business and their corner house in Neuer-Graben had been utterly destroyed in the attack. When she emerged from a shelter after the raid was over, she stood gazing in horror at the ruins of her family home. She saw a man in a helmet. It was her father. They fell into each other's arms and sobbed in despair. "Both my parents were completely destroyed," she said.

"They had lost everything they had worked all their lives for." Her father saved only the family's radio set. Everything else was gone. Her bitterness never faded: "That raid was so futile—it did nothing to shorten the war." (Hastings, 2004).

Amongst those who suffered from the air raids many shared a common hope that the bombers were symbols of hope. Michael Wieck, a sixteen-year-old, could not enter the city's air-raid shelters, because he was a Jew. He witnessed the RAF's "Christmas tree" pathfinder markers drifting towards their target to illuminate them for the bomb aimers.

Michael, after the war, goes on to recount that "I was not so critical of bombing then as I became after the war. We knew that the only thing that could save our lives was the victory of the Allies, and this seemed a necessary part of it. Schoolbooks, curtains, debris of all kinds rained half-burned from the sky. The heat was so enormous that many people could not leave their cellars. Everything was burning. Some people took refuge from the flames by jumping into the river. When it was over, the scene was like the aftermath of an atomic explosion."

Upon reflection he feels that the RAF's second raid on Königsberg seemed a catastrophe (Hastings, 2004).

Local Hitler Youth leader Hans Siwik, a former member of the Führer's bodyguard, was as appalled as Wieck, from a somewhat different perspective. Siwik was disgusted by the "immorality" of the British assault.

"It seemed crazy that people should destroy such a place. People in Königsberg were unaccustomed to raids. We didn't have a lot of flak. I was horrified by the idea of such vandalism." Yet worse, much worse, was to come.

Hans von Lehndorff watched the storks begin their annual migration southwards. It was difficult to resist the need to do likewise. "Yes, *you're* flying away! But what of *us*? What is to become of us, and of our country?" (Hastings, 2004).

East Prussians recognised that they were doomed to suffer Germany's first experience of ground assault, because they were nearest to the relentless advance of the Red Army.

The East Prussian Gauleiter was one of the most detested bureaucrats in the Third Reich, Eric Koch. Earlier in the war, as Reich commissioner in Ukraine, Koch had delivered a speech notorious even by the standards of Nazi rhetoric:

"We are a master race. We must remember that the lowliest German worker is racially and biologically a thousand times more valuable than the population here. I did not come to spread bliss. The population must work, work and work again. We did not come here to give out manna. We have come here to create the basis for victory." (Wistrich, 2001)

As the Soviet shadow fell upon the landscape of East Prussia that went beyond its eastern border Erich Koch its Gauleiter of the Nazi Party was delivering bombast and bile in increasingly strident tones regard the German supremacy on the battlefield that would save the province.

He made it quite clear that to even contemplate civilian flight or military retreat would invite the possibility of German defeat and would therefore be considered as treason. As citizens of the Reich, he declared that it was their duty to stand fast and hold onto every inch of Prussian soil.

There would be no evacuation.

By now the German citizens knew the significance of flight and defeat enshrined in the Yalta agreement that once defeated, the province would be ceded to Poland, in compensation for eastern Polish lands which were to become part of the Soviet Union.

Additionally, 16 million ethnic Germans throughout eastern Europe would be deported to the new post-war frontiers of Germany. Roosevelt was recorded as early as 1943, "...he thought we should make some arrangements to move the Prussians out of East Prussia the same way the Greeks were moved out of Turkey after the last war," recorded Harry Hopkins in 1943. "While this is a harsh procedure, it is the only way to maintain peace and, in any circumstances, the Prussians cannot be trusted." (Hastings, 2004).

While Churchill asserted the justice of this pioneer exercise in "ethnic cleansing" to the House of Commons on 05-Dec-1944, "a clean sweep will be made," he said. "I am not alarmed by the prospect of the disentanglement of populations, nor even by these large transferences, which are more possible in modern conditions than they ever were before. The disentanglement of populations which took place between Greece and Turkey after the last war, was in many ways a success," he declared to the British Parliament (Hansard, 1944).

The purpose was clear, compulsory migration would ensure that Germans could not in the future act aggressively on the interests of their ethnic brethren in Eastern Europe, and Prussia, would be dismembered. There would be no more German minorities elsewhere.

The first Soviet incursions into East Prussia took place on 22-Oct-1944, at Nemmersdorf and several other border hamlets. Five days later, General Hossbach's 4th Army retook the villages.

Very few citizens survived. Women had been nailed to barn doors and farm carts or been crushed by tanks after being raped. Their children had been killed. Forty French POWs working on local farms had been shot.

The Red Army's behaviour reflected not casual brutality, but systematic sadism rivalling that of the Nazis. "In the farmyard stood a cart, to which more naked women were nailed through their hands in a cruciform position," reported a Volkssturm militiaman who entered Nemmersdorf with the Wehrmacht.

"Near the Roter Krug, a large inn, stood a barn and to each of its two doors a naked woman was nailed through the hands, in a crucified posture. In the dwellings we found a total of 72 women, including children, and one man, 74, all dead, all murdered in a bestial fashion, except only for a few who had bullet holes in their heads. Some babies had their heads bashed in." (Hastings, 2004).

Even the Russians displayed subsequent embarrassment about what had taken place. Moscow's official history of the Great Patriotic War of the Soviet Union, usually reticent about such matters, conceded: "Not all Soviet troops correctly understood how they had to behave in Germany. In the first days of fighting in East Prussia, there were some isolated violations of the correct norms of behaviour." (Hastings, 2004).

In reality, of course, what happened in October in East Prussia was a foretaste of the Red Army's conduct across Poland and Germany in the awful months to come.

Perhaps it had its roots in the by now infamous Berlin Sprtspalast speech by Goebbels in Feb-1943 he called for *totaler Krieg* and more ominously mentioning the "Ausrotten" (extermination) a reference.

Any lingering doubts that may have existed within the minds of East Prussian citizens were crushed by Koch and Goebbels who the events at Nemmersdorf into a propaganda campaign that recorded in every gruesome detail the atrocities committed by such barbarism hoping that it would steel the hearts of East Prussia's defenders.

Posters of the victims were distributed throughout the province and film newsreels shown in every cinema. This prompted many women to acquire cyanide capsules, and a few succumbed to their immediate use.

A ban on civilian evacuation remained in place apart from villages on the borders which were being turned into fortresses, as poster appeared decreeing that anyone who took flight from their home would be executed as a traitor.

Cattle began to roam free across the land that had by now succumbed to the early frosts and snow flurries of winter. A harbinger of the coming terror they were in many respects the first refugees, as the provinces defender grew more anxious by the day as their doubts began to realise the magnitude of the task before them.

the province by now was placed at the junction of two Soviet armies, who were being assigned to thrust towards Berlin, with Rokossovsky more or less on eastern border while Zhukov rubbed along the southern border.

East Prussia was not Zhukov's priority, but he needed Rokossovsky to protect his right flank towards Berlin. As Rokossovsky protected Zhukov's flank his army would thrust across the province with Zhukov on his left flank and together they would assail the Vistula and head straight into the heart of Germany. In the meantime, Rokossovsky brough pressure to bear on the eastern border to tie down German forces and prevent them from being withdrawn to Zhukov's front.

The Russian armies attacking East Prussia under Chernyakhovsky to the north and Rokossovsky to the east possessed overwhelming superiority. They outnumbered the

Germans by ten to one in regular troops, seven to one in tanks, twenty to one in artillery.

Throughout the winter of 1944 running inti 1945 the Russians had amassed 3,800 Russian tanks and assault guns along the border of East Prussia. While Chernyakhovsky would move in from the north and seize Konigsberg; Rokossovsky would move from the east and south and head for Danzig and at the same time protect Zhukov's right flank as he moved west directly for Berlin.

When the first Russian troops swept forward, they met fierce resistance. The Germans took every advantage they could, based upon known local geography and the fact that they would now be fighting on their own territory for the first time. Taking up positions in in the cellars of houses commanding crossroads and key strategic points.

German propaganda had been painted in huge letters on many buildings, in the days before the Red Army crossed the border, to which the political officers of the Red Army held meetings designed to promote hatred of the enemy, through discussion based on "How shall I avenge myself on our German occupiers?" and "An eye for an eye."

It worked; this was a genie that once out of the bottle proved impossible to put back in. alarmed at the bloodbath this created they tried to reign in the Soviet soldier's world view, it was far too little too late to change an ethos cultivated over years of struggle. "Hatred for the enemy had become the most important motivation for our men," wrote a Russian historian. "Almost every Soviet soldier possessed some personal reason to seek vengeance." (Hastings, 2004).

To the Russian soldiers entering East Prussia there was a sense of bewilderment as to why the Germans want ed to invade Russia when there was comparative wealth all around them in the form of prosperous towns, villages, and well-ordered and productive farms.

Lieutenant Gennady Klimenko said, "German villages looked like heaven compared with ours. Everything was cultivated. There were so many beautiful buildings. They had so much more than we did." Vladimir Gormin shared his enthusiasm, "Great country! So clean and tidy compared to ours!" (Beevor, The Fall of Berlin, 1945, 2002).

Understandably, the political officers in the Red Army became alarmed at the changing mind-sets of the soldiers and the ideological impact it may have, particularly as they had spent years promoting the benefits of socialist economics over that of fascism. In time they channelled Russian rage towards the wealth of the Germans in stark contrast to relative Soviet destitution gained by Nazi invasion, theft, and plunder.

Once on German territory the invaders found wealth and booty beyond their wildest dreams, and they began to loot on an epic scale to the extent they began to compete with each other on how much largesse they could acquire and send back to family in the Motherland.

They looted and pillage on a scale that went way beyond German worldly good and chattels to include the civilian population itself, particularly women and young girls. It was in Jan-1945 that Soviet soldiers began to rape women on a scale that went way beyond the need for casual sexual gratification. It was wonton, gratuitous, indefensible, but designed to tyrannise an entire population as a form of indemnity.

Corporal Osminov spotted in a billet one day a soldier lazily playing a piano with his toes, while staring fascinated at his own image in a huge gilt mirror placed on the opposite wall.

Civilians foolish enough to remonstrate were simply shot and their homes put to the torch. Once some Russian women, forced labourers, appeared at Red Army HQ, trying to explain the difference between good and bad local Germans. An officer said roughly, "We don't have time to start classifying fascists." (Hastings, 2004).

Very soon Red Army soldiers were sifting through the debris of the Hitler HQ at Rastenberg, The Wolf's Lair from which Hitler and his High Command had plotted and planned the invasion of Russia nearly four years earlier. One Russian idly flicked through a discarded telephone directory with an entry for the Fuhrer, Dial "1".

Many were fascinated by the eery silence of many German villages as they kicked down doors and found ovens still hot and food on the table. The only people left behind were forced labourers and a growing number of POWs, many French, Italian and some British who had been abandoned along with the livestock.

Booby traps were endemic. These had been set by the military once the civilians had left the property for the unwary Soviet keen to acquire the spoils. Very soon the invader learned to open doors tied to a long piece of rope from a safe distance.

However, an enemy that was as deadly as the Germans was alcohol to which the Russian soldier was terrifyingly vulnerable. It was this vulnerability that was to answer the sometimes-bewildering whimsicality with which they would treat the conquered local populations. On one occasion the Russians captured a railyard where they found a tanker wagon full of neat spirit, no doubt made from sugar beet. The men were very soon reduced to an almost helpless stupor before the Germans counter attacked. The unit only narrowly avoided disaster.

The Red Army did not behave with universal brutality. In one village, local people were praying in church, awaiting their end, as the first occupiers arrived. The villagers were astounded when instead a Soviet officer brought them bread. One German woman marvelled, "The Russians have been here half a day, and we are still alive!" Forward units often behaved in a punctilious, even kindly fashion, but warned local inhabitants, "We can vouch for our people, but not for what is coming behind," the great undisciplined, wantonly barbaric host which followed the spearheads (Hastings, 2004).

Boys and old men were dragooned into the Volksstrum in their thousands for active duty in defence of the Fatherland.

Eric Koch the Gauleiter of East Prussia had ordered the formation of "Hitler Youth battle groups" from the ages of 13 to 16. They had been hastily armed with aging WW1 weaponry and dressed in various type of ill-fitting worn-out uniforms that had been cut for fully grown men and not mere boys. Comical yes but horrifying as their eyes filed with unease and expectation. It could not be expected that at a distance Soviet soldiers could tell the difference between your and professional soldiery.

The only thing that they could be distinguished by was the school satchels some carried packed with food that their mothers had prepared.

Was Germanic heroism or was it some dark insanity?

Most professional soldiers viewed it as the latter, with a fair degree of disgust at the wasteful dissipation of innocents.

Who would ever be able to judge this absolute sacrifice?

In one action a group was deployed to dig anti-tank ditches. Next day the company were in trucks with a single anti-tank gun to occupy positions beside a sunken road and sighted their guns. After a long, shivering wait, they saw Russian infantry advancing towards them, with three T-34s following.

They began firing at the advancing infantry but soon the aged weapons began to jam as soldiers jumped from foxhole to foxhole, helping to clear them. The nearest Russians came within yards of them before, to the Germans' surprise, pulling back in failing light.

The children fell asleep in the snow where they lay.

Early next morning, the Soviet advance recommenced, this time supported by accurate mortar fire. The commanding officer had once told the Führer that he yearned for the opportunity to win a medal suddenly found that his interest in decorations had now faded. "The issue wasn't about winning; it was about surviving; it was about delaying the Russians long enough for the refugees to escape."

He hardly knew the names of any of his boys, he simply addressed them as "you." In the middle of the morning, a truck-full of panzer fausts arrived. No one knew how to use them. They fired some twenty without effect before a lucky shot hit a T-34, which brewed up.

Russian mortaring was causing casualties. They could only use strips of torn shirt to bandage wounds.

After hours of indecisive firing, there was a muffled roar of armoured vehicles behind them. A Panzer officer dismounted and gazed in amazement at the children.

"What the hell's all this?" he cried in some disgust.

He told the commanding officer and his boys to make themselves scarce. They had six killed and fifteen wounded. "The boys were traumatised." "Their patriotism had shrivelled away." His own enthusiasm for combat had also waned.

As they marched towards the coast among the throng of refugees, he told his company to throw away their weapons and try to find civilian clothes. "They were all from towns the Russians now held. I could not send them home."

The officer kept his own uniform, and with a handful of boys eventually secured space on a naval supply ship leaving Pillau. It may be assumed that he was able to exercise his authority as a Party functionary. After two days at sea, he reached the temporary safety of Stettin (Hastings, 2004).

Towards the end of January most of East Prussia was by now in Soviet hands apart from two enclaves, one around Königsberg and the other in the Vistula delta, both joined by the Frisches Haff, a 100km long sandbar that separated the Vistula Lagoon from the Gulf of Danzig in the Baltic.

The fortunes of the battlefield, and of the precarious escape routes, seesawed violently, tragically, through ten weeks that followed.

One illustration of the brutality of the conflict in East Prussia was illustrated towards the end of Jan-1945 at a Soviet assault towards Konigsberg's rail line to Pillau. The engine was halted by a T-34 on the tracks. The passengers jumped out when Red Army soldiers started firing on the carriages. Russian infantry then embarked on a familiar orgy of looting and rape.

To the south and west Rokossovsky started his advance on 14 Jan and cleared most of East Prussia while Chernyakhovsky was still hammering at the gates of Königsberg.

At the irresistible force the Russians represented German commanders pleaded with Berlin to allow 4th Army between Danzig and Königsberg to withdraw, to avoid envelopment. Inevitably, Hitler refused. Guderian told the commander of Army Group North, Hans Reinhardt, that 4th Army would have to maintain its existing positions.

"But that's quite impossible," protested its commander.

"It means everything is going to collapse."

"Yes, my dear Reinhardt," said Guderian wearily.

When at last a modest withdrawal was authorised, it was too late (Guderian, 2015).

However, Stalin was losing patience with Chernyakhovsky's failure to quickly take Königsberg. From the comfort of the Kremlin in Moscow he ordered Rokossovsky's to pivot north towards the Baltic coast and cut East Prussia from the Reich.

On the 22-Jan Rokossovsky's army carried out a sweeping pincer movement along the southern border and then North up the Vistula valley towards Marienburg along the Warsaw-Danzig railway axis to achieve this objective.

By the 29-Jan Rokossovsky's troops were forcing the defences of Elbing some 30km from Danzig. They reached the coast along a 25km to close the Soviet ring around the Germans 4th Army with Chernyakhovsky's armies to the north and the Germans in between (Anon, The Argus, 1945). Within days, Zhukov was driving towards the Oder with Pomerania on his right flank and Rokossovsky crosses the Vistula and drives towards Danzig.

At the shock of two Soviet fronts smashing into East Prussia wrought havoc among millions of German soldiers and refugees. This only served to open a wide gap between Rokossovsky and Zhukov, who was appalled to find his right flank exposed, the result was that any possibility that Zhukov could have reached Berlin "on the run" in February had gone.

It was the Stavka's worst strategic decision of the last phase of the war and ultimately of course, Stalin.

I don't think Zhukov ever forgave him.

Rokossovsky's forces became embroiled in a long succession of battles along the Baltic coast. In all these the Soviets triumphed, yet they seemed strategically irrelevant.

Once Berlin fell, surviving pockets of German resistance could be addressed at leisure. By sending Rokossovsky north, Stalin importantly weakened the drive for Hitler's capital.

Rokossovsky's tanks crashed into 4th Army to the south-west of Königsberg and into hundreds of thousands of trekking refugees.

On 21-Jan, Soviet spearheads began shelling throngs of fugitives struggling to escape through Elbing towards the Reich. On 23-Jan they entered Ebling, temporarily halting the refugee trek. Having suffered substantial casualties from local defenders, the Russians were obliged to withdraw. They did not enter the town again for a fortnight. Only the Frisches Haff lagoon and the sea offered a passage for refugees.

With considerable courage, the German commanders on the Baltic decided to defy Berlin in order to save 400,000 troops and the great mass of civilians milling helplessly across thousands of square kilometres of snowbound countryside, searching for a path westwards.

On the moonlit night of 26-Jan, 4th Army launched a counter-offensive which drove back the Russian and broke through to Elbing. Once again, a land passage for the refugees was open.

Reinhardt of Army Group North was sacked for his disobedience, as was 4th Army's commander, Hossbach.

Hitler was wholly uninterested in the plight of his suffering people. Hundreds of thousands of fugitives, however, had cause to be grateful to the generals. Across the entire front from Königsberg to Warsaw tanks, artillery, infantry, machine-guns were contesting ground occupied by throngs of civilians and POWs fleeing westwards, and the merciless winter weather.

The plight of East Prussia's fugitives was worst of all. Women and infants huddled upon columns of carts laden with possessions, figures shuffling through the snows became doomed extras in the drama of the conflict.

Russian attitudes towards the refugees ranged from indifference to deliberate brutality. When advancing T-34s met trekkers, the tanks smashed through their midst as mere battlefield flotsam. Again and again, Russian artillery and machine-guns raked columns of trekkers or blocked their flight. Cold and hunger also killed huge numbers. To this day, surviving East Prussians place the heaviest burden of blame for their fate upon Gauleiter Koch, who denied them licence to flee before the Russians came (Beevor, The Fall of Berlin, 1945, 2002).

But Soviet gunfire was directly responsible for the slaughter of tens of thousands. The Russians' policy owed little to military necessity and everything to the culture of vengeance fostered within the Red Army over almost four years of Russian propaganda.

Once the Soviet commitment to fire and the sword became evident, the German army in East Prussia performed extraordinary feats of courage and sacrifice, to hold open paths to safety for the civilians.

Russians said, "Remember what Germany did in our country." It was indeed true that for each German killed by the Red Army could be counted the dead of three, four, five Russians killed by the Wehrmacht, the Luftwaffe and the SS in their glory days.

Yet few modern readers can escape a revulsion in contemplating the fate of the East Prussian people in the first months of 1945.

Given that there had already been agreement it can hardly be a surprise that the Russians remained untroubled by the plight of refugees that the western allies had unwittingly contributed too.

Waltraut Ptack was only thirteen in early 1945 when all she and her friends talked about was suicide when the Russians came. For her and her family it was a doom-laden Christmas indeed that lacked all the usual festivities. Especially so as her eldest brother Günther had been killed fighting on the western front.

On 23-Jan, the Ptack's left their home just a few hours before the Russians arrived, towing a family sled. Waltruat pleaded to take her doll. Like everyone else on the trek the shed their goods at the side of the road to lighten the load they had to drag through the snow and the bitter cold. Passing trains carried only troops to the front and the wounded back.

At one point a soldier took pity on the misery of the Ptack children. He allowed them to climb on a freight train, which crawled through the countryside for many hours, stopping repeatedly.

Then they heard that the Russians were in Elbing.

They were shunted eastward again.

After a few kilometres, all the passengers were ordered off.

They stumbled for a few kilometres to the edge of the Frisches Haff. Through the days that followed, they scavenged for food and sought a path to safety, as Russian artillery fire grew steadily closer. They slept in barns, cowsheds, or abandoned houses.

On a truck about to cross the Frisches Haff they managed to get aboard; they arrived a Military Police checkpoint where there was a bitter exchange of words as the MPs insisted on the sixteen-year-old son join the Volkssturm. In settlement the father had to exchange the place of the son at the prospect of almost certain death.

They never saw their father again.

Next morning, the skies cleared, the sun shone, and the Soviet Air Force came. They watched the bombs leave the aircraft above, so small in the air, and then saw huge explosions all around them, blasting holes in the ice and killing many people who stood upon it. The aircraft maintained a shuttle all through the daylight hours, "Many, many people died that day" (Hastings, 2004).

The family managed to scramble onto a freighter that took them to Danzig. They then trekked from Danzig along the coast of Pomerania and spent the rest of the war in an abandoned seaside villa.

Another more aristocratic family resided at Wildenhoff, some way between Königsberg and Elbing on the Count von Schwerin estate. They shared their last Christmas with a various collection of Russians, Poles, and French POW's who had worked the estate for the past four years. They gave each other small gifts and the French prisoners sang Christmas carols for the last time.

After many years of German victories, the cellars of Wildenhoff were well stocked with anything from malt whisky to champagne. The festivities were very definitely over as von Schwerin went to the front at the beginning of Jan-1945, two weeks later he was killed in action.

The were living on a volcano and with each passing day the urge to flee the coming onslaught grew. Eventually the urge was irresistible, the family papers were walled up in the cellars along with treasure that had been saved in the aftermath of the RAF air raids on Königsberg the previous autumn. Gauleiter Koch promised to evacuate the treasures should the Russians approach but none of that came to pass.

He had his own problems.

A Ukrainian woman art historian was billeted with them as curator of the art treasures, which included a priceless hoard of icons looted by the Wehrmacht from Kiev. She refused to abandon her cherished charges.

"When the Russians come," said the Ukrainian, "I shall set fire to the whole place and everything in it."

Finally, they left the estate for the railway station where a train took them to where they had a cousin at Braunsberg, only to find that he himself was about to depart on his own onward journey west. As a group they were one of the first to make it across the ice of the Frisches Haff, on 24-Jan. Soldiers helped them with the wagons. They manged to escape westwards into Germany proper. The horrors of their war were not yet ended, but they had left behind the nightmare of East Prussia.

They never saw Wildenhoff again.

Further west in Germany itself the news from East Prussia hung like an albatross as a portent of that that was approaching.

As fleeing East Prussians arrived in Berlin news of the horror that was unfolding began to spread through the Berlin population. The death, the cold freezing temperatures in the open, the callous disregard for life exhibited by the Soviet Army. Babies being carried by mothers that were long dead from cold and malnutrition, attended by the growing amount of graft being exhibited by German soldiers and Nazi apparatchik as discipline was tested to destruction.

As a scorched earth policy soldiers were shooting cattle, horses, and also resorting to looting and pillaging of vacant property and sometimes before they were even vacated.

Berliners set up soup kitchens on railway station platforms and clothing dispensed to replace those lost in flight. A cruel irony is that a great deal of the clothing given out was itself the product of a plunder from those sent to the death camps.

"Berliners are receiving the first visible warning that the Red Army stands before the frontiers of the Reich," wrote the German correspondent of Stockholms-Tidningen on 24-Jan.

"Columns of trucks crowded with refugees and baggage and bags and sacks roll through the streets on their way between one railway station and another. Most of the refugees are typical German peasants from the East, and only women and children, no men. They peep wide-eyed from under their headscarves at the ruined streets of the capital they are now seeing for the first time in their lives."

Yet Berliners did not receive the easterners with sympathy.

For four years, the people of East Prussia, Saxony and Silesia had lived in tranquillity, while the cities of the west had been bombed to destruction. More than a few Berliners were by no means displeased now to see their smug fellow countrymen from the east dragged down into the common misery.

Schadenfreude, indeed.

The Wehrmacht estimated that 3.5 million ethnic Germans were already in flight, and this number increased dramatically over the weeks ahead.

In mid-January in Berlin, said Paul von Stemann, "We expected the Russians to arrive any day. The East was like a flood which had broken all dikes. Berlin sat back and prepared itself for the flood to roll over it, only hoping that it would be short and sharp" (Hastings, 2004)

At Yalta on the evening of 06-Feb, in a spasm of compassion Churchill said to his daughter Sarah: "I do not suppose that at any moment of history has the agony of the world been so great or widespread. Tonight, the sun goes down on more suffering than ever before in the world." (Hastings, 2004).

Churchill knew little, when he spoke, about what was taking place in East Prussia. Yet its people's fate formed a not insignificant part of his vision.

The winter was so bloody cold as I repeatedly said to Wilf, "We're all prisoners now".

Chapter 6: The Fall – Disintegration of the Third Reich

On the afternoon of 11-Jan-1945, Generaloberst Guderian received the news he had been dreading. His intelligence chief confirmed that the great Soviet winter offensive was to begin the next morning. Only two days before, Guderian had warned Adolf Hitler: "The Eastern Front is like a house of cards. If the front is broken through at one point all the rest will collapse. (Guderian, 2015)"

Guderian was by now the head of the OKH, having fallen in and out with Hitler on a number of occasions. Guderian was now responsible for the Eastern Front. He had feared from the start that Hitler's Ardennes Offensive the previous month would leave his forces in the east severely weakened in the face of the Red Army.

Stalin did not trust his western Allies, especially Churchill. He had made a habit of rubbing in the fact that British and American armies had suffered few casualties in the war against their common enemy while the sacrifices of the Red Army had been enormous. He even pretended that he had advanced the date of his winter offensive in order to save the Americans in the Ardennes. This was untrue. The German attack in Belgium had been halted on 26-Dec.

Stalin's real reason for bringing forward the date was due to meteorological forecasts. A thaw was predicted for later in January and the Red Army needed the ground to remain frozen for its tank armies to charge forward to the river Oder.

The Soviet's winter offensive began on 12-Jan on Konev's 1st Ukrainian Front south of Warsaw, advancing from the Soviet bridgeheads west of the Vistula towards Upper Silesia. Over the next two days, the 2nd and 3rd Belorussian Fronts assaulted East Prussia, and Zhukov's 1st Belorussian Front began its operation towards Berlin from Warsaw. Once crossings had been secured over the Vistula around Warsaw, there was little to stop the 1ˢᵗ and 2ⁿᵈ Soviet Tank Armies. Their headlong advance by day and night meant that all orders from the führer's HQ were 24 hours out of date by the time they reached German divisions.

The front collapsed even more rapidly than Guderian had feared. By now there were still some 8 million German civilians fleeing for their lives. Hitler made things worse by his meddling, and on 31-Jan the first Red Army soldiers were creating bridgeheads across the frozen Oder 100km from Berlin.

It seemed that the whole civilian population was on the move, and it was. Although they had a day or two head start, they were clogging up the road and railway networks for 100km around.

We were soon to catch up with them.

We left the farm in fairly good spirits, but apprehensive about the conditions we were marching in and the growing awareness that the Russians were on the move. As we marched west, we could see the Soviet front at night lighting up the winter sky, the sound was like a rolling thunder under a starlit sky that made it all the more surreal.

We took what we could with us, but within 20km we were beginning to abandon the heavier baggage simply to lighten the load under very extreme conditions. One thing I did hold onto was an enamel milk pail filled with pork fat that I found in the cellar of the house.

We marched down the country lanes between the different farms around Schadwalde and as we passed each farm more men joined the column. Within a couple of hours, we reached the main road between Marienburg and Neuteich where we merged into a column of British POWs coming up from our camp at Willenberg. By now our column had grown to more than 800 men.

We then turned north to Neuteich and then west through Damerau to the main bridge that crossed the Vistula carrying a road and railway from Marienburg to Dirchau on the west bank.

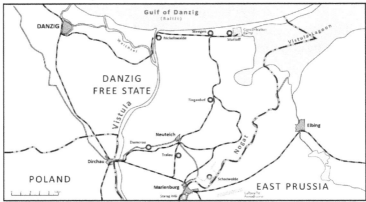

Map 16: Crossing the Vistula.

As we approached the bridge it was absolute chaos as civilians mixed with POWs going west and German soldiers moving east to face the Soviet invasion.

It was pandemonium.

German troops struggling through the snow, thousands of German civilians with carts piled high with their possessions, staff cars towing armoured vehicles to save fuel, SS and German police with revolvers drawn shouting at everybody. And in this melee, we could also see German engineers working on the bridge placing charges getting ready to blow the span.

We were halted and the commanding German officer in charge of our column set off to arrange a time for crossing the bridge.

He came back, it was not good news.

They were about to blow the bridge with us stuck against the east bank of the Vistula.

We watched as the officer and his staff group had a conference, heads bowed looking over maps pointing in one direction and then the other.

Great!

At this rate we are going to be in the front-line between Fritz and Ivan.

A couple of guards joined the group and the officers stopped and listened to what they had to say.

The guards had found a small ferry just down river from the bridge that was plying small groups of people across the river.

The whole column turned and marched along the riverbank. The ferry was simply a platform by which the ferry men pulled the platform back and forward across the Vistula. The river at this point was 300m wide; and it looked like 20 people at a time were being put onto the platform and pulled to the opposite bank.

It took about 10-12 hours to get us all onto the west bank and by now it was dark, and the temperature had plummeted.

However, the Germans were keen to keep us going and get us as far away from the river as possible, so we set off in the dark heading north towards Danzig. We marched for 3 hours through the dark on the road towards Danzig and by now it was too late for the guards to see where they were going.

We were in the village of Langenau and it was deserted; all the houses had been evacuated. So, they put us into the houses. We just crashed out on the floor exhausted but thankfully inside in the relative warmth, so we broke out some bread we were carrying and dipped it into the bucket of pig fat, lovely.

The next day we started the march, and we walked all day; it was snowing and there was already a foot of snow half melted and frozen on the roads. By the time darkness came, we had reached a small settlement and the only accommodation was a barn with straw in it and a small farmhouse. Some lucky ones got into the house that was empty while the rest of us were put into the barn.

We learnt a lesson there. When you took your boots off at night your socks were wet and when exposed to the freezing temperature even in the barn your socks and toes would freeze. The dreaded danger of frostbite.

In future the boots would stay on.

Some of us slept in a stable with the horses – it was warm in there.

By the end of the second day on the march we had put some 80km between ourselves and the farm at Schadwalde.

Just 48 hours after we left the farm the Russians attacked Marienburg and took position along the south bank of the Nogat.

Twice in that first week we had to move off in the middle of the night because the Russians were down the road. The Germans billeted us wherever there was a building suitable. During this time, we were joined by many more British POWs and a thousands of Russian POWs.

One night for six hours we marched through a blizzard, the Russians leading. They were dropping dead on the side of the road as they walked. Of course, they had not had the protection of the Red Cross parcels and they had been subjected to a deliberate ploy of starvation. After three weeks with very little food, probably some bread and a cupful of steamed potatoes three or four times a week we were clear of the Russian advance and were able to rest for one day.

The Russian POWs were no longer with us.

We were hanging about one morning as we were being called to order ready for the day's march ahead when one of our mates struck up a song. The lyrics were all a bit improvised, but the tune was well known to us, when Darky came up with a line to start us off:

"Somewhere in Poland mother dear.
And I followed that up and sang,
Why are we walking about in the snow?
Darky followed up with,
It's colder here than over there,
it's 45 below."
I've since heard that on the wireless. What we did was base
our little ditty on "Oh It's A Lovely War" Sung By Courtland &
Jeffries, first published in 1918.

On the 31-Jan, we came to Stolp, just to the north of Danzig,
and marched into an evacuated German artillery barracks.

In just seven days we had marched over 250km in the most
appalling weather conditions.

Stolp was Polish originally, we could see where they had
changed the Polish Eagle for the German Swastika.   In the
barracks I met Duncan Smith from Tarbert in Argyll and he
wasn't very well.   And as I was going through the door I looked
down at the end of his bed, his feet were black, frost bite.

I inquired afterwards how he got on and I was told that both
his feet had been amputated.

That happened often.

We were told to pack and be ready to move off in one hour.

The Red Cross monitored the evacuation of POWs
throughout the period as the allies closed in on Berlin from both
the east and the west.

On 18-Feb, the British and American governments received
a situation report from Robert Schirmer, the Red Cross official
in north Germany. He was likely to have seen columns of
marchers through Pomerania. His report described three main
POW evacuation routes to the west:

The "northern route" included POWs from Stalag XXI-B,
Stalag XX-A and Stalag Luft IV. Many of the men in Stalag
Luft VI, the camp closest to the Russian advance, were

transported to Stalag XX-A by train in July 1944, and so took part in the evacuation from there.

Schirmer estimated that 100,000 POWs were marching through the northern route (Rennell, T. Nichol, J, 2003) via Gross Tychow, between Koslin and Stargrad, then onto Stettin. In interpreting Schirmer's description, Nichol and Rennell emphasise that the various groups of POWs were distributed across an area of more than 1,300 km²), with some still far behind on roads to the west of Danzig.

The reality was that it was much less organised than it might first appear.

A "central route," started at Bankau, near Kreuzburg in Silesia to Görlitz, and ended at Stalag III-A at Luckenwalde, 30km south of Berlin.

The "southern route", from Stalag VIII-B at Teschen (not far from Auschwitz) which led through Czechoslovakia, towards Stalag XIII-D at Nuremberg and then onto Stalag VII-A at Moosburg in Bavaria (Rennell, T. Nichol, J, 2003).

Our direction of travel was not consistent, as we would sometimes travel in circles and end up at a previous stopping point; we often zig-zagged. The German did this for a number of reasons, mostly operational as other columns were in the same area marching west in an increasingly shrinking area of occupation.

By now the Eastern Front had collapsed and the Soviet attack on Berlin, under Zuchov was now rampant. The initial thrust headed straight for Frankfurt an der Oder and arrived there on the 10-Feb.

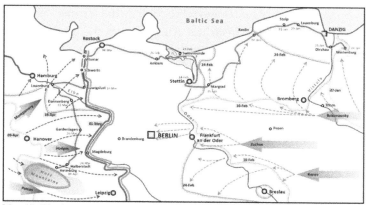

Map 17: The Soviet Breakthrough to Berlin.

Zhukov's left flank was supposedly guarded by Rokossovsky, but in reality, there was very little resistance, so Rokossovsky began to perform a series of flanking sweeps north towards the Baltic coast between Danzig and Stettin.

It was like playing "whack-a-mole." We were hurriedly marched in turn with each of Rokossovsky's sweeps north keeping just ahead as the Soviets swept by behind us to reach the Baltic coast, which they reached on the 24-Feb separating the encircled German 3rd and 4th Army in Danzig and East Prussia from those defending Berlin on the River Oder.

The Germans provided farm wagons for those unable to walk when they could. However, with few horses available, having been requisitioned by the military, teams of POWs pulled the wagons through the snow. Sometimes the guards and prisoners became dependent on each other, other times the guards became increasingly hostile.

Passing through some villages, the residents looked on in sullen silence whether in pity or anger, who knows; and in others, the civilians would share their last food.

Some groups of prisoners were joined by German civilians who were also fleeing from the Russians. Some POWs who tried to escape or could not go on were still being shot by guards.

By the end of January, the Russians had established a front line that ran parallel to the route we were on from Stolp to Stettin, some 80km to the south, where we would cross the River Oder on the Baltic Coast. Three weeks later in mid- February that distance had narrowed to 40km. The Russians were closing in on us and we knew they were not far away as our column continued to march west, we could hear the Russians coming from the south and passing behind us heading north.

As we approached Belgard we could see the distant horizon light up at night with flash of artillery fire, and we started to think of liberation in equal measures of excitement and foreboding as who knows what the circumstances of that likely hood would turn out to be. As we moved through Belgard the sick and wounded prisoners were taken aboard trains along with others who came from nearby Stalag Luft IV where we ourselves were then billeted.

By mid-February the Russian Offensive threatening Stalag Luft IV. We left in three separate sections: A, C, and D. our group was Section D, last in, last out it seems, by now we had grown to approximately 2,500 men. Sick and wounded continued out of the camp and were taken on the last trains out of Belgard. The remaining POWs set off on foot again.

We suffered tremendous hardship during the long march as we marched long distances in bitterly cold weather on starvation rations as we kept one step ahead of the Russians.

At the end of each day, exhausted we dropped down in filth and squalor and often slept in open fields or barns.

In open fields we were reduced to scavenging and foraging for what little scraps of crop had been left from the previous harvest. A frozen cabbage here, frozen sprouts on the stalk there. Anything for mean survival.

Clothing, medical facilities and sanitary facilities were utterly inadequate.

By now many of us were suffering leaflet dropping from malnutrition, exposure, trench foot, exhaustion, dysentery, tuberculosis, and other diseases.

On 18-Feb, we arrived at Stettin, the capital of Pomerania, on the Baltic coast just as the Russians repeatedly broke through to the Baltic coast behind us.

We had covered 280km from Stolp in just three weeks.

Hunger was back to plague us yet again.

In Stettin we had never before seen such destruction on this scale. The RAF had visited Stettin on a number of occasions targeting the armament works in and around the city; and supporting infrastructure for what the Germans were doing in nearby Swinemunde. In whole areas of the city there stood the skeletons of buildings, empty, eerie, rising 8-10 stories above the streets in the city centre. The RAF's main raids had happened in April 1943 and again over two consecutive nights in August 1944.

The destruction all around us was total, at least half of the city was just mountains of rubble (RAF put estimates at 53% of the city).

As we marched (shambled) up a steep hill, there was a tipper truck slowly driving up the hill beside us and it came to a halt at a corner shop just ahead of us.

It was full of CARROTS!!!

Hunger makes you do strange things, of course, and I was tempted. The lorry driver was in a shop, and he knew what was about to happen as he watched me climb up the side of the lorry onto the top and kicked as many carrots as I could off for the boys and jumped off the other side before anybody could do anything about it.

The carrots had disappeared in the pockets of greatcoats within seconds before the guards realised something was happening. They just restored order and barked commands to move along.

By now the lorry driver was on the pavement wistfully smoking a cigarette watching us as we marched by.

We crossed the Oder into an area that by now had some tens of thousands of prisoners meandering along the north German coast to the west. The great mass of prisoners was now resting in the area between New Brandenburg and Swinemunde. The rear guard was still on the roads west of Danzig. These prisoners would continue their march westward until they reached us in the region of Hamburg.

The rations by now consisted of one 1ltr of hot water and three potatoes daily, plus 200gr of bread every five days (when available). By now frostbite, exposure, malnutrition, dysentery, and pneumonia were commonplace.

We were to cross the Oder estuary by ferry.

But when we reached the ferry for some reason it wasn't working. There was a country road to our right with a pine plantation on one side and scrub the other side. It was freezing cold. We tried to light a fire.

The guards came and put it out, so I lay down in the middle of the road and fell asleep.

In some places we simply dropped and rested on the road where we halted. An hour later we were called to order for another march, but I had a problem.

I was literally stuck to the road.

My body heat had melted the ice on the road and then froze again. I couldn't get up.

My mates unbuttoned my greatcoat and pulled me free of it, but I wasn't leaving that behind. Suddenly the sun broke through the leaden sky, and I was able to rescue the coat.

Carrying on without it invited certain death.

We marched until about 2 o'clock in the morning and this time there were fires in the plantation with guards running about trying to put them out. In the end they gave up and just joined us. We had a great time because there had been a thinning of the plantation, and the foresters had left the cut timber behind thankfully for us to burn to see us through the night under the canopy of the trees.

The next day the ferry was working again, and we eventually got across, 20 at a time.

We were on the island of Swinemunde.

We reached a small village near a large bridge that would eventually take us off the island to the town of Anklum 15km south of the bridge. Again, we spent the night on a deserted farm and one fellow found that there was still a horse left on the farm, and they decided to take the horse with them.

Before moving off the road towards the farm the guards made us line up on the side of the road allocating groups to various buildings.

I thought to myself, I was at the end of my tether.

I said to my mate, "I'm not going any further."

"You canny do that"

To which I replied, "Watch me".

There was a plantation, just 10m away to the side of the road. I waited until the guard's back was turned. And I ran into the plantation.

As I'm running between rows of trees, I heard somebody running behind me and I thought it was a guard.

If he stops and aims his rifle at me. I've had it.

So, I crossed from one row to another and turned around. It was one of my mates and another one following him.

We waited in the woods until all the guards and the rest of the men were away up the road, they hadn't missed us.

Once the column moved off, we ventured out and we started to idle along in the same direction not really sure what to do next.

It was a strange sensation walking along free from the barking commands of officers and guards, and we felt giddy with the newfound sense of freedom we had so unexpectedly snatched from our captors.

For the first time since Jun-1940 I actually felt free.

It was all very up-lifting.

Maybe it was this heady sense of abandonment and discretion that emboldened us as we watched a German anti-aircraft unit come along the road and we just walked straight past them. We then walked up the road for 2km and came to a fork in the roads when we saw a Jerry soldier coming up the road. It was a bit of a hill, and he was labouring hard pushing the bike.

We stopped him and asked him if there was a village and some houses down that road?

Oh yes, yes.

There are houses down there and he asked us what we wanted, and we told him that we had been in a column and that we had blisters on our feet and hadn't been fed for days and gave him a real old sob story.

He went into the back of the bike, and he had a wee box on it between two panniers. Opened the box and inside, a half loaf and a big lump of cheese. He gave us that, jumped on his bike, and went on his way.

The Germans by now knew the war was lost and where they could we were shown kindness.

The German soldier said there was a village down that fork of the road.

We followed his direction, and we came to a village right enough. By now it was getting dark and we're looking for some place to sleep.

We saw this house and barn.

I said, "Let's go in there."

I went straight into it. But one of the mates says, "Let's ask the farmer if we can sleep in his barn for the night."

I knocked the door and told him what had happened to us and, "that we had blisters on our feet, and we'd lost our column," and all that.

He took us in, and they gave us a feed.

His wife made coffee and bread and cheese again.

On one wall he had a very full bookcase.

The shelves were groaning under the weight of every Charles Dickens book that you could think of.

I asked him if we could sleep in the barn for the night. And he says, "Well, my barn's full because today we were threshing, but my neighbour's barn is empty, you can ask him."

"I'll send my daughter with you," she was only 12 or 14 years old, "and I'm quite sure he'll let you sleep in his barn for the night."

The neighbour tuned out to be the village policeman, the crafty old git!

They put us in the cells for the night.

The next morning, when we got up, we got coffee bread and a bit of cheese.

Across the road from them was another prison camp. But it was a French camp, so we were taken across there. He said, "They'll take you in there, and we'll tell them all about you and whatnot".

So that's what we did. We stayed there until dinner time about 12 o'clock the next day dining on pea soup.

After we had finished the French cook in there said, "It's time to go".

"Go where?", I asked.

We were shown outside and there was a horse wagon with a tarpaulin over the top of it and we were loaded into the back of it with a German soldier driving it with one horse. He couldn't see us because the tarpaulin also came right down between us in the back and the soldier in the front, but the back was open.

It was a cobbled road, and we felt every bump, not square cobbles they were rounded cobbles.

He never told us where we were going.

The road was on a bit of a rise and at the top of the rise there were some other houses. Halfway up I was looking around, and I jumped out of the wagon, and rolled into the ditch, then the other two did the same thing.

And he drove on and he never knew it. I often wonder what happened to him, or how he felt once he got to where he was going.

Probably sent to face the Russians.

We waited until he went out of sight and then went to the nearby village where we found the village hall. It had obviously been used for prisoners or troops, because there was straw on the floor and there were big blackout frames with black paper in them to blackout the windows.

The shutters were all down and hanging by their hinges and the door had been kicked in. We found a boiler stove and we lit it and decided that it was going to be our home until somebody else said no.

We were five days in there.

A tipper truck came one day with two soldiers in it and ordered us out.

One of them drove the lorry and the other one came in the back with us to keep an eye on us with weary resignation.

He was dead from starvation.

He was a chap getting on in years, in his fifties; he must have been a territorial or regular soldier.

We were put to work in the railway station in Halberstadt just to clean it up doing odd jobs for a couple of days.

And then the air sirens went.

Everybody evacuated the place, and we were taken up a country lane when two RAF Typhoons with rockets bombed the railways themselves.

Straight after that raid leaflets were dropped.

The leaflets were asking for Halberstadt to be declared an open city by Sunday; they had six days.

Six days later, nothing.

On the following Monday in the late morning, the sirens went again.

The guards took us away and marched us into a field about 2km away.

We could hear the drone of the engines, and just before noon the first bombers appeared over the city and, after targeting with smoke signals, began dropping 504 tons of high explosive and 50 tons of incendiary bombs from a height of 6,700 meters (Freeman, 1981).

We counted twenty plus aircraft, then another flight of a similar number, and so it went on and on and on.

There were about 500 bombers, and they flattened the place.

The whole 500 didn't drop bombs on Halberstadt, they were coming for other towns. I would say there was about 250 bombers that dropped bombs on Halberstadt, and I'll never forget it.

Six bomber groups attacked the city from the south from 11:31 to 11:54 a.m. in several waves, undisturbed by flak fire, and they destroyed the city centre.

The incendiary bombs were filled with a total of 50 tons of a mixture of gasoline, viscose and magnesium dust. Liquid, stick and phosphorus incendiary bombs were also used.

The initial high explosive bombs shattered the roofs, cracked the windows, and tore open the walls of the houses. Then by means of fire caused by the highly combustible incendiaries, the densely built-up medieval town descended into wildfires that destroyed most buildings. A firestorm developed from the individual fires in the city centre. Rescue and fire-fighting work was hindered by harassing low-flying aircraft. About 25,000 people were left homeless by the bombing.

According to the 8th Air Force's war diary, the total bomb load was 595 tons (Freeman, 1981).

We were in a field on the side of a small hill with a clear view looking down on the railway station, a couple of hundred metres away there was a sausage factory with lots of goods wagons in railway sidings beside it.

The factory was reduced to rubble and the wagons beside it all took direct hits. It was quite mesmerising watching the wagons levitate about 10m off the ground and then suddenly explode. A lot of the content came in our direction, and it rained down tins of sausages all around us.

Of course, they disappeared as fast as they were hitting the ground.

Then, in the railway sidings at the station, we looked on as a row of goods wagons took a series of direct hits, the bombs this time seemed to explode about 100m from the ground. From where we stood in the field you could see the bombs coming down and the earth appearing to rise up to meet them.

As these wagons exploded their contents were sent high up into the air. This time cigars rained down on us; they were a lot less danger than flying sausage tins.

We watched the raid with a compelling fascination. Everything seemed to be happening in slow motion as great clouds of smoke, dust, and debris rose into the air and came crashing down.

In the field as we were bombarded by tins of sausages of various shapes and sizes, many of them had burst open due to the blast. So, there we were sat in a field in the middle of an air raid eating German sausage. And just as the sausage factory took a direct and we were feeding off that triumph, we were then bombarded with cigars from the goods wagon that suffered a similar fate, but we were in no mood to celebrate as the carnage we witnessed was just too awful to contemplate.

And just as we were enjoying our good fortune, we were all suddenly gripped by a deadly fear that rooted us all to the spot. A steam engine in the railway station took a direct hit and from the plume of fire, ash, and steam there came towards us an engine axle with the wheel still attached.

It seemed to rise about 50 metres into the air in a graceful arc that we couldn't take our eyes off, before we realised that it was heading straight for us in the field.

Rooted with fear it landed and buried itself in the soft earth about 50m away from us.

After the raid was over the guards took us back to our factory loft where we were billeted, and as we ambled along the railway line there were bombs with just the fins sticking out of the ground, that hadn't gone off.

The city burned for three and a half days (Friedrich, 2005). The streets were largely blocked by debris. Many bombs with long detonators exploded unforeseeably during clearance work.

The transport system no longer existed: The station had been destroyed, tram rails and overhead lines destroyed, the streets no longer passable. Gas, water and electricity were down, as was the telephone network.

It took 15 years to clear all the debris. About a third of the original 1,500 half-timbered houses were destroyed, especially the houses with a unique architectural position in the upper town.

After the air raid we were taken out of Halberstadt on the 10-Apr, and we were back on the road again!!!

But that did not last long.

We marched for 15km to the little village of Heimburg at the foot of the Hartz Mountains

We also noted that there was a significant reduction in the number of German guards we had with us.

Suddenly the guards gave every impression that we were released up to a point because they stopped and told us that if we wanted to go into any of the houses, just to go in and chase the folk out, take over you're free.

But within half an hour, Germans in the Hartz Mountains attacked leading American units that we did not even know were in the area. And we were caught up on the edge of the fighting. The Germans were from the 11th Army under Hitzfeld and Lucht who were being encircled in their mountain redoubt by Americans under General Hodges coming in from the west.

A lot of our boys went into the barn, there was a lot of sheep in the barn, and they chased the sheep to one end when the barn took a direct mortar hit.

I think there were about 20 killed in there.

The Germans withdrew as suddenly as they had appeared.

But we stayed another night there and in the morning the Jerry guard who was with us, asked some of us if we would volunteer to go with him to try to meet the allies and say where we were. Just about 10 minutes after that we heard the roar of tanks.

They were American tanks.

Part of General Patton's crew.

We had been liberated.

For us now the war was over.

We were taken from Heimburg by the Americans in alphabetical order.

I was on my last legs, as were many others, I wasn't alone.

If I had been left to go by alphabetical order, I wouldn't be here today.

The reason I'm here is when the first lorry was nearly full one of the medical orderlies suggested, "Would some of you fellows first on the list, stand down and wait and let these folks go who look in worse shape?"

And I was one of the ones that got onto that first lorry.

The lorries took us to Hildesheim, which had been captured just days before. There was an aerodrome there, but the first thing that they did was to put us through a tent where we had to take off our clothes and there was a machine blowing DDT that smothered us in the stuff.

Then you got your clothes back similarly smothered.

Once we got out of that hut, they started giving us something to eat. And I remember getting a slice of bread that was heaped with peanut butter.

I ate that, but for some strange reason I wasn't hungry.

Then they took us to the aerodrome, which was only yards away where there were many Dakotas sitting with their engines running and ready to go.

It was time to go home.

They put us into the leading three Dakotas, and I was as sick as a dog as I was getting on, everything that they gave me to eat I brought up again and that's the last I remember until I woke up in the John Radcliffe Infirmary in Oxford.

While I was in a coma flying back to Oxford the end game was playing out in Europe.

The reason for Stalin's dash to Berlin was to hold all the cards with Churchill and Roosevelt to secure all Polish territory agreed at the Yalta Conference. With the Potsdam Conference coming up Stalin wanted a strong hand in the bargaining that would inevitably take place. Stalin intended to impose on Poland his puppet "Lublin government" and treat the Armia Karimova, or Home Army, which was loyal to the Polish government-in-exile, as "fascists," despite their heroic and doomed uprising against the Germans in Warsaw the previous year. He greatly exaggerated the influence of German forces still inside Poland as a justification for oppression of non-communist Poles.

Irrespective of their wartime efforts in resisting Nazi occupation or assistance to the Red Army, those found with weapons were arrested by Red Army secret police. Stalin claimed that he had to secure his rear areas to ensure the resupply of his fighting formations.

The agenda for the Yalta Conference, between the 'Big Three' set out the mapping of a post-war Europe where Stalin took every opportunity to divide the British and the Americans.

He knew that Churchill wanted to secure freedom for Poland while Roosevelt's priorities were to establish the United Nations and persuade Stalin to attack Japanese forces in Manchuria and northern China.

The American president felt that he could win Stalin's trust and even admitted to the Soviet leader that the western Allies did not agree on the strategy for the invasion of Nazi Germany. Roosevelt suggested that General Eisenhower should establish direct contact with the Stavka supreme command of the Red Army to discuss plans. Stalin encouraged the idea to uncover what the American view was while giving nothing away himself.

Stalin made clear his casual disregard for the smaller nations in order to advantage the future border security of the Soviet

Union. In general, Stalin was taking an interest of Slavic peoples wherever they were in central Europe and across the Balkans. However, it was to Poland that Stalin reserved his greatest interest was more acute as time and again had proved that the plains of Poland seemed to only exist as a corridor through which Russia was invaded from the west.

Stalin was building a series of 'buffer' states along his wester border with 'friendly' governments as a buffer to future invasion.

Churchill soon realised that he was out on a limb. Roosevelt, suffering from extreme ill-health, showed little interest, and to Churchill's horror, Roosevelt announced without warning that American forces would be withdrawn from Europe. The Americans simply wanted to finish the war. They showed little interest in the post-war map of Europe.

All Churchill could ask for was free elections in Poland, but Stalin's insistence on a government "friendly to the Soviet Union," suggested it would be under Moscow's control.

Ever since the breakout from Normandy, led by Patton's 3rd Army in August 1944, British influence ran aground on the rocks of Montgomery's vanity. He repeated his attempts to be appointed ground forces commander had only made things worse. The American's were having none of it, especially so when he asserted that he had saved the situation in the Ardennes.

General Marshall, the American chief of staff, was furious, and Eisenhower told Churchill that none of his generals was willing to serve under Montgomery in future. "His relations with Monty are quite insoluble," Brooke wrote after a meeting with Eisenhower on 06-Mar. "He only sees the worst side of Monty" (Anon, 1945: The Race for Berlin, 2021).

Montgomery lost the American 9th Army from his command, and the British were side-lined in the north. All his hopes of leading the advance on Berlin from the west were dashed. He was ordered to head for Denmark via Hamburg. Churchill's desire to reach Berlin and "shake hands with the Russians as far to the east as possible," was ignored.

Eisenhower, who had started to believe in an Alpine Redoubt to which the remaining German forces would withdraw, intended to send the bulk of his forces across central and southern Germany.

Stalin assured Eisenhower that "Berlin has lost its former strategic importance" and that the Soviet command would send only "second-rate forces against it." The bulk of the Red Army would join up with Eisenhower's armies further to the south. They would not start their advance until the second half of May. "However, this plan may undergo certain alterations, depending on circumstances" (Anon, 1945: The Race for Berlin, 2021).

It was the greatest April Fool in modern history.

During the first week of April, the British 2nd Army reached Celle 40km north-east of Hanover, while the US 9th Army, led by Simpson, was beyond Hanover and heading for the river Elbe. The 1st US Army was heading for Leipzig (200km south-west of Berlin) and Patton's 3rd Army was in the Harz Mountains on its way to the Czech border. By 12-Apr, the British were approaching Bremen and the American 9th Army had bridgeheads across the Elbe.

Simpson wanted his divisions to head straight for Berlin, but on 15-Apr Eisenhower stopped him there to avoid casualties. In fact, Simpson's forces would have faced little resistance since the best German formations faced east awaiting the onslaught from the rivers Oder and Neisse, which began the next day.

But Eisenhower had made the right decision for the wrong reasons. Stalin was so determined to have Berlin that almost certainly he would have turned his long-range artillery and attack aircraft on US forces, claiming that the Americans were responsible for the mistake. And Eisenhower was determined to avoid clashes at all costs.

Churchill wanted Patton to take Prague to pre-empt a Soviet occupation, but Eisenhower refused on Marshall's advice.

On the German side Hitler was informed late in the day that, with the approval of Heinrici, that Steiner's attack was never launched. Instead, Steiner's forces were authorised to retreat. In response, Hitler launched a furious tirade against the perceived treachery and incompetence of his military commanders in front of Keitel, Krebs, Jodl, Burgdorf and Martin Bormann.

Hitler's tirade culminates in an oath to stay in Berlin to head up the defence of the city. Hitler orders Wenck to attack towards Berlin with the 12th Army, link up with the 9th Army of Busse, and relieve the city. Wenck launched an attack, but it came to nothing.

On 23-Apr, Göring sent a radiogram to Hitler's bunker, asking to be declared Hitler's successor. He proclaimed that if he received no response by 10 p.m., he would assume Hitler was incapacitated and assume leadership of the Reich.

Furious, Hitler stripped him of all his offices and expelled him from the Nazi Party.

Speer makes one last visit to Hitler, informing him that he (Speer) ignored the Nero Decree for scorched earth.

Himmler by now, ignoring the orders of Hitler, made a secret surrender offer to the Allies, (led by Count Bernadotte, head of the Red Cross), provided that the Red Army was not involved. The offer was rejected and when Hitler heard of the betrayal on the 28-Apr, he ordered Himmler shot.

By now the Armies of the 1st Belorussian Front and the 1st Ukrainian Front had linked up in the initial encirclement of Berlin, and on 25-Apr Soviet and American troops first made contact on the river Elbe, near Torgau.

With the tightening encirclement of Berlin, on the 30-Apr Hitler and his wife Eva Braun committed suicide with a combination of poison and a gunshot. Before he died, he dictated his last will and testament. In it Joseph Goebbels was appointed Reich Chancellor and Admiral Dönitz was appointed Reich President.

The British occupied Bremen on 27-Apr after a five-day battle. Montgomery, to Eisenhower's frustration, crossed the lower Elbe in his usual methodical way to take Hamburg. Then news arrived that the Red Army was making a dash for Denmark ahead of him. The 11th Armoured Division rushed on to Lübeck on the Baltic coast and British paratroopers seized Wismar just two hours before Rokossovsky's forces reached the town (Anon, 1945: The Race for Berlin, 2015).

Denmark was saved, but Poland, to Churchill's bitter regret, was not.

General Krebs begins to negotiate the surrender of Berlin with the Soviets. Krebs was not authorised by Reich Chancellor Goebbels to agree to an unconditional surrender, so his negotiations with Chuikov ended with no agreement.

The fighting in Berlin continued, on 02-May the Soviets capture the Reichstag building and installed the Soviet flag. The Battle of Berlin finally ended when General Weidling, commander of the Berlin Defence Area, (and no longer bound by Goebbels's commands), unconditionally surrenders the city of Berlin to the Soviets, while German troops in Denmark, Northern Germany and The Netherlands surrender to Montgomery.

On the 07-May Germany surrenders unconditionally to the Allies at the Western Allied GHQ in Rheims, France at 02:41am. In accordance with orders from Reich President Dönitz, Jodl signed for Germany.

Om 08-May, it was declared Victory in Europe Day: The ceasefire takes effect at one minute past midnight.

Germany surrenders again unconditionally to the Soviet Union but this time in a ceremony hosted by the Soviet Union. In accordance with orders from Dönitz, Keitel signs for Germany.

The Soviet Union officially pronounced 09-May as Victory Day.

Himmler was arrested by Soviet troops, attempting to pass himself off as a common soldier and handed to a British interrogation centre on 23-May. Himmler died of suicide via cyanide pill.

Stalin's intention to impose a Soviet government in Poland had become clear at the end of March when 16 Polish representatives of the government-in-exile in London were arrested despite safe-conduct passes. In May Soviet foreign minister Molotov brutally informed Edward Stettinius, the American secretary of state, that they had been charged with the murder of 200 members of the Red Army, a preposterous accusation (Beevor, The Fall of Berlin, 1945, 2002).

Further indications of communist repression in Poland convinced Churchill that something had to be done. Within a week of Germany's surrender, he summoned his chiefs of staff to ask them to study the possibility of forcing back Soviet troops to secure "a square deal for Poland." The offensive should take place by 01-Jul, before Allied troops were demobilised or transferred to the Far East.

Although the discussions were conducted in great secrecy, one of the Whitehall moles reporting to Beria, the Soviet police chief, heard of them. He sent details to Moscow of the instruction to Montgomery to gather up captured German arms in case they were needed to re-arm Wehrmacht troops. The

Soviets, not surprisingly, felt that their worst suspicions had been confirmed.

Operation Unthinkable, was a mad enterprise.

British soldiers, grateful for the Red Army's sacrifice, would have had the greatest difficulty obeying such orders. And the Americans would surely have rejected the plan. The chiefs of staff all agreed that it was "unthinkable." "The idea is of course fantastic and the chances of success quite impossible," wrote Brooke. "There is no doubt that from now onwards Russia is all powerful in Europe."

Churchill was forced to face the inevitable fact that his impoverished country had lost almost all its power and influence in a dramatically changed world. Britain had helped liberate the western half of Europe at the cost of abandoning the eastern half to a Soviet dictatorship that would last for another 44 years.

On the 05-Jul the UK went to the polls in a general election and a new Labour government won by a landslide victory. Labour played to the concept of "winning the peace" that would follow the war. Possibly for that reason, there was especially strong support for Labour in the armed services, which feared the unemployment and homelessness to which the soldiers of the First World War had returned.

The Labour appeal to the electorate was as much to do with recession and austerity through the 20s and 30s as it was with its clear support for reform and reconstruction. The people were looking to build a new, like the same public spirit after WW1. The result was due more to positive support for Labour and renewal rather than an anti-Conservative vote (Fellows, 2020).

It was to be one of the greatest reforming governments in British history.

Churchill was out of power.

Back at the John Radcliffe, I began to come round.

There was another chap, the first thing I saw when I woke up, I realised I was in a hospital ward.

It was nothing but beds.

There were beds along both sides of the ward and above each bed was an electric light on a long cable.

I'm looking across at a fellow on the other side and thinking he's having a shower from the electric light above him.

Either he was suffering from shell shock, or I was hallucinating.

That was the first thing I saw when I woke up anyway.

After a couple of days, they gave me nothing to eat and then one day I woke up and there was a glass of water beside my bed.

The next day it was milk then milk along with 9 tablets.

What they were I had no idea, but I always remember one would be a size of a thumb nail. It was black

It turned out to be charcoal.

I was allowed nothing else to eat.

Just to take these tablets, and that carried on for two more days. And then my diet switched to an egg and that stayed down.

I left the Radcliffe on 01-May.

After about three weeks it was time to leave.

I had no clothes because the clothes I had they probably burned them.

These old clothes were with me all the way through from Marienburg. I'd become quite attached to them. I got one new battle dress during the five years that I was a prisoner and one pair of boots, that's what they took from me in Oxford.

I was given a new battle kit, a new Balmoral to finally replace the one the German soldier had stolen at Forges les Eaux.

Two of us were taken by car to the railway station.

At every main station in Britain, there was an army office of Railway Transport Officers (RTOs). The Oxford office at the station had an officer and a couple of men that manned it. The taxi man handed us over to an RTO. He took us to his office and phoned somebody who came and took us to the train, put us in a compartment and locked the door so that we wouldn't be disturbed between Oxford and Bletchley.

We had to change at Bletchley where the RTO met us and opened the door and let us out, put us with a third soldier on another train, locked the door, and left us.

We travelled to Crewe, the train stopped, and an RTO opened the door to let the others go and told me I had to stay in the train.

One of the other fellows travelling with us was on his way to Plockton on Skye via another route.

Nobody else got into my carriage all the way to Carlisle.

An RTO met me at Carlisle and transferred me onto a train for Carstairs, when it got to Carstairs an RTO met me and handed me over to a taxi. And the taxi took me home.

I was finally home.

One of the worst jobs that I have ever done was once I came home.

David Arnold, who was killed beside me at Forges-le-Eaux, was from the wee village of Templin near Lochmaben, Dumfriesshires in the Scottish borders, we all knew him as Davie.

I never really knew much about him because we were all put together into to makeshift companies and divisions, we were from all over the place.

I had to tell his mother and stepfather the incident of that day, they wanted to know all the ins and outs of how he was killed.

And we were still prisoners.

Epilogue

I wasn't demobbed until 1946. Since being discharged from hospital I was put on the reserve list for the Far East.

Really!!!

I left the farm on the 24-Jan and left the Radcliffe on the 01-May 1945. My discharge was Aug-46, just after I had arrived in Glenbranter in Jun-46.

We had hardly been under cover or fed properly throughout the route march across Germany back to the west.

Since then I often think of some episodes that come back to me now. I'll wake up during the night and think here we are again.

But there were some interesting things I saw and witnessed, not least of which was the human character, British, German, and Ukrainian. We also had some good laughs.

I still think of Marienburg and the life we had there as POWs and have often wondered what happened after we left on the long march. Over the years I have picked up bits and pieces of the story on how Marienburg fell.

I read a piece about Marienburg by Bonisch and Wiegrefe for Spiegel International in 2009: In 1944, the Nazis had declared Marienburg, then a city of 30,000, a "stronghold," along with other cities on their eastern front. Thousands of men dug trenches and built bunkers. Two divisions were sent in to defend Marienburg, and the leadership wanted to evacuate civilians, to be brought back into the city after it had been successfully defended.

As the Red Army approached Marienburg on 25/26-Jan there were only about 2,000 men standing ready. The city was swarming with refugees trying to cross the Nogat River on their way west. Groups of people jammed the streets leading to the bridges. In the train stations, others fought desperately over the last seats on the trains.

German soldiers supposedly searched homes for elderly people on the morning of 25-Jan, in order to bring them to safety. But it's impossible to know how many civilians were still in the city when the Soviet army arrived. The last civilian transport departing from Marienburg on 25-Jan.

Soviet troops entered the town on 27-Jan and from the end of January until the beginning of March laid constant siege of the castle as they fought off a few German counterattacks. On the 09-Mar German troops retreated from the castle and gained access to a German redoubt in the Vistula estuary.

Soldiers on both sides carried out a grim battle, which probably cost thousands of lives. Afterward there was talk of sharpshooters with at least 50 tank kills and of sustained fires in the castle, set by the Soviets. On the night before 10-Mar the German group holed up in the castle withdrew.

West Prussia, according to Allied plans, was supposed to become Polish, but in those first weeks, there was not yet a Polish administration and the city was under the Soviet army's control.

The Soviet army was under orders to detain Germans in the conquered eastern territories who were capable of working. They would then be put into forced labour either there or in the Soviet Union. There was a collecting point in Marienburg, our old Stalag XX1B at Willenberg, where Soviet troops held not just Germans but also Poles.

The living conditions in these camps are known to have been terrible in general, but there are no witness accounts available from Marienburg in particular. After the war, the Russians took almost every one of the men. The older ones returned to the city after six weeks, but of the younger men no one came back.

The situation in the region was chaotic at that point. Refugees who had been overrun by the Red Army were now being sent back to their hometowns. Meanwhile, Polish settlers arrived to settle the country's new territory, at the behest of the provisional communist government.

Many Germans were suffering from hunger, and many are known to have died of typhus in the summer of 1945. Others survived and later left for West Germany (von Georg, Puhl, & Wiegrefe, 2009).

I didn't keep in touch with those that I spent my time within East Prussia or on the Long March. Like many of them it was an episode in our life that we simply wanted to try to move on from, looking to a better future than the one we just had.

There was one fellow I did keep in contact with, Callum MacLean.

I spent a while at Redford Barracks in Edinburgh, before I was demobbed, with a chap who had been with us on the long march, and he told me that the German who murdered Clicks Mackenzie stood trial. I don't know how they managed to get him; God only knows how they done it. It appeared that the German was tried and executed.

I don't think it's had any effect on me but it's there all the time. And especially when a person like me is on their own, your mind wanders back or something will crop up, maybe something that you're doing, oh I remember that things like that crop up and no, it doesn't have any great effect on me.

I had just returned home to where I was on the estate, and it had been turned into a market garden with a new owner. There used to be eight of us in the garden all together.

When we came back after the war, anybody that was in work when they got called up had to be paid £30 by their former employer if there was no work to return to, which at that time was quite a lot of money.

There was no work for me, and I never seen any sign of the £30 they owed to me upon demobilisation.

Most private estates after the war were finished. It was only the very rich that could hang onto them because they couldn't make them pay their way. Most private estates couldn't afford pre-war lifestyles. The estate tried to market itself as best it could, but the owners couldn't afford to employ anybody. And that's where on return we lost out.

So, I said to the Old Man that I wasn't going back to gardening, and I was going to go to join the Forestry Commission.

That's how I came to Glenbranter.

I came to Glenbranter late 1946, there were thirty-six of us and we all came from all over Lanarkshire, Stirlingshire, some even local, and two from Tighnabruaich. We were housed in the old POW camp that converted to a Royal Navy navigation training station in preparation for D-Day landings. The idea was that we would go to the Forestry School and study for an exam to enter the Forestry Commission.

After seven years in the forces, you didn't think for yourself, you just did as you were told, so it was a shock to get turned out and de-mobbed and then adjust your mind to think for and look after yourself.

We were told that Glenbranter was the only place. Of the 36 that sat for the exam three passed and the rest of us didn't.

Some of the questions on the exam paper I remember such as:

What did they call the chair that was put on an elephant's back?

A sink with two tops in it of a certain diameter how long will it take to empty the sink?

I mean, really?

That's the sort of questions that were asked.

There was one fellow there, the exam was supposed to be a two-hour exam. He'd done the whole thing in half an hour, and he passed the exam.

I stayed in the Forestry Commission without going through the school exam again.

I also returned to the football. Before going to Glenbranter I was in Dornoch staying with my sister. The local amateur side Dornoch Rangers asked me to play for them. I stayed with them until the end of the season despite not really being fully match fit.

We started a football team at Glenbranter playing in the summer league in Dunoon, and had a few games against Dunoon Athletic, another amateur side in the Scottish league.

There was one fellow with us who played for the Athletic and he played for Glenbranter as well. A mate of his told us that if we could fix a team, we could win the summer league. If we won, they would hold a dance in Dunoon, and bring George Young who used to play for the great Glasgow Rangers and fellow players down to the winners' dance at Dunoon.

And they did.

So, these were happy days.

Eventually I settled down in Glenbranter where I met Ann, she stayed with her mum and dad at Bridgend Cottage in Glenbranter. We married in Strachur church on 13-Sep-1948. We have three boys who all grew up in Glenbranter and left home to follow work and their careers.

We both worked for the Forestry Commission until Ann was asked to run a new restaurant for Marnie MacLachlan the chief of the Clan MacLachlan, whom I remembered from these few days we were in Rouen in May-1940. The restaurant was a huge success, and Ann worked there for 10 years.

Sadly, Ann died just a few days short of our 55th wedding anniversary.

I now have more grandchildren and great-grandchildren than I can count, and they all seem to take turns when in the district to pop in and say hi.

In 2019 the family organised a clan gathering for my 100th birthday. They came from all over the world, and it was a great occasion.

I even got a birthday card from the Queen.

Imagine?

I'm still pottering about doing bits and pieces, looking after my beehives, and still keeping active with the local beekeepers' association.

Was I blessed, was I just lucky, or was it fate?

Probably all of that.

Working on the farm at Schadwalde probably saved my life as it had done for many others who worked the farms in the area. It gave us easy access to fresh food and kept us strong and healthy for the trauma that lay ahead of us. The Eichenbergers helped; they were good to us on the farm.

In 1978 I took retirement from the Forestry Commission and became a gardener again for the NHS in Dunoon. I maintained the hospital grounds in Dunoon, and those of Finnartmore respite care home at Kilmun where I based myself in a potting shed and large greenhouse there.

One day I was listening to the wireless around 1991, after the reunification of Germany following the fall of the Berlin Wall, when a programme started on a news story about a group in Germany who, as archaeologists, were working on the identification of Germans killed during the flight of refugees from the East as the Russians advanced on the winter of 1945.

A particular reference that caught my attention was an item on one roadside exhumation at Schloppe where they had identified the remains of a little two-year-old girl, the name given was Eichenberger.

It was like a lightning rod. Completely unexpected and sent a shiver down my spine and brought back all my memories of that winter.

Could this be Marie, the same little girl who left the farm at Schadwalde on 23-Jan-1945 along with her mother, two siblings, and the Ukrainian girls?

One can only speculate, as Schloppe is just over halfway on the direct route between Schadwalde and Frankfurt-an-der-Oder, via Dirschau the nearest crossing point on the Vistula to Schadwalde.

I wonder.

The price of war exacts a heavy toll.

All my comrades are now gone, and I often think about them, the Eichenbergers and the Ukrainian girls.

Whatever did happen to them all?

Bibliography

Alexander, M. S. (2007). *After Dunkirk: The French Army's Performance against 'Case Red', 25 May to 25 June 1940.* London: SAGE.

Alexander, M. S. (2007, April). After Dunkirk: The French Army's Performance against 'Case Red', 25 May to 25 June 1940. *War in History, 14*(2), 219-264. Retrieved Jun 30, 2021

Anon. (1945). *The Argus.* Melbourne: The Argus. Retrieved January 30, 2022, from https://trove.nla.gov.au/newspaper/page/28938

Anon. (2006). *Operation Bagration: Soviet Offensive Of 1944.* Retrieved December 16, 2022, from HistoryNet: https://www.historynet.com/operation-bagration-soviet-offensive-of-1944/

Anon. (2013). *1939: Key Dates.* Retrieved November 16, 2021, from United States Holocaust Memorial Museum: https://encyclopedia.ushmm.org/content/en/article/1939-key-dates

Anon. (2015). *1945: The Race for Berlin.* Retrieved January 30, 2022, from History Extra: https://www.historyextra.com/period/second-world-war/1945-the-race-for-berlin/

Anon. (2016, June 15). *Beauman Division.* Retrieved June 15, 2021, from Wikipedia: https://en.wikipedia.org/wiki/Beauman_Division#CITEREFKarslake1979

Anon. (2021, November). *1945: The Race for Berlin.* (BBC, Editor, & Immediate Media) Retrieved 2021, from History Extra: https://www.historyextra.com/period/second-world-war/1945-the-race-for-berlin/

Anon. (2022, July 26). *Operation Bagration.* Retrieved July 28, 2022, from Wikipedia: https://en.wikipedia.org/wiki/Operation_Bagration

Anon. (n.d.). *The Treatment of Soviet POWs: Starvation, Disease, and Shootings, June 1941-January 1942.* Retrieved November 22, 2022, from United States Holocaust Memorial Museum: https://encyclopedia.ushmm.org/content/en/article/the-treatment-of-soviet-pows-starvation-disease-and-shootings-june-1941january-1942#germans-reject-geneva-convention-0

Atkin, D. (1990). *Pillar of Fire: Dunkirk 1940.* London: Sidgwick & Jackson.

Beevor, A. (2002). *The Fall of Berlin, 1945.* New York: Viking.

Beevor, A. (2004). *Berlin: The Downfall 1945.* London: Penguin.

Butler, B., & Bury, J. P. (1960). *Documents on British Foreign Policy 1919-1939: Chapter VIII, The Plebiscites in Allenstein and Marienwerder January 21 - September 29, 1920* (Vol. X). (M. E. Lambert, Ed.) London: HMSO.

Chen, C. P. (2008). *World War II Database: Your WW2 History Reference Destination.* Retrieved December 16, 2022, from Library of Congress: https://www.loc.gov/item/lcwaN0005634/

Cohen, E., & Gooch, J. (1990). *Military Misfortunes: The Anatomy of Failure in War.* New York: Free Press.

Craenen, J. E. (Ed.). (2012, December 18). Retrieved January 05, 2022, from Catalogue of Monuments of Dutch Colonization in Poland: https://papers.academic-conferences.org/index.php/eckm/issue/view/9

Deutsche Verwaltungsgeschichte Westpreußen, K. M. (2020). *Malbork.* Retrieved June 2021, from Wikipedia: https://en.wikipedia.org/wiki/Malbork#cite_note-12

Ellis, L. F. (1953). *The War in France and Flanders 1939-1940.* London: HMSO.

Evans, R. (1942-1943). The 1st Armoured Division in France. *The Army Quarterly, 45-47.*

Fellows, N. (2020, September 01). Why Did Attlee Win the 1945 General Election? *Modern History Review, 23*(1), pp. 1-3.

Forczyk, R. (2017). *Case Red: The Collapse of France.* London: Bloomsbury.

Freeman, R. A. (1981). *Mighty Eighth War Diary.* London, New york, Sydney: Jane's.

Friedrich, J. (2005). Operation Sardine. The destruction of Halberstadt. (M. Ahrens, Interviewer) Halberstadt.

Guderian, H. (2015). *Panzer Leader General Heinz Guderian.* (C. Fitzgibbon, Ed.) New York: Da Capo Press.

Hansard. (1944, December 15). Poland. *Hansard House of Commons, 406,* pp. 1478-1578. Retrieved from https://hansard.parliament.uk/commons/1944-12-15/debates/7644a864-82be-4411-bf09-a39480c1915e/CommonsChamber

Hastings, M. (2004). *Armageddon: The Battle for Germany, 1944-45.* New York: Knopf.

Holocaust Encyclopedia. (2020, March 23). *Lebensraum.* Retrieved February 20, 2022, from United States Holocaust Memorial Museum: https://encyclopedia.ushmm.org/content/en/article/lebensraum

Jackson, J. (2003). *The Fall of France: The Nazi Invasion of 1940*. New York: Oxford University Press.

Karslake, B. (1979). *1940 The Last Act: The Story of the British Forces in France After Dunkirk*. London: Leo Cooper Ltd.

Le Miroir Des Sports. (1932, July 23). Kaye Don Bat Le Record Du Monde. *Le Miroir Des Sports*(663), p. 95. Retrieved January 24, 2022, from https://gallica.bnf.fr/ark:/12148/bpt6k97965989/f14.item

Linklater, E. (2007). *The Battle for Abbeville 3rd - 6th June 1940*. Retrieved August 20, 2021, from 51st Highland Division: https://51hd.co.uk/accounts/abbeville_linklater

Lovin, C. R. (1969, October). Agricultural Reorganization in the Third Reich: The Reich Food Corporation (Reichsnährstand), 1933-1936. *Agricultural History, 43*(4), pp. 447-462.

Macrae, R. A. (2007). *War Diary of Captain R.A.A.S. Macrae 27 May - 10 Jun 1940*. Retrieved August 20, 2021, from 51st Highland Division.

Martin, R. E. (1929, June). The Speediest Craft Afloat. *Popular Science Monthly*, pp. 19-20, 146. Retrieved April 05, 2020, from https://books.google.co.uk/books?id=XSgDAAAAMBAJ&pg=PA20&dq=Popular+Science+1931+plane&hl=en&ei=XeARTe7ZJ4alnQf84KjpDQ&sa=X&oi=book_result&ct=result&redir_esc=y#v=onepage&q&f=true

Mawdsley, E. (2019). *The War for the Seas: A Maritime History of World War II*. New Haven, CT: Yale University Press.

Moore, R. (2020, March 01). *German Occupation and Alliances*. (B. Warnock, Editor) Retrieved November 28, 2021, from The Holocaust Explained: https://www.theholocaustexplained.org/life-in-nazi-occupied-europe/occupation-case-studies/

O'Donaghue, H. (1996-1999). *German Tanks, Forges-les-Eaux*. Imperial War Museum (Art.IWM ART 17112), London.

O'Neill, R. (2010). *World War II Europe 1939-43*. (R. Havers, Ed.) New York: Rosen Publishing.

Rennell, T. Nichol, J. (2003). *The Last Escape: The Untold Story of Allied Prisoners of War in Germany 1944-1945*. Penguin.

Romano, C. (2014, July 21). *Revanchism and its costs*. Retrieved November 01, 2021, from The Chronicle of Higher Education: https://search.proquest.com/docview/1550803988

Saul, D. (2018). *Churchill's Sacrifice of the Highland Division, France 1940*. London: Sharpe Books.

Shelton, D. L. (2005). *Encyclopedia of Genocide and Crimes Against Humanity.* (D. L. Shelton, Ed.) Detroit, Michigan: MacMillan Reference.

Smith, H. (1981). *Smith's Story of the Mennonites.* Newton, Kansas: Faith and Life Press.

Streit, C. (2000). *Soviet Prisoners of War in the Hands of the Wehrmacht.* (H. Heer, & K. Naumann, Eds.) New York: Berghahn.

Sullivan, W. (1972, March 27). The Einstein Papers. A Man of Many Parts. *The New York Times,* 1. New York.

Thompson, J. (2009). *Dunkirk: Retreat to Victory.* London: Pan Books.

Trouillard, S. (2020, June 21). *The Nazi massacre of African soldiers in French army, 80 years on.* Retrieved March 22, 2021, from France 24: https://www.france24.com/en/20200621-the-nazi-massacre-of-senegalese-soldiers-in-french-army-80-years-on

United States Department of State. (2022, April 24). *German Federal Archive (Deutsches Bundesarchiv).* Retrieved from Wikipedia: https://commons.wikimedia.org/wiki/File:Bundesarchiv_Bild_102-17049,_Joseph_Goebbels_spricht.jpg

von Georg, B., Puhl, J., & Wiegrefe, K. (2009, January 23). Death in Marienburg: Mystery Surrounds Mass Graves in Polish City. *Spiegel International.* Retrieved October 19, 2021, from https://www.spiegel.de/international/europe/death-in-marienburg-mystery-surrounds-mass-graves-in-polish-city-a-603131.html

von Mellenthin, F. W. (1977). *Panzer Battles, 1939-45.* (L. C. Turner, Ed.) Futura.

Wistrich, R. S. (2001). *Who's Who in Nazi Germany.* London: Routledge.

Wyatt, W. J. (1876). *The History of Prussia* (Vol. II). London: Longmans, Green.

Yeliseenko, A. (2012, August 06). *Casualties of the USSR.* Retrieved DEcember 16, 2022, from AxisHistory.com: https://forum.axishistory.com/viewtopic.php?t=188391&start=45#p1721837

Yves, P. J. (2010, May 10). *Chronology Of Mass Violence in Poland 1918-1948.* Retrieved December 28, 2021, from SciencePo: https://www.sciencespo.fr/mass-violence-war-massacre-resistance/en/document/chronology-mass-violence-poland-1918-1948.html

Index

In the early hours of the morning of June 3rd 1940, General Harold Alexander was alongside the quay at Dunkirk as he lifted a megaphone and called "Is anyone there? Is anyone there?" There was no reply. He had directed the evacuation and was the last to leave Dunkirk.

The very next day Churchill stood at the dispatch and gave his "We Shall Fight Them on the Beaches" speech.

Tradition tells us that the dramatic events of the evacuation of Dunkirk, in which 300,000 BEF servicemen escaped the Nazis, was a victory gained from the jaws of defeat. Rather than telling the tale of those who escaped, Peter Smith reveals a story of those sacrificed in the rear-guard battles.

For us the Battle for France was not over. In June 1940 there were still 41,000 British soldiers fighting the Germans alongside their French allies. Mounting a vigorous counterattack at Abbeville and then conducting a tough defence between the Somme front and the Seine, Peter was fighting a very uncertain battle for mere survival for an even more uncertain future.

Peter Smith tells his own story and captures the drama of those military operations and subsequent capture by Rommel's 7th Panzer Division (the infamous 'Ghost Division') who moved with clandestine stealth towards their objectives.

Nothing prepares a man for war and there can be little doubt, Peter was not prepared, even less so for a life as a POW. "I lost my freedom on June 8th 1940 when we were told it was every man-for-himself and didn't re-gain it until April 1945 when I was rescued by Americans near Halberstadt, having walked 1,600km along the Baltic coast from East Prussia."

Silent for nearly 80 years, Peter tells his story about his five lost years: the terrible things he saw at Thorn, Stuttoff, Stettin and Halberstadt; working on farms, Peter experienced first-hand the East Prussian way of life; his period in solitary confinement for 'stealing apple'; the disintegration and collapse of a whole way of life in East Prussia in the face of the Soviet invasion; and the terrible Long March, when 80,000 British POWs were forced to trek through a vicious winter westwards across Poland, alongside 2 million East German refugees as the Soviets approached.

"We were all prisoners, as POWs, and refugees alike embraced a dance with death in the coldest winter for 50 years as we all trudged west; and similarly the German Army as it battled to save its population."

Peter's story is also about friendship, of physical and mental resilience and of compassion for everyone who suffered. It was a difficult march undertaken in unimaginable wintery arctic conditions, where lack of food, the cold, and death were constant companions.

ISBN 978-1-80424-122-6

Lightning Source UK Ltd.
Milton Keynes UK
UKHW020723171222
414082UK00011B/1289